Exploring Health Careers

Second Edition

EXPLORING HEALTH CAREERS

SECOND EDITION

MAUREEN MCCUTCHEON

Delmar Publishers

an International Thomson Publishing company I(T)P®

Albany • Bonn • Boston • Cincinnati • Detroit • London • Madrid
Melbourne • Mexico City • New York • Pacific Grove • Paris • San Francisco
Singapore • Tokyo • Toronto • Washington

Cover photos courtesy of: (top & right): Images copyright © 1997 PhotoDisc, Inc.; (top center): Louise Simmers; (bottom center): USDA

Delmar Staff

Publisher: Susan Simpfenderfer
Acquisitions Editor: Dawn Gerrain
Developmental Editor: Andrea Edwards Myers
Project Editor: Eugenia L. Orlandi

Production Manager: Wendy A. Troeger
Production Editor: Carolyn Miller
Marketing Manager: Katherine Slezak

COPYRIGHT © 1999
By Delmar Publishers
an International Thomson Publishing Company

The ITP logo is a trademark under license.

Printed in the United States of America

For more information, contact:

Delmar Publishers
3 Columbia Circle, Box 15015
Albany, New York 12212-5015

International Thomson Publishing Europe
Berkshire House 168-173
High Holborn
London, WC1V 7AA
England

Thomas Nelson Australia
102 Dodds Street
South Melbourne, 3205
Victoria, Australia

Nelson Canada
1120 Birchmount Road
Scarborough, Ontario
Canada, M1K 5G4

International Thomson Editores
Campos Eliseos 385, Piso 7
Col Polanco
11560 Mexico D F Mexico

International Thomson Publishing GmbH
Konigswinterer Strasse 418
53227 Bonn
Germany

International Thomson Publishing Asia
221 Henderson Road
#05-10 Henderson Building
Singapore 0315

International Thomson Publishing—Japan
Hirakawacho Kyowa Building, 3F
2-2-1 Hirakawacho
Chiyoda-ku, Tokyo 102
Japan

1 2 3 4 5 6 7 8 9 10 XXX 03 02 01 00 99 98 97

Library of Congress Cataloging-in-Publication Data

McCutcheon, Maureen.
    Exploring health careers / Maureen McCutcheon.—2nd ed.
      p. cm.
    Includes bibliographical references and index.
    Summary: Discusses all facets of each health care specialty within acute care, clinic, and office settings.
    ISBN 0-8273-8533-1
    1. Medicine—Vocational guidance. 2. Allied health personnel—Vocational guidance. [1. Medicine—Vocational guidance. 2. Allied health personnel—Vocational guidance. 3. Vocational guidance.] I. Title.
    R690.M354   1998
    610.69—dc21   97-26075
                                                CIP
                                                AC

Contents

Preface

Exploring Health Careers, Second Edition, was written primarily to help students determine the health care career most suited to their individual goals by learning the specifics of each role and the factors that affect professional performance. It may be used effectively in any health occupations or general career exploration course, or in a health career training program.

The text has been written from the perspective of health care specialties or departments within acute care, clinic, or office settings. Following Chapter 1 on job skills, each chapter presents all facets of a specialty, including terms, career descriptions, professional skills, and procedures performed that would be encountered by students anticipating joining that specialty or interacting with professionals in that field. This approach prepares students to experience that specialty of health care.

The text presents two types of information: job skills and health care careers. Chapter 1 identifies job skills that contribute to the successful performance of health care workers. The subsequent chapters on health care specialties are presented in alphabetical order. Organizational charts, educational requirements, desired personal characteristics, job satisfaction, career advancement, employment opportunities, and work hours are covered.

Added features in the second edition include chapters on veterinary medicine and vision careers. Salary ranges have been updated and demonstrate the relationship of education to monetary reward. The School to Work section relates how academic subjects apply to tasks on the job. General examples are given in the "Job Skills" chapter, with specific examples detailed in individual chapters. The Biography section tells the stories of people who have achieved health care careers, and the What's New section identifies advances in the field. Addresses and fax numbers of professional organizations and review questions also are part of each chapter. Students can access most professional organizations on the Internet. After www., enter the initial letters of the organization's name, followed by .org/. (For example, http://www. AAS.org/)

Program expectations and student responsibilities are clearly stated in the chapter objectives. An introduction to the structure and function of some body systems and a glossary are provided in the appendices.

An *Instructor's Guide* is available that offers information on establishing a staff-mentored program, problem-solving situations, the student selection process, and possible pitfalls and solutions in clinical areas. Examples of class schedules, quizzes, and tests are also included.

The author, Maureen McCutcheon, received a bachelor of science degree in nursing from Saint John College in Cleveland, Ohio, and a master's of education from Kent State University. She has worked at the Cleveland Clinic Foun-dation, Cook County Hospital, the New York Hospital, Memorial Hospital for Cancer and Allied Diseases, and Lakewood Hospital. She has been a staff nurse, a nursing supervisor, and an instructor in staff development, in LPN and RN schools and for the Red Cross. She wrote this textbook as a result of teaching a health occupations course for the Lakewood school system based at Lakewood Hospital. She is also the author of a medical/surgical textbook for LPNs.

The Diversified Medical Occupations program that the author developed for the Lakewood school system, and that inspired this textbook, won an award for creativity and excellence from the Ohio Board of Education in 1996.

Acknowledgments

I wish to thank the administration of the Lakewood school system for recognizing the need for a medical careers program and allowing me the autonomy to create and develop the course. In particular, I wish to thank: Dr. Daniel M. Kalish, Superintendent of Schools; Alan Penn, Director of Vocational Education; Judith Sellers, Former Director of Vocational Education; Sarah Sweeney, Personnel Administrator; William McNamera, Assistant Principal; and special colleagues Eileen Ptacek, Carol Litzler, and Joseph Ertler.

I wish to thank the administration of Lakewood Hospital for hosting the medical careers program, encouraging staff mentors, supporting the educational goals of the program, and nurturing community youth: Jules W. Bouthillet, Chief Executive Officer; Gail Bromley, M.S.N., R.N., Vice President of Clinical Services; Susan Ridell, Director of Volunteer Services; James L. Stewart Jr., M.D., Vice President of Medical Affairs; John Bolan, Director of Human Services; Joy Kovar, Employee Relations Manager; Barry Dore, Compensation/Benefits Manager.

In addition to the mentors and medical photographer, I wish to thank the following staff who reviewed the manuscript associated with their specialty and allowed photographs to be taken in their departments. They made substantial contributions to the development and accuracy of information.

Biometrics Department: Ilse Hazners, B.S.; Judy Kinder, R.C.T.; Sharon Suter, R.EEG.T.

Communication Disorders Department: Theresa S. Dawson, M.A., CCC-SLP, Supervisor of Speech Pathology

Dental Office: Marie A. Albano, D.D.S.; Richard H. Haug, D.D.S., Director of Oral and Maxillofacial Surgery at MetroHealth Medical Center

Dietary Department: Bonny Ayers, R.D., L.D., Assistant Dietary Director/Clinical and Patient Services

Emergency Department: Sue Jachnick, B.A., R.N., Clinical Nursing Coordinator, Emergency Room; Matt Burke, EMT—P, Supervisor, EMS

Medical Laboratory: Rosemary Kirchner, M.T. (ASCP), Chief Medical Technologist

Medical Library: Jo Ann Hudson, Director; Ann Mancuso, Assistant Librarian

Medical Photography: Steven Robertson

Medical Records Department: Janet Griffin, A.R.T., Assistant Director

Mental Health Department: Grace Herwig, M.S.N., M.B.A., R.N., Clinical Nurse Specialist, Psychiatry

Nursing Department: Rosalie DeBlase, R.N., M.S.N., Clinical Nurse Specialist, Critical Care; Barbara Soltis, R.N., M.S.N., C.R.R.N., Certified Rehabilitation Nurse, Certified Nurse Consultant; Cynthia D. Sansom, A.C.S.W., Director of Social Service Department

Occupational Therapy Department: Sandy Dadante, O.T.R./L, Manager of Occupational Therapy; Matthew Kohl, O.T., Cleveland Clinic Hospital

Pharmacy Department: Scott Jamieson, R.Ph., Director of Pharmacy

Physical Therapy Department: Carol Bieri, P.T., Director of Rehabilitation Services; Judith Bryan, P.T., Skilled Nursing Unit

Radiology Department: Joan Ellsworth, R.T., MRI Technologist; Judy Wilms, R.T., MRI Coordinator; Dennis Schisler, R.T., MRI Technologist

Respiratory Therapy Department: Mary Ann Marsal, B.A., R.R.T., Chief Respiratory Therapist

Support Departments:

Admitting: James Yaeger, A.A.M., Admitting and ER Registration Manager

Business: Julie Abouserhal, Office Coordinator of Patient Accounting

Central Service/Storeroom: Tim Kirwelnz, Material Handler

Surgery Department: Mary Jane Wolf, R.N., Director of Surgery

Veterinary Medicine: Dr. William Fenner, D.M.V., Assistant Dean of Admissions, College of Veterinary Medicine, Ohio State University; John Swartz, Senior Medical Photographer

Vision Careers: Michele Miller, Director of the Ophthalmic Technician Program, Lakeland Community College; Mike Hartnatt, Instructor; Kathy Uhl, Optician, Pearle Vision; Anne Pinter, C.R.A., Lakewood Hospital Eye Clinic

Thanks also to:

Kristen Purdy, B.S., R.N., Teacher, Diversified Medical Occupations program, Lakewood school system, who photographed students in action at Lakewood Hospital.

Cheryl Seredy, Video and Media Specialist at Cleveland MetroHealth Medical Center, for her assistance with photos.

Louise Simmers, Author, *Diversified Health Occupations*, Delmar Publishers, for her fine advice.

Special thanks go to the professionals at Delmar Publishers for their foresight, encouragement, and able assistance in the development, preparation, and publication of this project: Dawn Gerrain, Acquisitions Editor; Andrea Edwards Myers, Developmental Editor; Carolyn Miller, Production Editor, and Cristin Day, Project Editor at Shepherd, Inc.

I also wish to acknowledge my indebtedness to past and present reviewers for their thoughtful comments and creative recommendations that added immeasurably to the writing and usefulness of the manuscript.

First Edition Reviewers

Peggy A. Grubbs
Health Occupations Instructor
Hillsborough County School Board
Tampa, Florida

Judith Mabrey
Health Occupations
Putnam County Vocational School
Cookeville, Indiana

Faye Munoz
Tri-Cities Regional Occupation Program
Whittier, California

Luetisha Newby
Health Occupations Education Consultant
Michigan Department of Education
Vocational-Technical Education Service
Lansing, Michigan

Virginia Rullman
Diversified Cooperative Health Occupations
Instructor/Coordinator
D. Russel Lee Career Center
Hamilton, Ohio

Linda Stutzman
Health Occupations Coordinator
EHOVE Career Center
Milar, Ohio

Second Edition Reviewers
Gwen Barnett
North High School
Evansville, Indiana

Donna Butts
Hart/Mexico AVTS
Middletown, Missouri

Johnny Beth Nolan
Carroll County Vocational Technical Center
Huntingdon, Tennessee

Regina St. George
Newnan High School
Newnan, Georgia

Allison Shroff
Tulsa Technology Center
Tulsa, Oklahoma

And finally, I thank those special people in my life who offered continuing encouragement throughout the project: Margaret Saunders McCarthy, M.A.; John Joseph McCarthy, M.A.; Ruthanne Dillhoefer, M.A., M.Ed.; Maureen McCarthy, M.S.N., R.N.; Kevin McCarthy, Ph.D.; and my children—Kelly, Casey, and Kate.

Exploring Health Careers, Second Edition, is dedicated to future health care professionals, students who want to learn about health care occupations, and to their teachers and mentors who nurture that interest and help to make it a reality.

Introduction

*W*elcome to the world of health care! At the beginning of a career quest, several topics need to be considered. First is area of interest. If you decide on health care, the next step is to choose a specific career. The following questions and answers may help you to determine a career course.

How can I decide what career I want to select?

One of the most effective methods of determining a career is to spend time working or volunteering in the area of general interest. Talking with professionals about their jobs, observing the duties they perform each day in their work site, and discussing the personal characteristics and academic courses that are needed to attain success in that field are ways to learn about a career. A survey program about hospital health careers offered by a high school, technical school, college, or re-training program is ideal for an extended on-the-spot experience.

Another way to discover career interests is to read about a job setting such as an emergency room or surgery. Think about all the career professionals that interact in that setting, and learn about the skills performed there and how much education it takes to become each one of those professionals. Then determine if you like the work and how much time, money, and effort you are willing to invest to prepare yourself for that career. This textbook was written to help you evaluate health care careers. All the careers in a particular field of health care are presented in a chapter.

Why choose a health care career?

A career in health care is advantageous for several good reasons: worthwhile work, job satisfaction, position availability, and the opportunity to work with people of all ages in every area of the country. Other reasons include the variety of specialties, interaction with professional people, feelings of involvement with work, pride in a role, feeling of team spirit, membership on a professional team, opportunity to specialize, and ability to use ingenuity, leadership, and entrepreneurship. Health care careers can serve as a springboard to other professions and management positions.

Health care is dynamic and exciting work. New procedures and instruments are continually being developed, so careers do not stagnate. New illnesses and treatments are constantly being recognized. Research in science, biotechnology, and human behavior continues to result in discoveries that affect health, health care, and communication.

How safe are care givers?

Universal standards to protect care givers from illness and infection have been developed by the Centers for Disease Control in Atlanta, Georgia. Infection control measures continue to be developed from research on bacteria and viruses, their habitats, and modes of transmission. Standards include recommended tests and vaccinations for tuberculosis and hepatitis B. Care giving practices include when to wear protective clothing, such as gloves, masks, gowns, goggles, hats, and shoe covers, and proper hand-washing techniques.

Generally, measures are recommended to protect care givers from contact with the body fluids of blood, sputum, emesis, urine, and stool. Also, protective measures are necessary to protect patients from the bacteria and viruses of other patients.

What is included in each chapter of this textbook?

Chapter objectives, commonly used medical terms, and goals are meant to be reviewed before associating with department professionals to better understand their work and discussions. Compare the credentials of your mentors with those listed in the Education and Credentials section, the organizational chart with the Career Hierarchy, and the approximate range of their annual incomes with the Range of Annual Incomes. (Salaries vary widely between geographical areas of the country and between suburban and inner-city facilities. Wages are usually higher on the East Coast, West Coast, and inner cities, and lower in the southern states and suburban facilities.)

The Career Description section delineates tasks that sum up a role or profession. Compare them with job descriptions in the work site. Some health care workers have greater responsibility than others, depending on state laws and facility policies.

The Skills section describes tests, procedures, and processes. These will change as technology develops and communication techniques improve.

The Biography section relates the story of how one person achieved a career discussed in that chapter. You will see how some people have had to overcome a variety of obstacles to achieve success. Also, you will see that some people have more than one career in succession.

A Career Search can be facilitated by contacting career-related organizations at the addresses provided. Fax numbers have been provided where available. Please note that telephone area codes are subject to change; it may be necessary to call your telephone company's Information Services Department to obtain the new number.

The What's New section relates current developments in the field. Progress in health and health care is unfolding every day as researchers announce new findings and develop medications, treatments, and machines to improve health and patient care.

The School to Work section demonstrates how academic subjects are applied in the workplace. For example, courses such as anatomy and physiology, chemistry and physics are particularly applicable in careers related to diagnosing and treating illness. Mathematics, for example, is used in direct health care and pharmacy, as well as in business careers in health care.

Review Questions will help identify important information. These are the facts that will help in making career decisions.

What education programs are offered to become a health care worker?

Many educational programs, offered in a variety of settings, lead to certificates, diplomas, and degrees. From lowest to highest, they go from certificates and diplomas to associate, bachelor, and master degrees, to medical, osteopathic, and nursing doctor degrees, and doctor of philosophy degrees.

Where are health career programs offered?

Health career programs are offered as on-the-job training and in high schools, vocation or technical schools, junior or community colleges, four-year colleges, universities, graduate schools (at universities), and medical, osteopathic, and dental schools.

When I graduate from a program, will my education be complete?

In many careers, graduates of an accredited program must pass a state or organizational board exam to be permitted to practice. This license or certificate may need to be renewed. This may require continuing education, a process designed to ensure career practitioners have up-to-date knowledge. Some programs require an internship of supervised practice before the right to practice independently.

What are the legal implications of health care?

Patients have a right to expect that they will be cared for safely by qualified people who are pleasant, caring, and knowledgeable. Certain tasks are not to be done by workers until an accredited educational program has been completed and required exams passed. People in a training program must be extremely careful to carry out only those tasks they were taught, only when properly supervised, and only when given permission to do so by the instructor and professional staff.

Will I be expected to remain in the same career all my life?

Health care is unique in offering a variety of specialties within a career as well as encouraging members to use one career as a stepping stone to another career. Some programs may recommend or require experience in another health care career before an applicant will be accepted.

How will the changes in health care delivery affect me?

Health care is a dynamic system that will continue to change. It is also a business. Personnel, medications, equipment, treatments, medical procedures, and facilities are expensive. In the search for a method of health care delivery that will help people to remain healthy and will care for them when they are ill at a reasonable cost, many systems will be tried. Managed care, health maintenance organizations, Medicare, and Medicaid are a few approaches to delivering health care. Generally, the roles of health care workers will remain the same. Work sites, responsibilities, scope of practice, job titles, team members, and methods of reimbursement may change, but the basic concepts of health care will not.

HOSPITAL ORGANIZATIONAL CHART*

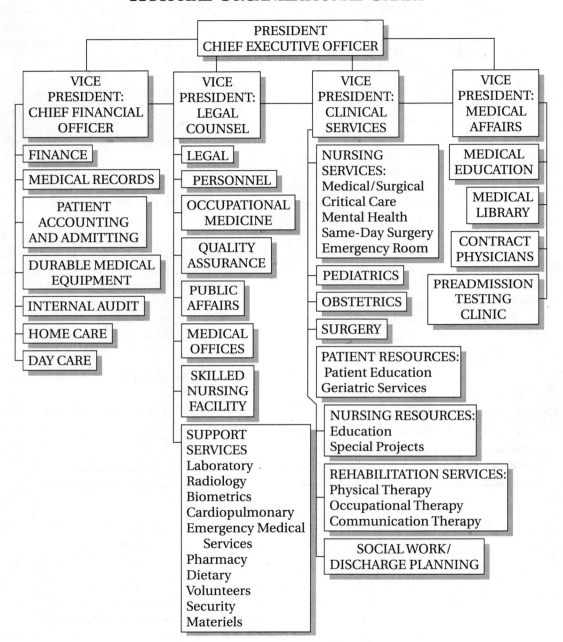

*Other kinds of health care facilities have similar structures depending on the services offered to the public.

JOB SKILLS

Objectives

After completing this chapter, you should be able to:

- ❏ Identify work habits that are important to employers.
- ❏ Apply specific job skills to health care workers.
- ❏ Describe the steps of the problem-solving process.
- ❏ Compose a résumé and cover letter.
- ❏ Complete a job application.
- ❏ Gain interview skills.
- ❏ Recognize how academic subjects apply in the workplace.

Key Terms

Employability skills

Attitude	Attendance	Communication
Problem solving	Confidentiality	Universal precautions

Résumé

INTRODUCTION

Valued staff members bring certain characteristics to the work site that enhance their usefulness on the job. Most health care workers have these characteristics (Figure 1–1).

Staff members with a positive attitude and good job skills are fine representatives of the health care agency.

Employers depend on their employees' good work habits and, **employability skills.** Good work habits include a positive attitude, regular attendance, punctuality, responsibility, dependability, communication techniques, and ability to set goals and follow directions. Other desirable work habits include taking pride in one's work (Figure 1–2), being able to

Figure 1–1 *Dependable employees come to work every day.*

Figure 1–2 *Good employees take pride in their work.*

solve problems, and exhibiting team spirit.

PRINCIPLES AND PRACTICE

Professional people in health care usually have good job skills. They have learned these favorable work habits and put them into practice every day. Listed below are 1) explanations of job skills as they relate to health care workers, and 2) methods to improve each skill.

Positive attitude

Attitude is the most important job skill. An employer values workers who look on the bright side of things, who want to work, and who are willing to learn. Enthusiastic workers are a real asset on the job and a positive influence in the workplace (Figure 1–3). Workers who look at the negative side of every situation have a depressing influence on the rest of the employees. Working with complainers can make everyone feel unhappy. When workers feel unhappy or argue with each other, less work gets done and mistakes may be made.

Practice:

- Be thankful that you are in the health careers program.
- Compliment yourself on what you have learned and how well you have worked on the job.
- Praise a classmate for a job well done, an answer well spoken, or a problem well solved.
- Feel good about being at your job site.
- Want to learn.
- Try to do good work every day. Understand that every task is helpful in the

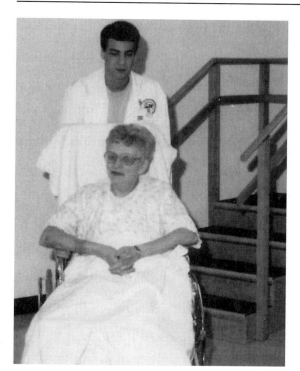

Figure 1–3 *A positive attitude creates a workplace where people look forward to being.*

health care system and ultimately to patient care. Every task is important— even those that do not involve direct patient care.

• Appear interested and eager when you arrive at the clinical practice site. Mentors are happy to teach interested students.

Attendance

Workers must come to work to qualify as good workers. They need to come to work every day. If workers do not come to work when scheduled, other workers may become angry because they will be overworked and patient care will suffer. Workers with good **attendance** may have

to do the absent workers' jobs plus their own. Soon, workers with regular attendance feel burdened and may seek employment elsewhere. Workers do well to come into work even during their time off to relieve a team member who is ill or to help team members if the unit becomes very busy and scheduled staff is not sufficient.

Practice:

• Come every day to the work site. Even if you feel tired or irritable when you wake up, get dressed and report to work. Of course, if you feel sick or have a fever or an upset stomach, you will not want to expose patients to your illness.

• Decide that you want to have a good attendance record and care about being a team member (Figure 1–4).

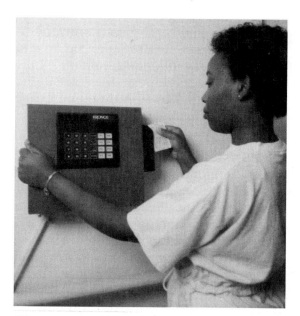

Figure 1–4 *A health care worker must report to work on time and maintain a good attendance record.*

Punctuality

Workers need to come to work on time every day. In many health care facilities, patient care continues twenty-four hours a day, seven days a week. When an eight-hour or twelve-hour shift is over, workers are ready to go home. Relief workers need to arrive before their shift is scheduled to begin, so they will be ready to work when it starts. This allows for a smooth transition between shifts and uninterrupted patient care. When workers arrive late, irritation and angry feelings may result. To avoid jeopardizing patient safety and to ensure efficient care, on-duty workers must wait until relief workers arrive and get organized for their shift.

Practice:

- Come on time every day. Organize your life so that you arrive early for work every day.
- Do not depend on others, family members or classmates, to wake you up and drive you to work or school.
- Arrange your work at the job site so that you can leave on time and arrive promptly for class.

Responsibility

Valued workers can be depended on to fulfill the duties of their job every day. These workers are reliable. The employer knows that reliable workers make good decisions. Though workers have a degree of freedom of choice at a job site, good workers do not take advantage of them. Running errands to many departments, using the facility telephone, and parking in restricted lots present freedoms and decision-making opportunities. Good workers feel responsible to the employer and do not take advantage of such freedoms. They accept the responsibility that freedom brings. They go directly to departments when running errands, and do not stop to visit with friends. They understand that telephone lines are for business and do not use the facility phone for personal calls. They respect the facility's parking restrictions.

Practice:

- Call the teacher if you are unable to work or will be late.
- Follow directions (Figure 1–5).
- Ask questions when in doubt.
- Conduct yourself with maturity at the work site. Do not shout at classmates, push and shove one another, or chase friends through the facility.
- Dress in your uniform every day.
- Speak respectfully to co-workers and classmates. Do not gossip or discuss your personal life when you are on the job.

Dependability

Valued workers are worthy of trust. The employer knows that dependable workers will be on the job performing properly each day. Dependable workers do a good job every day without needing to be supervised. They are motivated to do their best.

Practice:

- Report directly to the work site and appear eager to work and learn.
- Remain at your workstation until it is time to leave. Do not leave your workstation to visit friends.
- Work when on the job; do not waste time or do other projects. Always try to do a good job.

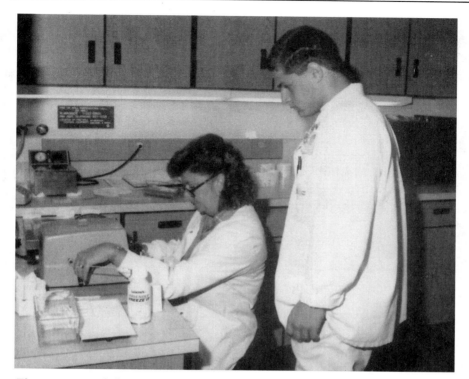

Figure 1–5 *Ability to follow directions is important for patient safety.*

- Respect the privacy of patients and co-workers.
- Complete homework, notebook, and class tasks on time—but not on the job.

Communication skills

An employer expects a worker to be honest and polite. Listen to directions and ask necessary questions. It is good to ask questions if you do not understand. It is not good to make sarcastic remarks about rules, methods, or tasks. Remember that you are a "guest" of the health care agency. You have limited rights. Your experience in health care is different from that of your co-workers. Be sensitive to others' feelings. If you do not like the work, feel good that you have learned something about yourself. But be careful how you share that information with your mentors to avoid hurt feelings. Be tactful and polite when speaking.

Practice:
- Ask questions when you do not know what to do (Figure 1–6).
- Admit mistakes to the appropriate people.
- Speak respectfully to professionals in the workplace.
- Think before you speak. Say what you really want to say. Look at the person when you speak. Tell the truth.
- Talk loudly enough to be heard. Listen carefully.

Figure 1–6 *Ask questions if you do not know what to do.*

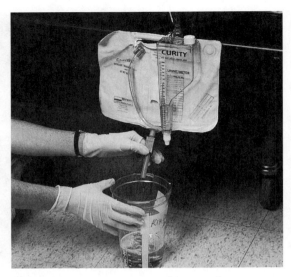

Figure 1–7 *Carry out tasks exactly as taught.*

• Do not sit unless you are asked to do so.

Follow directions

Workers need to follow the rules of the job and the guidelines of the program. Rules ensure a safe environment and an effective, efficient workplace. Follow the rules precisely. Carry out tasks exactly as they were taught (Figure 1–7). If you feel rules should be changed, follow the process for doing that. Do not just do what you want to do.

Practice:
• Report when you are coming on and off duty.
• Park where you are instructed to park. If you ride the bus, wait where you are told to wait until the bus arrives.
• Speak softly in the halls.
• Eat only where that is allowed.
• Wear your uniform every day.

• Do not smoke or chew gum in the facility.

Pride in work

An employer wants workers who are proud of their jobs. Workers who feel good about a job well done will strive to continue this quality performance. Workers like to work in a job that they can be proud of and perform well. If workers do not like the work or do not perform well, they need to seek other employment.

Practice:
• Enjoy completing assigned tasks accurately. Tell yourself that you are doing a good job.
• Record the aspects of your job that you especially like and that you perform well.
• Write down compliments that you receive.

Pride in the health careers program

Professional people in the workplace are aware that the health careers educational program is special. They know that students are carefully selected. Many wish that a health careers program had been available to them when they were in school. The actions and words of each student in the workplace reflect on the entire class. This means that the attitudes of the professional workers toward the entire program will be based on each individual student's job performance and work skills.

Practice:

- Dress like your professional mentors (Figure 1–8).
- Speak politely, using correct grammar.
- Pay attention when a patient or professional talks to you. Look at the person speaking to you.
- Show respect for the patients, the program, the job site, the employer, and the staff.
- Walk, do not run in the halls.
- Stand tall and straight; keep your hands out of your pockets and your feet on the floor.
- Wear a clean lab coat or uniform, minimal makeup, small pieces of jewelry, and no fragrances.
- Remember that in a health care facility, there is no smoking, no rowdiness, no loud voices, and no gum chewing.

Teamwork

Ideal workers care about others and are sensitive to their hopes, feelings, and needs. They reach out and help one an-

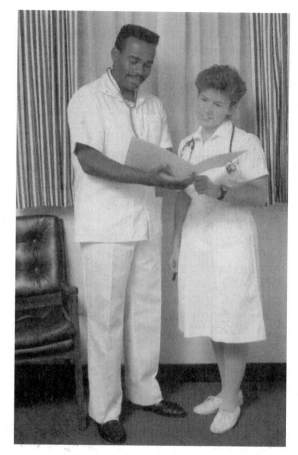

Figure 1–8 *Good employees take pride in their appearance.*

other. They are not argumentative. They do not say nasty things about their fellow workers.

Teammates work together to get the job done (Figure 1–9). When their tasks are finished, they ask how they can help with their teammates' work. They exchange days off to help another team member. They come to work on their day off if a team member is ill. They think about the needs of others and the goals of the facility. They are willing to work.

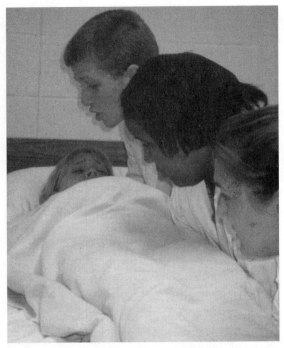

Figure 1–9 *Teammates work together to get the job done.*

Practice:

- Think about how your comments influence others. Make only positive comments to classmates and professionals. Do not say anything negative or hurtful about another's clothes, relationships, or habits.
- Become aware of how patients, staff, and classmates feel. Then avoid doing and saying things that will cause them to feel sad or angry.
- When your assigned tasks are completed, ask for more work. Ask how you can help other workers.

Self-discipline

Workers who manage themselves are assets to the workplace. These workers are in control of their lives and can concentrate on their jobs (Figure 1–10). They can do what needs to be done to accomplish their goals. They do not wait for others to manage their lives. They get up on time, get themselves to their job, and accomplish their tasks. They do their homework on time and study every night. Life's tasks do not overwhelm them and take them by surprise. They have a plan and they go about carrying it out.

Practice:

- Set your alarm to get yourself up. Use a battery clock so that if the electricity fails, you will not be late for work or school.
- Study every night.
- Come to work or school ten minutes early each day.

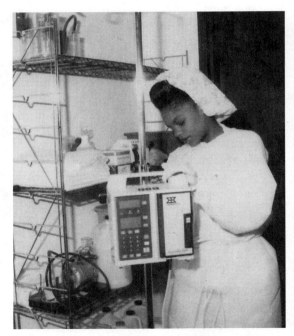

Figure 1–10 *Concentrating on the task at hand is important in health careers.*

- Launder your uniform yourself; do not depend on someone else to do it.
- Stand with good posture in the clinical site, unless you must sit to accomplish assigned tasks.
- Get enough rest.

Works well with others

Valued employees respect other people and allow others to be themselves. These workers are pleasant to everyone at work. They do not participate in arguments or take sides. They act as peacemakers on the job. They do not talk about boyfriends or girlfriends on the job, brag about expensive gifts they have received, or talk about home or school problems.

Practice:

- Be pleasant and courteous to classmates and people at the job site.
- Offer your class notes to a student who was absent. Take the time to help another student with a skill or terms that you know.
- Encourage others to be kind.
- Do not criticize or complain about others.

PROBLEM-SOLVING PROCESS

Problem solving is the process used to make decisions. Every activity involves a decision by the doer. For example, getting out of bed, eating breakfast, and going to school are three actions requiring decisions. Some actions become so automatic that they no longer seem like choices. But they are choices, whether the doer takes a long time to decide or acts without thinking about it. The process of making decisions also becomes automatic.

Steps of problem solving

The process of problem solving may be described with different terms, but it remains the same. While learning the process, write out each step. The seven steps of problem solving are represented by GILMAEC, an acronym for the following:

G —Gather data
I —Identify the problem
L —List possible actions
M —Make a plan
A —Act
E —Evaluate
C —Change the plan

1. **Gather** data; assess the situation. Problem solving is what good detectives do. Just like Sherlock Holmes, each person can learn to solve problems. The more information the problem solver learns about a situation, the better chance a good decision can be made. There are many sides to a story and many facts in every situation. So review all aspects. Write a list of the facts of the case. The list should have at least six facts.

2. **Identify** the problem. This is the hardest step and takes the most time. It is often difficult to separate the real issue from the facts and the actions of the characters in the situation. A problem is rarely an action. An action is usually a symptom or sign of a problem. For example, a student may be rude to a nurse at the hospital. Although that behavior is not acceptable on the job, the problem is not rudeness. The rudeness is a symptom of the problem. The problem is immaturity. This immaturity resulted in a job performance that

lacks the skills of responsibility and appropriate communication.

The problem-solving process is constantly being used in health care. For example, a doctor uses a symptom as a guidepost leading to the real diagnosis, the real problem. A fever may be a sign of infection, the real problem. Numbness may be a sign of poor circulation, the real problem. Headaches may indicate high blood pressure, the real problem. Nurses and therapists use this process, too. For example, when a person does not want to walk after surgery, the real problem may not be that she cannot, but that she needs adequate pain medication.

3. **List** all possible actions, even if some may not seem like good choices. When the list is complete, evaluate each action. List at least six action choices.

4. **Make** a plan, that is, select an action. Think about the consequences of each action before making your choice. Then choose the action that will result in the most desirable outcome.

5. **Act.** Do it. Carry out the plan.

6. **Evaluate** the action. Was it effective? Did it achieve the goal? Is there a better way?

7. **Change** the plan if a different action would be more effective. Continue steps 5 through 7 until the problem is resolved or the situation improved.

Problem-solving steps must be followed in order. Eventually, small decisions can be made quickly and without the doer being completely aware of each step, such as deciding whether to take the 7:30 A.M. or 7:45 A.M. bus. Big decisions require conscious problem solving, that is, carefully going in order through each step of the problem-solving process. Examples of big decisions are choosing what college to attend or determining whether you are ready to have a baby.

Health care workers make many important decisions about patient care every day. Sometimes those decisions must be made quickly, such as when a patient experiences a cardiac arrest. Sometimes decisions take longer because many facts need to be gathered. The public has a right to expect that health care workers follow the problem-solving, decision-making process. The public expects health care providers to make the right choices for their well-being.

Solving a problem using GILMAEC

Put your self in this situation: You are a student in the health careers program driving to your hospital job site. You need to decide where to park.

G—Gather data. You need to park the car and go to the hospital classroom, dressed in your uniform, on time for class. The hospital has two garages, one north and one south. Students have been directed to park in the north garage, which is one block away. They are not to park in the south garage, which is connected to the hospital and reserved for outpatients and visitors, many of whom are elderly. Students park for free in the north garage. The teacher stamps their garage tickets to show they are entitled to free parking. Other parking options are metered spaces on the street in front of the hospital, and a surface lot outside the emergency department marked for "ER patients only." Class begins at 8:00 A.M. It is now 7:53. It takes seven minutes to walk from the north garage to the hospital, but only three minutes from the south garage. You need four minutes to get your uniform out of your locker. It is raining.

I—Identify the problem. Where should you park so you can get to class on time and follow the program rules?

L—List actions. Park in the north garage, as students have been instructed to do, receive free parking, and be late to class. Park in the close, convenient, but off-limits south garage and pay for parking. Park in the south off-limits garage and trick a hospital employee into stamping your ticket to receive free parking. Park at a metered place on the street and leave the work site to feed coins to the meter twice during the morning. Park in the emergency department lot marked for "ER patients only."

M—Make a plan. Park in the south garage attached to the hospital, avoid the rain, and be on time to class. Ask an employee to stamp your ticket to avoid the parking charge.

A—Act. You park in the south garage. You then pressure an employee in the emergency room to stamp the ticket so you can avoid the parking charge, and you hope the teacher does not find out.

E—Evaluate. You evaluate as positive arriving to class on time and getting free parking. You realize a negative consequence when the teacher assigns you to after-school detention after she discovers that you parked in the south garage and led an emergency room employee to be-lieve that you were qualified for free parking there.

C—Change the plan. In the future, park in the north garage, even if it is raining and you will be late to class.

Critical thinking is the process of solving problems and making decisions. Following the GILMAEC steps will help the user become more proficient in this process.

Patience

Workers in health care need to have self-control and tolerance for others who may be under stress because of illness, pain, or disability. They need to understand that the people they serve are always treated with respect and kindness. Personal feelings of anger and frustration are never expressed to the patients or staff. Complaints of this kind can be reported to the appropriate person in authority, such as the unit manager. Physical or verbal abuse of patients is never tolerated and may result in the worker being suspended or discharged.

Practice. Ignore or respond without showing anger or frustration to criticisms and argumentative statements of family members and friends. If necessary, leave the area until your control returns. Others may stop trying to provoke your anger when you don't respond with anger, especially if you were quick to answer in the past. Tolerance can be learned, practiced, and polished.

Empathy

Empathetic workers are an asset on the health care team. Empathy is the ability to put yourself in another person's place and experience how this individual thinks and feels. How would you feel if you were in pain all the time? Who would help you care for your family and pay your bills if you were disabled? Remember that patients have lives and responsibilities outside of the facility where you work. Understand that sometimes they become overwhelmed with their concerns and respond in negative ways without meaning to be difficult or unpleasant (Figure 1–11).

Practice. Consider why people act the way they do. Think about why an individual makes a nasty or provocative comment to another. Is that person trying to provoke an angry response, or is he so troubled about a problem that he lashes out verbally? Try to put yourself in that person's place to determine motivation. Behavior is more tolerable when you can consider a person's point of view and motivation.

Acceptance of criticism

An employee's work, behaviors, attitudes, and team contributions are reviewed and evaluated periodically by the worker's immediate supervisor. This process identifies areas of achievement, positive attributes, and interaction with team members. It also reviews unacceptable flaws in workplace behaviors, breaches in agency policy, and inaccurate performance of procedures. The evaluation includes recommendations for improvement, specific guidelines on how progress will be measured, and a time table of when the employee needs to have made these improvements to keep her job.

Needed improvements that are identified in daily performance and in these periodic evaluations sometimes come as a surprise to workers, especially those who think that they are outstanding performers. Hostility can result if the worker has limited insight into her own performance or resents constructive criticism. Remember, all workers in a facility are evaluated, and all have some areas where their performance could be improved. The evaluation should be a positive experience, not a crusade to find fault. Look at this evaluation process as a learning experience and gain from it. It isn't easy to accept criticism of performance and work habits, but facilities must employ the most talented workers for each job and help them become better. The entire

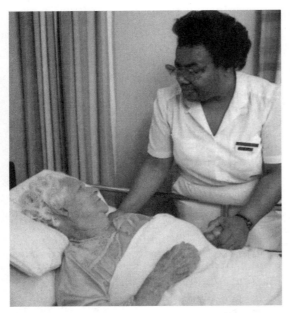

Figure 1–11 *An empathetic worker is an asset to the health care team and valued by patients.*

facility and individual employees profit from each worker giving his or her best to the job.

Practice. Avoid feeling personally attacked when a person of authority corrects your behavior or academic work. This is not meant to be a personal insult to you. Behaviors and school work can be improved, and you can learn from this experience if you are open to it. Listen to the comments and think about them. Then take appropriate action to improve.

Conflict resolution

In every workplace, differences arise between people. Understand that you do not have to like everyone you work with, but you must get along with them. Harmony in the workplace allows workers to feel good about their jobs and concentrate on carrying out their tasks. Disharmony, antagonism, hostility, and arguments cause disruptions and bad feelings. Much time and energy is wasted on them. Disharmony and negative attitudes cause workers to feel uncomfortable about coming to work. In an argumentative setting, workers focus more on taking sides than on patient care. The end result is poor quality patient care and loss of business.

When conflict arises between you and another person, try to deal with it in a positive, constructive way. Both of you can learn something. Talk to the person privately and peacefully about how those comments or actions affect you. Avoid being accusatory. If you are not comfortable meeting with this person alone, ask someone in authority (a teacher, counselor, or supervisor) to be present to keep the meeting constructive, positive, and objective. Ask the other person for a possible solution. Be sure to include the suggestions of the other person when developing a solution. Lay out a tentative resolution to the conflict, then plan another meeting to evaluate progress. Work toward maintaining a positive atmosphere in the workplace. Leave the door open for future negotiations. End on a positive note. Some facilities have conflict resolution committees that can mediate problems between workers or between employees and administrators.

Practice. Next time a sibling, classmate, or fellow worker makes a negative comment to you, think about how, when, and where you might respond. Practice what you would say to that person when the situation arises. Ask for a private conversation and relate how those comments affect you. See if the person is willing to change. Keep the meeting objective. Ask what you do that causes the person to make those comments. Together work to build a more positive relationship.

Self-motivation

Valued workers function well on their job because they want to do quality work. They willingly volunteer to take on extra tasks. They are eager to learn new skills and seek ways to improve their performances. They are imaginative and creative in how they carry out their duties. They make the most of their abilities and continually strive to do better. People who want to improve and actually carry out a plan are self-motivated.

Everyone is born with different mental and physical abilities. Self-motivation can help you to make the most of what you have but will not increase your innate capacity. Admission to some careers requires specific abilities plus a certain grade point average in high school and in prerequisite courses. Some fields are highly competitive to enter in school and to get employment in after graduation. Being self-motivated, and doing your best will help you stand out if your qualifications match those needed for a particular career.

Practice. Think about how you can improve your school work, work skills, and family relationships. Choose one area to work on. Trying to focus on too many at one time can lead to failure.

Tact

A thoughtful, refined manner of speaking is essential in the workplace. Patients and family members are particularly sensitive to communication with health care workers. Speaking with grace, patience, and diplomacy is comforting, especially when persons are upset, angry, or fearful. Carefully articulate in a slow rhythm, loud enough for elderly patients, anxious family members, and busy co-workers to hear and understand. Negative statements about physicians, procedures, or other workers are never acceptable. Reply to angry statements by acknowledging the person's feelings, but do not agree or make any negative remarks. Workers are expected to speak politely and to use good grammar. Swear words and foul language are not acceptable.

Practice. Listen to the speech pattern of others. Notice how people who use swear words and foul language frequently repeat these words. This habit limits the imagination and bores the listener. Repeating foul words does nothing to inspire or stimulate interesting ideas. Work toward omitting foul language from your vocabulary. Emulate a person whose speech you admire. Words are fun. Play with them. Learn new ones. Make up words to use as expletives instead of those old, worn-out swear words. Foul language is not acceptable in the workplace. It is crude and rude. To prepare yourself for situations where a person is upset, learn a few phrases that you can use so you will remember them when needed. These phrases should indicate that you understand how the person feels without giving an opinion. For example, "I can see that you are upset," "I'm sorry that you are having such a hard time," or "This is a difficult situation for you." Report patient complaints to your supervisor so the situation can be addressed.

Competence

People receiving health care have a right to expect that workers are proficient in problem solving and skill performance. Their lives and rehabilitation depend on it. Workers who are not capable bring harm to patients and lawsuits to facilities. Incompetent workers have no place in health care. Patient care and safety is the number one concern of health care workers. Health care is a team effort. Members need to work together for the good of the patients.

Practice. Recognize areas where you need to perform more accurately. This could be in school work, sports, language, or style. Decide who is the best person to help you and how you will ask for that help. To avoid harming someone in the workplace, be sure you are capable of carrying out your assigned tasks. If you are not comfortable with the procedure, ask the appropriate person to review the procedure with you or accompany you while you perform it.

Confidentiality

Every person has a right to privacy in all areas of life, especially in regard to personal health. Health care workers are privy to very personal information. For example, evidence of venereal disease can be detected by workers in the lab, impotence in a urologist's office, psychiatric diagnosis in the dietary department, cancer in radiology, and financial information in social work and admitting departments. With the use of computers in health care facilities, even more private information is available to workers. Personal information is secret and not to be shared with anyone, not even fellow workers. Gossip about private facts is harmful and can cost patients their job, marriage, or insurance coverage. People who come to a health care facility have a right to expect that their privacy will be strictly honored (Figure 1–12).

Practice. Remember to keep silent about a secret that a friend has told you, even when you know that it is big news and telling it would cause a colossal uproar. Do not tell anyone. You will be rewarded with a feeling of pride because you are responsible, dependable, and trustworthy.

Figure 1–12 *Confidentiality must be maintained with regard to health care records.*

Universal precautions

People who work in health care are at risk of infection and illness because they are in contact with individuals who are sick, harbor infectious agents, or carry pathogens in their secretions. Hand washing is one of the most effective ways of preventing the spread of organisms. People in some occupations are at higher risk of exposure than others because of the frequency with which they may encounter blood, body fluids, and airborne pathogens. Among health care workers who are at high risk are those who work in nursing and the medical laboratory. All patients, regardless of their diagnosis, are treated with the same careful measures: these are called **universal precautions** (Figure 1–13).

Body substance precautions (BSP) are the safety measures used to prevent

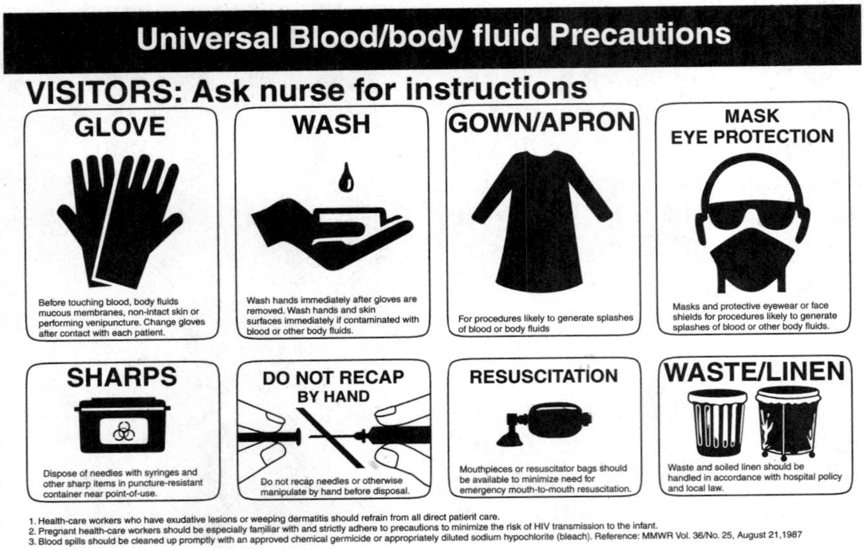

Universal Blood/body fluid Precautions

VISITORS: Ask nurse for instructions

GLOVE

Before touching blood, body fluids mucous membranes, non-intact skin or performing venipuncture. Change gloves after contact with each patient.

WASH

Wash hands immediately after gloves are removed. Wash hands and skin surfaces immediately if contaminated with blood or other body fluids.

GOWN/APRON

For procedures likely to generate splashes of blood or body fluids

MASK EYE PROTECTION

Masks and protective eyewear or face shields for procedures likely to generate splashes of blood or other body fluids.

SHARPS

Dispose of needles with syringes and other sharp items in puncture-resistant container near point-of-use.

DO NOT RECAP BY HAND

Do not recap needles or otherwise manipulate by hand before disposal.

RESUSCITATION

Mouthpieces or resuscitator bags should be available to minimize need for emergency mouth-to-mouth resuscitation.

WASTE/LINEN

Waste and soiled linen should be handled in accordance with hospital policy and local law.

1. Health-care workers who have exudative lesions or weeping dermatitis should refrain from all direct patient care.
2. Pregnant health-care workers should be especially familiar with and strictly adhere to precautions to minimize the risk of HIV transmission to the infant.
3. Blood spills should be cleaned up promptly with an approved chemical germicide or appropriately diluted sodium hypochlorite (bleach). Reference: MMWR Vol. 36/No. 25, August 21,1987

Figure 1–13 Universal precautions must be observed while working with all patients.

the transmission of organisms. To protect themselves, workers who come in contact with blood, body fluids, and airborne organisms wear protective clothing. This includes masks, goggles, gloves, aprons, gowns, and footwear covers (Figure 1–14). Not all types of protective clothing are worn all the time. The situation dictates how the workers will dress. Sometimes protective clothing is worn to protect patients. For example, respiratory therapists wear gloves to prevent patients from contracting infections from other patients. The gloves are changed after the therapist has handled equipment used by a patient. Body substance precautions include carefully disposing of all needles and sharps in puncture-proof, sealable containers and placing grossly soiled disposable materials in red plastic bags that will be handled in a special way.

Other hazardous substances that might be encountered in a health care setting are radioactive materials and toxic chemicals. People who work in areas where those substances are present are given special instruction.

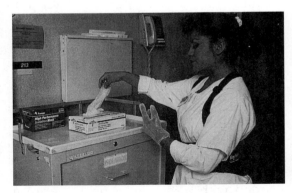

Figure 1–14 Gloves should be worn whenever contact with blood, body fluids, mucous membranes, or broken skin is possible.

WORKPLACE READINESS

During high school and after graduation are important times for employment because they usually mark the beginning of your job history. Your job performance evaluations and references from previous employers will be the basis on which you will seek future jobs or admission to college. Having learned employability skills, you are now ready to enter the job market. To be successful in obtaining a job, you will need guidelines on writing a résumé, cover letter, and job application; tips on interviewing; and clues you can use for the first day on the job. Keep in mind that as a new worker, you will begin at the bottom of the job ladder in both tasks and pay. After you prove yourself, you will be given more responsibility and pay.

Résumé

A **résumé** is a one-page summary of academic achievements and job history in outline form. It creates an impression of you. If you are seeking a first job, you have no job history, but you do have an academic record.

Begin your résumé by placing your name, address, and telephone number at the top. Then state an objective or job desired. Next, list your schools, years attended, and ultimate outcome, just as you would on a job application. List the most current school first, then go back in time. If you have held a paid or volunteer position, begin with the latest. Be truthful. These may be checked and verified. Be sure to include a section on honors, offices held, and volunteer activities. List your special skills if they are appropriate to the job; for example, entering computer data or taking vital signs. If you have helped pay for any college courses, include a statement such as, "Assisted with the cost of post-secondary education."

Attach a list of three references from teachers, counselors, or employers. Avoid using relatives. Again, be sure these people have agreed and will give you a good reference. If you were fired from a job, do not give that employer as a reference. Type or print out from a word processor your résumé on quality paper. Spell correctly. When responding to a newspaper advertisement, send your résumé and a cover letter to the person at the address given.

Cover letter

The cover letter is is an opportunity to introduce yourself in narrative form. It should be on one page in proper business format. Use correct grammar and spelling. Address the letter to the person and department given in the advertisement or call the facility and ask the name, proper title, and department of the person to whom you are to send the letter. State your purpose for writing the letter. Express interest in the job. Explain why you are applying for the job. If responding to a newspaper advertisement, state the name and date of the publication in which the ad appeared. If referred by an employee, state that person's name and job title. Include a brief overview of your educational and work histories and a little information about yourself. Explain how you became aware of this position and what motivated you to apply. Describe why you are a good candiate for this job. Do not repeat information.

Avoid wordiness; the details are on your résumé. Conclude by clearly stating when and how you can be contacted. Mail this cover letter with your résumé and list of references to the appropriate person.

Job application

An employer identifies certain personal qualities and technical skills needed for each available position. Be sure that your interests and qualifications match those stated in the advertisement. Job applications may be the only tool used by a company to identify the candidates who will be called to interview. The job application represents you. Complete it carefully and totally, front and back. Follow the directions. Use neat, legible penmanship and good grammar. Spell correctly. List previous jobs, beginning with the latest. For each, include the address of the company, your hourly wage, dates of employment, and the reason you left it. Complete the education section with your schools and years attended, major area of study, and type of diploma, certificate, or degree earned. Include honors and awards you have received, such as perfect attendance awards, National Honor Society, organization or class offices, honor or merit roll. List three references other than relatives who have agreed to recommend you. For each reference, include their name, occupation, workplace or home address, and phone number. Be sure your references remember you and will give you a good recommendation. Teachers and previous employers write good references (Figure 1–15, pp. 20–21).

Interview

Here is your chance to make a good impression in person. Before the interview, attend to personal grooming. Shower, shampoo, wear a deodorant, and brush your teeth. People asociated with health care need to be clean. Avoid eating raw onions and garlic or smoking before the interview. Since most health care facilities are smoke-free, nonsmoking applicants may be preferred. Fresh breath is especially important, but do not chew gum. Wear clean, unwrinkled clothes and a minimum of jewelry. Avoid short shorts and skirts. Use makeup and fragrances sparingly. Read about the facility to know something about it. Prepare a written list of questions you need to have answered during the interview. For example, "How many hours per week does this job entail?" Have ready a response to the questions, "Why do you want to work here?", "Why should we hire you for this job?", and "What do you look for in a job?" When preparing, make a list of the personal assets and outstanding job skills that you would bring to the job so you can discuss them during the interview.

Arrive early, with pen, notebook, CPR certification card, and hepatitis B vaccine verification, if applicable. You will need a photo ID, such as a driver's license, and your social security card, birth certificate, passport, or immigration card to prove that you are eligible to work in the United States. Bring the completed application and list of references, if not previously submitted.

When you meet the interviewer, shake hands and call that person by name (Figure 1–16, p. 22). During the interview, look directly at the person speaking. Appear pleasant, interested, and eager to work. Listen to the interviewer. Answer questions appropriately and briefly using good grammar. Be polite. Take notes to remember major facts. Be willing to start small to learn the job, gain experience, and hone skills. Avoid criticizing a former employer. Keep a positive attitude. Do not discuss your personal problems. Review the job description, uniform requirements, and potential for advancement. Do not ask about holidays or vacation until the end of the interview and then only if you have not been informed. If you want the job, avoid telling the interviewer what you are not willing to do, such as work weekends and holidays. Thank the interviewer at the end of the appointment. Ask when a decision will be made about filling the position. Many prospective employees may be interviewed before a decision is made.

After the interview, write a brief note to the interviewer. Include some of your impressions of the facility and the job. Express your gratitude for the time the interviewer spent with you. Say how much you are looking forward to hearing if you have been accepted for the position. If you were hired at the end of the interview, write that you anticipate a long and productive association with the facility. Thank you notes indicate thoughtfulness and may play a part in your being hired.

First day on the job

Everyone has a first day on the job. It is the most difficult day because you don't know the people, the job, or the facility. You don't know if your fellow employees will like you or if you will like them. You are now part of a team that has for its focus the goals of the facility or company. If this is your first job, realize that for the first time in your life, you are not the center of attention as you were at home and in school. You will need to shift your focus from yourself to your team and its goals. To become a valued member of that team and gain an understanding of the work to be done, you will want to follow these guidelines.

1. Look interested and friendly. The staff wants you to like the job and workplace. Your facial expressions, polite pattern of speech, attention, and willingness to work will determine how much they will like you.

2. Think about and talk about the department's work, associated careers, and patient care. Do not talk about your dates, prom clothes, family problems, or zits. Discussion of those topics is burdensome to other employees.

3. Introduce yourself to those you do not know. Maintain a positive attitude even though you may be irritated that you need to ask so many questions to function safely and well.

4. Choose your words carefully. Profanity and grossly descriptive words are not welcome in the workplace. Be polite. Say "please" and "thank you" appropriately.

5. Learn the tasks assigned. Ask if you are unsure. Admit errors and work toward correcting them. Don't ruminate about them; just don't repeat them.

6. Request chores to be a part of the team. When you finish one, ask for another. Build on your knowledge. What you do today, you can do tomorrow. Go ahead and do it. Look for things to do. Answer the department telephone by giving the department name and your name, and then asking, "May I help you?" Take complete messages.

HOSPITAL APPLICATION

Employment Application

Date _____

Position applying for _____

AN EQUAL OPPORTUNITY EMPLOYER M/F/H

□ Full Time
□ Part Time
□ PRN (as needed) # Hours _____

Last Name	First	Middle	Social Security No.	Other Name Worked Under

Address: Number and Street	City	State	Zip	Home Phone	Alternate Phone

In case of emergency contact: Name _____ Phone _____ Relationship _____

How did you learn about this hospital? □ Newspaper □ Career Day □ Friend □ Live in the area □ Other: _____

What shifts can you work?
□ Day □ Rotating □ Evening □ Night

Will you work other shifts? □ Yes □ No

Will you work on call? □ Yes □ No

Will you work weekends and holidays? □ Yes □ No

Upon offer of employment, can you submit verification of your legal right to work in the U.S.? □ Yes □ No

If employed and you are under 18, can you furnish a work permit? □ Yes □ No

Do you have any physical or mental limitations which would prevent you from performing any of the duties of the job for which you are applying? □ Yes □ No If YES, what can be done to accommodate your limitations? _____

Have you ever been convicted by any court of any offense? □ Yes □ No (Omit minor traffic violations and any offense which was adjudicated in a juvenile Court. Existence of a criminal record does not constitute an automatic bar to employment.) If YES, give details: _____

EDUCATION

Did you either graduate from High School or obtain a GED Certificate? □ Yes □ No If no, number of years at school. _____
Name and address of High School _____

COLLEGE, TRADE, PROFESSIONAL, OR OTHER SCHOOLS AFTER HIGH SCHOOL

Name	Street Address	City	State	Major	Degree

LICENSE / CERTIFICATION / REGISTRATION

Show title, date expires, serial number and which state or agency issued it. If pending, give date expected: _____

SPECIAL SKILLS

Typing rate: _____
Shorthand rate: _____
Transcription: _____
Other: _____

	Yes	No
Medical Terminology	□ Yes	□ No
Word Processing	□ Yes	□ No
Computer	□ Yes	□ No

FOR OFFICE USE ONLY

ARRANGE INTERVIEW: □ Yes □ No	DATE OF INTERVIEW:	DATE OF PHYSICAL:	START DATE:	STATUS: □ FT □ PT □ CONT □ TEMP □ PRNA □ PRNB

TITLE:	JOB CODE:	DEPT. NAME/NO.:	SHIFT: □ DAY □ ROTATING □ EVENING □ NIGHT	HOURS PER PAY:	RATE:

EMPLOYMENT

List employment references. Begin with most recent employer.

1. Employer _____ From _____ To _____
   Address _____
   Title _____ Salary _____ Reason for Leaving _____

2. Employer _____ From _____ To _____
   Address _____
   Title _____ Salary _____ Reason for Leaving _____

3. Employer _____ From _____ To _____
   Address _____
   Title _____ Salary _____ Reason for Leaving _____

4. Employer _____ From _____ To _____
   Address _____
   Title _____ Salary _____ Reason for Leaving _____

List any Military Service: Branch _____

Have you ever been employed by this hospital? ☐ Yes ☐ No
Dates: _____ to _____ Title _____

May we contact your present employer for references?
☐ Yes ☐ No

PERSONAL/PROFESSIONAL REFERENCES

List two persons other than relatives and former employers whom we may contact for references.

1. Name _____ Phone _____
   Address _____
   Occupation _____

2. Name _____ Phone _____
   Address _____
   Occupation _____

PLEASE READ CAREFULLY

AGREEMENT: I authorize this hospital to investigate all statements contained in this application and to obtain evaluations from all former employers, schools attended, and personal references. If any misrepresentations or omission of fact has been made by me, or if the results of an investigation are unsatisfactory, I understand that my application may be rejected or I may be dismissed, if hired. I hereby release this hospital, any agent acting on its behalf, and any former employers from any liability for damage which may result from such investigation or the disclosure of information concerning my former or prospective employment.

I also understand that employment is contingent upon satisfactory completion of a pre-employment physical examination which includes a medically-approved laboratory test for the detection of narcotics and other substances, the presence of which may affect my performance as an employee. I am aware that my employment may be terminated with or without cause and with or without notice, at any time, at my option or at the option of the hospital. I understand that no one, other than the CEO of the hospital, has the authority to enter into any employment agreement for any specified period of time or to make an employment agreement that is contrary to the preceding statement.

After employment, I understand that I will receive a copy of the Hospital's Employee Handbook and that the rules and regulations discussed therein are subject to change by the hospital without prior notice to employees; therefore, the Handbook, as well as other policy communication tools, should not be viewed as terms or conditions of an employment contract, either expressed or implied.

I understand that this application will be considered only for open/posted positions which are available when the application is submitted.

Signature: _____ Date _____

Revised 7/92

Figure 1–15 Hospital Application.

Figure 1–16 *Shake hands firmly and smile when you greet an interviewer.*

7. Remember that patient care and safety is the number one concern. If you are not a licensed professional and do not know the patients, do not do things to and for patients without specific direction and permission.

8. Do not eat in patient care areas. Do not bring munchies from home, search the refrigerator for patient snacks, or rummage through the staff's lunch bags.

9. Do not sit unless you are on official break, eating lunch, or assigned to a task that requires sitting. Parking yourself in a chair sends a message that you are not willing to work. Only people who have worked more than four hours are entitled to a scheduled break.

10. Wear a friendly expression and stand tall, with your shoulders back and your hands out of pockets. Take a deep breath, straighten your clothes, and go to work. You will do well! Go to it!

Biography

When I was in high school, I registered for a career program in a hospital setting. Though I enjoyed the program and learned job skills, I found that the science component was too hard for me to learn. However, I really enjoyed the people. They had positive attitudes and a helpful spirit. After graduation, I went to work in a law firm. What a different atmosphere! It seemed to me that the exclusive goal of this firm was to make money. I was paid a good salary to work as a receptionist, but I just wasn't comfortable there. Over time, I came to realize that I needed a nurturing environment. I missed the climate of a health care facility. Employees there work to help others.

Since I had taken a computer course in high school, I was able to obtain a clerk position in a hospital dietary department. I enter data into the computer and generate menus with a word processing program. Though I make less money in health care, I am much happier. This is the beginning of my working life, so I have time to work my way up the career ladder. Using the hospital's tuition reimbursement plan, I take courses at the local community college. I hope to remain in health care because of the unique attitude of health care workers.

Career Search

School learning, media, career, or counseling centers and community libraries have books, computer programs, and Internet connections through which you can investigate various careers in health care. These materials explain entrance requirements, recommended preparatory courses, and the kind of roles found in various careers. Some programs list the schools in your area, state, and across the nation that offer education in particular careers. Some books and periodicals rank schools in order of excellence in preparing students for certain careers. In addition, many videotapes and CD-ROM programs show members of health careers in action.

To determine a career for yourself, your first step is to identify your interests. Discuss with your counselor the results of the Interest and Preference Inventories and the Student Profile of Employability Skills that you completed during the eighth, ninth, or tenth grade. Or arrange with your counselor to take a computerized test to determine your academic and activity interests and what areas of study and work are best suited to you.

The second step is to evaluate your overall abilities. Include your grade point average (GPA) and subject areas in which you received high grades (A's and B's). Then match your field of interest and your abilities to a few careers.

The third step is to get yourself on the scene to see those careers in action. Find out if your school has a shadowing, apprenticeship, or mentorship program. If not, try to get a volunteer position or low-level job in your area of career interest to see what employees really do on their jobs. By following this investigative process, you will be basing your career decisions on real experience and realistic expectations.

Schools have certain prerequisites that must be achieved before they will consider an applicant for a career program. These may include a minimum GPA and previous volunteer or work experience in the health field. Schools seek students who are capable of passing the courses. Because of limited space in programs, finite clinical sites, and limited job availability, an applicant's GPA, leadership qualities, work or volunteer experience, quality of application, and references are seriously evaluated.

The job market differs from year to year, depending on a variety of factors. It is important to select a career that will offer employment. To determine current job availability in your field of interest, review the *Occupational Outlook Handbook*, published every two years by the U.S. Department of Labor's Bureau of Labor Statistics. The school's learning center or public library will have a copy.

Range of Annual Incomes

As a new worker in any job, you will receive an hourly rate or yearly salary at the bottom of the range. You will remain there until you prove your worth to the company, which will be evaluated at your job review. If you have previous job or volunteer experience, you may begin at one step higher on the salary range. More employers give merit raises than give automatic annual raises to reward quality of work and other job skills.

Wages are influenced by several factors, including geographic location. In large cities, where the cost of living is high, hourly wages may be higher than in rural areas. Complexity of skills needed for the job, leadership requirements, and available workforce are some other factors that influence wages.

What's New

As in other industries, there is no money to spare in health care. Each facility needs workers who will give 100 percent of their energies and focus on task. Productivity and quality of work are key to keeping a job. The wave of the future is cross-training workers to perform more than one role. For example, health care associates, service care associates, equipment technicians, and unit secretaries are being cross-trained to perform each of these jobs; respiratory technicians are trained to do electrocardiographs (EKGs). Remember, the more you are capable of doing in a job setting, the more valuable you are to the facility and the more likely you are to keep your job.

School to Work

This section demonstrates how school-based learning carries over to work-based learning. That is, how the courses taken in school apply to the workplace. In this chapter, academics are applied to skills that will be used in all health care careers. Specific school-to-work applications will be included in individual chapters. Some skills are learned in a high school laboratory. Some may be learned in a mentorship or apprenticeship program or through volunteer service.

Academic Subject	Workplace Skills
Arts	—Create a poster.
	—Draw a graph or pie-shaped chart.
	—Diagram items.
	—Locate photographs on a topic.
Business	—Answer the telephone.
Time Management	—Schedule appointments.
	—Use time effectively and efficiently.
Communication	—Write formal business letters.
	—Use a fax machine.

Academic Subject	Workplace Skills
Business	—Assess client's history.
English	—Write accurate, understandable messages.
	—Read with understanding.
Computer Skills	—Enter data appropriately.
	—Interpret data.
	—Use a modem.
Word Processing	—Write business letters.
Economics	—Develop cost-containment measures.
	—Understand insurance plans and managed health care.
Bookkeeping Systems	—Enter data appropriately.
	—Collect overdue bills.
	—Transfer information to the business department.
Filing Systems	—Organize department files.
	—File charts and reports appropriately.
Career and Guidance	—Take a career interest inventory test.
	—Shadow, volunteer, or work with a mentor.
	—View a video on health care careers in this department.
	—Visit a community college or university on career day.
	—Obtain the catalogue of a college offering dental programs.
	—Write a paper stating the duties of specific health care careers.
Education Levels	—Research prerequisites for health care careers.
	—Describe the length and content of the education required for specific health care careers.
English and Communications	—Read and write medical documentation.
	—Interpret reports and manuals.
Medical Terminology	—Use correct medical terms.
Medical Dictionary, Glossary	—Locate correct medical terms.
	—Spell terms correctly.
	—Document completely and accurately.
Speech Class	—Express directions clearly and understandably.
	—Reinforce instructions.
	—Determine the understanding of the listener.
Health Education and Safety	
Universal Precautions	—Use careful techniques to avoid infecting yourself and others.
	—Wash hands often according to accepted technique.
	—Wear appropriate clothing.

School to Work—continued

Academic Subject	Workplace Skills
Health Education and Safety (cont'd)	
Cardiopulmonary Resuscitation (CPR)	—Know when and how to call for help.
Pathophysiology	—Recognize malfunctions of certain organs.
Pharmacology	—Understand effects of medications on the ailing body part.
Radiology	—Protect body parts and persons not to be radiated.
Social Sciences	
Culture	—Consider the practices of various ethnic groups when working with patients.
Education	—Talk on a level that all patients can understand.
Ethics	—Maintain patients' rights and self-determination.
	—Treat all patients with respect.
	—Use work time to work.
	—Exhibit loyalty to co-workers and the facility.
Gerontology	—Meet the special needs of elderly patients.
Group Dynamics	—Work with health team members for the good of patients.
	—Make a special effort to be pleasant in the workplace.
Growth and Development	—Understand patients' needs are different at various ages.
Health Care	—Wear protective clothing to safeguard clients.
	—Wash hands appropriately.
Human Relations	—Understand family dynamics.
	—Respect the religious practices of others.
	—Honor the cultural beliefs of others.
Law	—Maintain complete and accurate documentation.
	—Respect patients' confidentiality.
	—Comply with facility rules and regulations.
	—Operate within the guidelines of your job description.
	—Follow emergency procedures and protocols.
	—Administer emergency measures when needed.
Personal Hygiene	—Maintain clean hair and body.
	—Avoid wearing strong fragrances.
	—Have fresh breath and clean teeth.
	—Keep your hands away from your face.
	—Maintain a clean uniform.
	—Wear little jewelry, especially on your hands.
Mechanical Maintenance	—Observe and report hazardous conditions.
	—Notice and report equipment in need of repair.
	—Locate emergency electrical outlets.
	—Find firefighting equipment.
Body Mechanics	—Use proper techniques when lifting.

Academic Subject	Workplace Skills
Mathematics	
Accounting	—Bill clients and insurance companies.
Addition, Subtraction	—Post insurance and client payments.
	—Determine balances owed.
	—Prepare deposit slips and receipts.
	—Pay suppliers or authorize payment by another department.
Division	—Order supplies.
Science	
Anatomy and Physiology	—Identify body structures.
Biochemistry	—Relate normal range of chemical elements in blood.
Microbiology	—Apply universal precautions techniques.
Nutrition and Food Science	—Articulate the relationship of diet to disease.
Mental and Social Needs of Humans	—Understand that illness causes stress.
	—Administer thoughtful, supportive care.
	—Allow patients to vent feelings.
Psychology	—Keep the atmosphere calm and friendly.
	—Encourage patients' efforts toward healthy living.
Religion	—Respect all religious practices.
Teamwork	—Work well with others.
	—Maintain a positive attitude.
	—Respect others' efforts.
	—Cooperate with group efforts.
	—Help others.

Review Questions

1. Define six job skills and explain how each is shown in the workplace. Use three sentences for each. Include the "most important" job skill.

2. What is your best work habit? Explain how you developed it and how you show that skill.

3. What does each letter in the acronym for problem solving stand for? Apply the process by writing out each step in your decision to "get out of bed in the morning" or "to come to school or work."

4. Based on the guidelines in this chapter, list five items to be considered when writing a résumé, five when writing a cover letter, and five when filling out a job application.

5. List five things you will remember to do during your first day on the job. In one sentence for each item, explain why you chose these as important.

BIOMETRICS DEPARTMENT

Objectives

After completing this chapter, you should be able to:

- ❑ Explain the goal of the biometrics department.
- ❑ Describe each career in this department.
- ❑ Identify the required education and credentials for each career.
- ❑ Describe the skills performed in this department.
- ❑ Recognize how academic subjects apply in the workplace.

Key Terms

Pulse

Blood pressure

    Systolic   Diastolic

Diagnostic tests

    Electrocardiograph   Stress test   Ultrasound
    Echocardiograph   Electroencephalograph

INTRODUCTION

In the biometrics department, life-sustaining organs are visualized and their functions assessed. The physical condition and performance of the heart, blood vessels, brain, and nerves are recorded (Figure 2–1). Most tests are done by technicians and technologists and interpreted by physicians. Some are performed by physicians, who are assisted by technicians.

The division of duties and types of careers within departments may differ according to facility policy. When the department deals with all heart and lung functions, it is called the cardiopulmonary department. Biometrics and respiratory therapy may be divisions within that

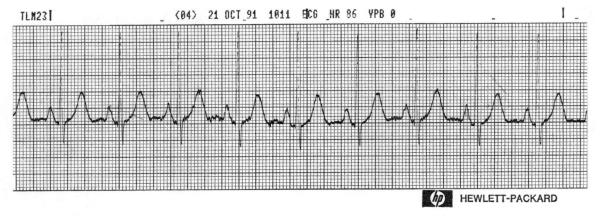

Figure 2–1 *An EKG strip showing normal sinus rhythm.*

department. The biometrics department conducts tests to measure heart, blood vessel, and brain function. The respiratory therapy (or pulmonary) department conducts lung function tests and performs treatments related to breathing.

GOAL

The goal of the biometrics department is to record accurate assessments of the heart, blood vessels, brain, and nerves and perform certain tests that will allow physicians to identify the physical condi-

tion and degree of function of cardiovascular and neurological structures.

CAREER DESCRIPTIONS

Biometrics offers several careers. Titles will vary according to the type of educational program completed, field of specialty, the employer's policy, and geographic location. Technicians may enter the field after a short on-the-job training program or attendance at a seminar. Technologists enter the field after a longer formal program, often in a college setting.

CAREER HIERARCHY

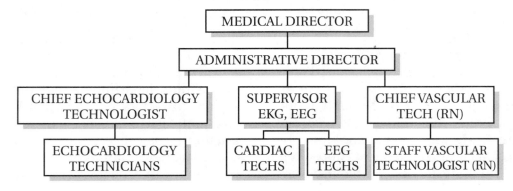

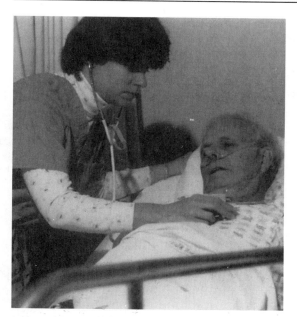

Figure 2–2 *The biometrics staff works with many types of patients.*

The biometrics staff works with patients of all ages, conditions, and levels of consciousness (Figure 2–2). They work with newborns and elderly, conscious and unconscious patients. They screen for circulatory problems and organ disfunction in well people. They also help to identify the effects of CPR on heart function in critically ill patients who were resuscitated after undergoing cardiac arrest.

Biometrics staff are important members of the health team. They help physicians determine abnormal physical status so that appropriate medications and treatments can be prescribed to help patients sustain or regain health.

Technicians in biometrics are electrocardiographic (EKG), echocardiographic (ECG), and cardiac. Technologists in biometrics are cardiovascular, electroencephalographic (EEG), and vascular.

Opportunities in biometrics

Employment opportunities vary. Biometrics staff work in hospitals, clinics, and physician offices. They work with ambulatory patients and in critical care areas of acute care institutions. EEG technologists can work in a neurologist's office, psychiatric facility, or the research department of a university, pharmaceutical company, or the military.

Work hours for cardiac technicians are in the day and evening of every day of the year; respiratory therapists often perform EKGs during the night in acute care facilities. Vascular and EEG technologists work Monday through Friday on the day shift. In clinics and physician offices, work hours are the day shift, Monday through Friday, with some evening and Saturday hours.

Career advancements include chief technologist and department director positions. Lateral moves include changing from office to hospital or clinic positions. Technicians can return to school to become technologists. Continuing education courses help to increase technical skills, increase responsibility, and enhance job security because the individual is able to do more and different kinds of tests. On a personal level, performing a variety of tests makes the job more interesting. With a bachelor's or master's degree, teaching may be an option.

Desired personal characteristics include good verbal communication skills, accurate work habits, ability to work in a stressful environment, and an aptitude for working with technical equipment. Other attributes include sensitivity to the needs of patients and professional staff, and being responsible, self-directed, and able to follow instructions.

Job satisfaction comes from performing an essential service, doing a job well, working closely with professional people, and continually increasing knowledge as technology expands and equipment is updated.

Biometrics roles

Cardiologists specialize in the diagnosis and treatment of cardiovascular diseases. A cardiologist serves as the medical advisor to the biometrics department, working with staff to perform certain diagnostic tests and interpreting those results. A summary of every test is written and sent to each patient's physician.

Electrocardiographic technicians are responsible for performing electrocardiographs, the most common test performed on the heart. The EKG traces electrical impulses from the heart onto special graph paper, showing the effectiveness of heart muscle contractions and the presence and extent of heart muscle damage. It is a health screening test, a tool to diagnose heart disease.

Technicians attach electrodes and manage the electrocardiograph machine to record a graphic tracing for interpretation by a physician, usually a cardiologist. Technicians review tracings for quality, screen the machine's computerized data, report serious or life-threatening heart rhythms, post the tracing paper, and file the printout. In the hospital, technicians are responsible for transporting the machine to patients' bedsides, attaching electrodes, and running EKGs even during cardiac resuscitation. In addition, technicians are responsible for the care and cleaning of the EKG machines and for maintaining supplies.

Cardiac technicians record electrocardiographs and attach leads for Holter monitor tests (portable EKGs). After the Holter monitor has been worn by a patient for twenty-four hours and the EKG recorded on tape cassettes, technicians run those tapes through a scanner to detect irregular heartbeats and record simultaneous patient activities that may have precipitated those arrhythmias. These records are then submitted to a physician for interpretation of heart function.

Cardiac technicians also work with physicians in stress tests and thallium scans. During stress tests, technicians run the computer and assist the physician with the nuclear scanner after thallium is injected into the patient. They also check cardiac pacemaker function by running an EKG-type test to determine if the pacemaker is controlling the heart rate properly.

Cardiovascular technologists perform diagnostic tests to obtain information about the structure and function of the heart and blood vessels. This information helps physicians diagnose congenital and acquired heart disease, coronary artery disease, causes of hypertension, and peripheral vascular disease. These tests include echocardiography, cardiac Doppler flow studies, stress tests, arrhythmia scanning, pacemaker function tests, and EKG procedures. Cardiovascular technologists teach patients about health maintenance and illness prevention.

Figure 2–3 *An echocardiograph uses a computer to evaluate cardiac function, reveal heart valve irregularity, and show defects or diseases of the heart.* (Photo by Marcia Butterfield, courtesy of W. A. Foote Memorial Hospital, Jackson, Michigan.)

Echocardiographic technicians (Figure 2–3) perform echocardiographs using sounds that are not audible by the human ear. The echoes of these ultrasound waves graphically picture structures of the heart. No radioactive materials are used.

Vascular technologists are trained to perform tests on veins and arteries. These tests include duplex scans and Doppler ultrasound. Qualifying for acceptance into a vascular technologist program may require working for one year in a health care facility, having a bachelor of science degree, or having another health care career, such as being a cardiac technician or nurse.

Electroencephalographic technologists are responsible for performing electroencephalographs, and nerve conduction

and evoked potential studies. Technologists work with sleep studies, recording brain activity and nerve conduction. Responsibilities include positioning patients, applying electrodes to the head, and setting controls on the instrument that traces brain activity on special graphic paper. Technologists are responsible for the quality of the tracing. They need to recognize when changes occur in patients and react appropriately.

Neurologists are physicians who specialize in the structure and function of the brain, spinal cord, nerves, and diseases associated with the nervous system. These physicians are responsible for interpreting EEGs, nerve conduction velocity, and evoked potential tests.

JOB AVAILABILITY

Opportunities in the field of biometrics are only fair. The U.S. Department of Labor estimates that the demand for EKG and cardiac technicians will decrease to the year 2005 because other workers are being cross-trained to perform electrocardiograph and Holter monitor tests. The need for cardiovascular and EEG technologists will grow slightly faster than average through the year 2005.

Keep in mind that this is a relatively small field. Consequently, jobs are not as abundant as those in other careers.

SKILLS

In a hospital setting, some tests must be available twenty-four hours a day, every day of the year. To ensure it has staff members who can carry out emergency procedures on all shifts, some hospitals

EDUCATION AND CREDENTIALS

CAREER	YEARS OF EDUCATION AFTER HIGH SCHOOL	DEGREE OR DIPLOMA	TESTED BY; LICENSED BY
Cardiologist (M.D. or D.O.)	4 yrs. college 4 yrs. medical school 3 yrs. postgraduate training	M.D. or D.O., Certificate	ABIM; registered by the state; ACLS certification
Electrocardiograph technician	3 months	Certificate OJT	Optional
Cardiac technician R.C.T. or C.C.T.	1 year (3 quarters)	Certificate	Optional
Cardiovascular technologist (R.D.V.T.)	2 years (5 quarters)	A.A.S.D. in cardiovascular technology	(Certification depends on specialty)
Echocardiographic technician R.D.C.S. or R.D.M.S.	2-year community college academic program, a hospital program, or 6-month preceptorship training program	A.A.S.D.	Optional; A.R.D.M.S.
Vascular technologist R.D.V.T.	Previous health care plus seminar or on-the-job training	Certificate	—
Electroencephalographic technologist R.EEG.T.	2 years	Associate or applied science degree or certification after hospital program	ABRET (optional)
Neurologist (M.D. or D.O.)	4 years of college plus 4 years medical school and 4 years postgraduate work	M.D. or D.O., Certificate in neurology	ABPN; State

Key to abbreviations:

A.A.S.D.—Associate of Applied Science Degree
ABRET—American Board of Registration of EEG Technologists
ABIM—American Board of Internal Medicine
ABPN—American Board of Psychiatry and Neurology
ACLS—Advanced Cardiac Life Support
AMA—American Medical Association
A.R.D.M.S.—American Registry of Diagnostic Medical Sonographers
C.C.T.—Certified Cardiac Technician
D.O.—Doctor of Osteopathy
M.D.—Medical Doctor
R.EEG.T.—Registered Electroencephalographic Technologist
R.C.T.—Registered Cardiac Technician
R.D.C.S.—Registered Diagnostic Cardiac Sonographer
R.D.M.S.—Registered Diagnostic Medical Sonographer
R.D.V.T.—Registered Diagnostic Vascular Technologist

train respiratory therapists to perform EKGs.

Skills learned include tests to measure heart function, identify structure and function of the heart and blood vessels, measure brain waves, and study the speed of nerve conduction. Each technician and technologist learns resuscitation procedures to support life in a cardiac arrest and safety measures to protect patients with grand mal seizures. Often, skills are performed in stressful situations since biometric technicians report to all hospital emergencies. Other skills include learning updated computer programs that accompany testing instruments and caring for equipment.

Biometrics tests

Pulse taking is the most basic test done on the cardiovascular system (Figure 2–4). Counting the **pulse** includes measuring the rate, rhythm, and strength of the heartbeat. Each pulse "throb" represents one heartbeat, one arterial "ripple" every time the heart beats. Characteristics of the pulse are indicative of the person's condition.

Blood pressure is the second most basic test done to measure the function of the cardiovascular system. It is the measurement of the force of the blood as it pushes against the walls of the blood vessels when the heart contracts and relaxes. **Systolic** pressure is the amount of force exerted against the wall of the vessel when the heart contracts, or beats. It is always the top number. **Diastolic** pressure is the amount of force exerted against the wall of the vessel when the

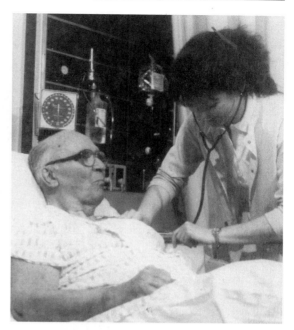

Figure 2–4 *Apical pulse taking.*

heart relaxes between beats. It is always the bottom number.

Diagnostic tests

An electrocardiograph is a graphic tracing of the electrical activity of the heart. A penlike instrument draws a graph on special paper as electrical currents move through the heart muscle. An abnormal pattern indicates heart damage.

A Holter monitor is a twenty-four-hour electrocardiograph (Figure 2–5). The patient wears five electrodes and a portable tape recorder for twenty-four hours. A diary of activities is simultaneously recorded. The test determines irregular heartbeats and patterns, and associates those whenever possible with the activity that occurred at the same time.

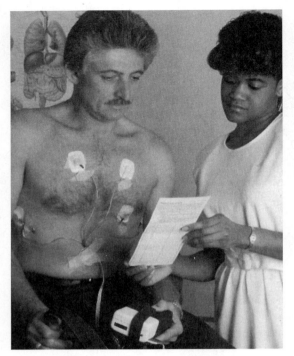

Figure 2–5 *Electrocardiograph technicians assist with Holter monitorings of the heart.*

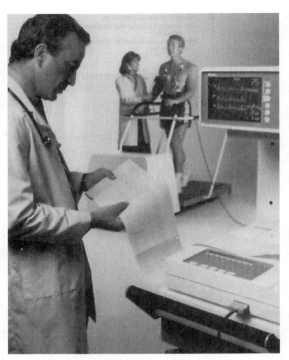

Figure 2–6 *Computers are used to perform stress tests to evaluate the function of a patient's heart during exercise.* (Courtesy of Siemens Burdick, Inc.)

An exercise tolerance test (stress test) is done by a physician assisted by a technician to determine the heart's response to various levels of exercise (Figure 2–6). The patient walks on a treadmill while the heart and blood pressure are monitored. The patient's physical activity rises as the treadmill gradually increases in speed. Depending on the patient's endurance, the physician may prescribe an exercise program, medication, or further testing.

An exercise tolerance test with thallium is a stress test plus an intravenous injection of a radioactive substance called thallium (Figure 2–7). This substance circulates through the blood vessels in the heart muscle. The concentration is measured with a scanner immediately after the exercise session and again when the heart is at rest. The physician compares the resulting scans for blood distribution in the heart muscle during exercise and when the patient is at rest.

Ultrasound is an examination that uses sound waves to detect normal and abnormal structure and function of a body part. Sound waves travel from the machine to the part of the body to be studied, bounce off the structure, and return to the machine. The returning sound waves create a picture of the structure on the computer screen. The use of sound

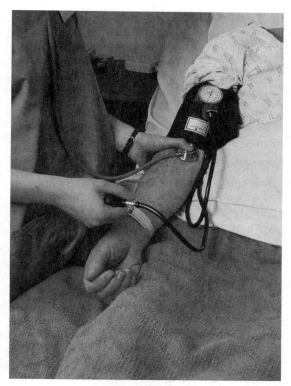

Figure 2–7 *Place the stethoscope over the brachial artery to listen for the blood pressure sounds.*

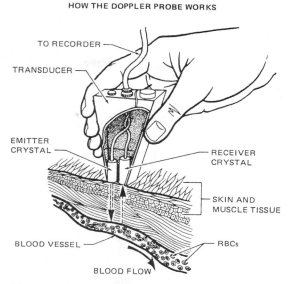

HOW THE DOPPLER PROBE WORKS

TO RECORDER

TRANSDUCER

EMITTER CRYSTAL

RECEIVER CRYSTAL

SKIN AND MUSCLE TISSUE

BLOOD VESSEL

RBCs

BLOOD FLOW

Figure 2–8 *Doppler ultrasound.*

waves is particularly helpful in locating abnormalities of blood flow and problems with blood vessel structure. It can detect plaque disease, arteriosclerosis, and aneurysms. Ultrasound tests are named according to the technique used or the part to be studied—echocardiograph, Doppler ultrasound (Figure 2–8), and duplex scanner. Ultrasound is especially effective in detecting blood vessel function (blood flow through the vessels), whereas arteriography (X ray of arteries) is effective in detecting blood vessel structure.

An **echocardiograph** is a test that uses sound waves to visualize the heart and valves. Sound waves travel from the machine, bounce off the heart, and return to the machine, forming a picture on the screen. The waves show the size of the heart's chambers. During the test, heart motion is recorded on videotape so it can be later reviewed to determine how well the heart functions. Also, the machine prints an image of the heart on paper. A Doppler ultrasound test is always done with an echocardiograph (Figure 2–9).

A Doppler ultrasound is a test that uses sound waves with amplification. The purpose is to detect the flow of circulation in blood vessels that are close to the surface of the body. Sound waves are sent toward a blood vessel where they bounce off blood cells as they pass through the vessel before returning to the Doppler instrument, where they are amplified. The presence of sound

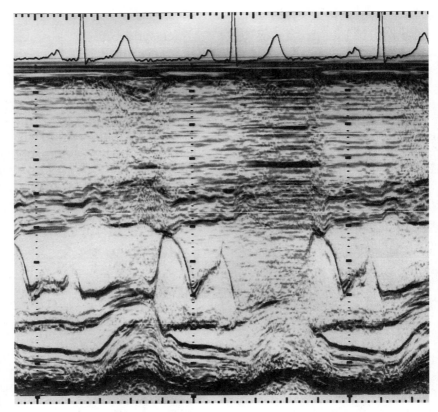

Figure 2–9 *Echocardiograph.*

indicates that blood is flowing through the vessel. A lack of sound indicates that no blood is flowing through the vessel. The reason for the lack of circulation cannot be determined by this test.

A duplex scanner combines echo images (sound waves) and the pulsed Doppler technologies to make a picture of blood flow in a vessel. The test shows blood flow and obstructions to blood flow in an artery or vein. In a vein, the test can show blood clots. In an artery, the test can show the presence of disease that impedes blood flow. It can also show blood flow through a replacement vessel after surgery. The actual sound generated by the Doppler instrument creates a permanent record.

An electroencephalograph is a graph of electrical impulses produced by brain activity. These brain waves are recorded by the electroencephalograph machine. Each part of the brain produces an electrical wave that has a distinctive rhythm and form. Variations in rhythm or shape of the wave indicate changes in brain activity. The physician determines the reasons for those changes.

An EEG measures how the nerve cells of the brain function. It does not measure thinking ability or intelligence. Electrical impulses do not pass through brain cells. There is no electrical shock to the brain. The EEG can be compared to the electrocardiograph for the heart because both tests measure the electrical activity of the body part. An EEG does not show structure; CAT and MRI scans are computerized visual procedures that show structure.

A nerve conduction velocity test measures the speed of a stimulus as it travels along the pathway of a peripheral nerve. Electrodes are placed along the nerve's pathway, then a small burst of electricity is applied. The electrodes pick up the speed of the electrical signal, and the machine automatically computes it.

Nerve conduction velocity tests are preformed by an EEG technologist and interpreted by a neurologist. They are used to diagnose peripheral neuropathy, carpal tunnel syndrome, degenerative diseases, and nerve disuse. They are also used to evaluate nerve function following injury.

In evoked potential (EP) tests, certain nerves are stimulated and the response of the brain is measured. Evoked potential tests are divided into three groups: brain stem, visual, and somatosensory. In visual EPs, a person looks at a flashing pattern or light, and the optic nerve is studied. In brain stem EPs, an auditory signal is given through headphones, and the auditory nerve is studied. Brain stem EPs are used to diagnose auditory tumors, damage after injury, multiple sclerosis, nerve disease, and peripheral nerve tumors. In somatosensory EPs, a signal is applied along the peripheral nerve to be studied, and the brain's response to it is recorded. EPs are usually performed by an EEG technologist and interpreted by a neurologist.

Biography

When I started college, I went to school full time during the day, so I needed a job where I could work evenings and weekends. I began working at a hospital as an orderly, an unlicensed care giver. When a position became available, I trained on the job as an EKG technician. After I married, I changed to evening classes and worked full time during the day at the hospital. Since my major was biochemistry, I developed an interest in, and was trained as, a dialysis technician. After I obtained a master's degree in biochemistry, the hospital sent me to a perfusionist program to learn to run the heart-lung machine used in open heart surgery. I love working in surgery. I have great responsibility. Patients could die if I do not pay attention every minute and do my job well. Surgeons respect my expertise as I respect theirs. They cannot perform open heart surgery without me. I feel that I am a valued part of the OR team. I made my way up the career ladder while I went to school, married, and worked full time. I am proud of my achievements as a responsible member of the surgical team.

Career Search

To discover more about a career and the roles of members in the biometrics department, contact the following organizations for online addresses, printed information, and videotapes.

American College of Cardiology
9111 Old Georgetown Rd.
Bethesda, MD 20814–1699
Phone: 301–897–5400
Toll-free phone: 800–253–9745
Fax: 301–897–9745

American Society of Cardiovascular
    Professionals
120 Falcon Dr.
Fredericksburg, VA 22408
Phone: 703–891–0079
Toll-free phone: 800–683–6728
Fax: 703–898–2393

American Society of
    Echocardiography
4101 Lake Boone Tr., Ste. 201
Raleigh, NC 27017
Phone: 919–787–5181
Fax: 919–787–4916

American Society of
    Electroneurodiagnostic
    Technologists
204 W. 7th St.
Carroll, IA 51401–2317
Phone: 712–792–2978
FAX: 712–792–6962

Society of Vascular Technology
4601 Presidents Dr.
Lanham, MD 20706–4365
Phone: 301–459–7550
Toll-free phone: 800–SVT–VEIN
Fax: 301–459–5651

Range of Annual Incomes

Cardiologist	$200,000–$300,000
Neurologist	$125,000–$170,000
Echocardiographic technician	$ 32,000–$40,000
Electrocardiographic technician	$ 18,000–$25,000
Electroencephalographic technologist	$ 19,000–$31,000
Cardiac technician	$ 20,000–$26,000
Cardiovascular technologist	$ 28,000–$39,000
Vascular technologist	$ 28,000–$39,000

What's New

The trend in health care is to hire multiskilled persons. To meet this need in the biometrics field, community colleges have expanded their EKG technician programs into cardiac technician programs.

Cardiac rehabilitation is an exercise program conducted by a nurse and a physical therapist, exercise physiologist, or fitness instructor for persons recovering from heart attacks and heart surgery.

They develop and teach individual activity programs. They conduct group sessions that include warm-up, aerobic, and cool-down exercises. They monitor patients to determine exercise tolerance and watch for symptoms that indicate adverse effects. They motivate persons to continue their rehabilitation program.

Sophisticated electronic devices are being developed and implanted in persons with heart problems to improve cardiac function. Pacemakers are devices that control the rate and strength of heartbeats. Pacemakers with defibrillators are devices that shock the heart into regular rhythm during episodes of ventricular tachycardia (rapid irregular heartbeat). Registered nurses in biometrics or cardiac clinics monitor the functions of these appliances and reprogram them when necessary to maximize their effectiveness.

School to Work

Specific school-based learning that applies to skills in this department is detailed here. Some of these skills may be learned in a high school laboratory, a mentorship or apprenticeship program, shadowing experience, or a college career program.

Academic Subject	Workplace Skills
Arts	—Perform diagnostic tests according to procedure. —Mount EKG strips in charts. —Enter computer printouts in charts.
Business Time Management Communication	 —Schedule appointments to avoid overlapping patient visits. —Answer the telephone. —Instruct patients about the procedure to be done. —Call patients to schedule a meeting with their physician.
English Computer Skills	—Alphabetize reports. —Enter data to run the test. —Report life-threatening test results immediately. —Fax results to the appropriate physician. —Check for electronic messages.
Word Processing	—Write a cover letter to the physician to accompany the test results.
Career and Guidance Education Levels	 —Research prerequisites for each career in this department. —Describe the length and content of the education required for each career.

School to Work—continued

Academic Subject	Workplace Skills
Mathematics	
Fractions	—Take blood pressures.
Calculation	—Measure the EKG strip.
Science	
Anatomy and Physiology	—Identify the normal structure and function of the cardiovascular system.
Biochemistry	—Be aware of the necessary levels of certain elements in the blood.
Microbiology	—Clean equipment between uses with patients.
	—Use disposal equipment.
Nutrition and Food Science	—Understand the relationship of diet to heart disease.
Pathophysiology	—Identify arteriosclerosis in vessels and its effects on circulation.
Pharmacology	—Understand the effects of cardiac medications.

Review Questions

1. What is the goal of the biometrics department?
2. What is the difference between pulse and blood pressure?
3. What is the purpose of a stress test?
4. Explain the difference between the electrocardiograph, an echocardiograph, and an electroencephalograph.
5. What is the job outlook for members of this department?

COMMUNICATION DISORDERS DEPARTMENT

Objectives

After completing this chapter, you should be able to:

- ❏ Define department goals.
- ❏ Explain the difference between speech-language pathologists and audiologists.
- ❏ Describe several careers within this department.
- ❏ Identify required education and credentials for each career.
- ❏ Understand the skills performed in this department.
- ❏ Recognize how academic subjects apply in the workplace.

Key Terms

Function

Speech	Language	Hearing

Conditions

Dysphonia	Stroke	Stutter
Cleft palate	Paralysis	Hearing loss
Laryngectomy	Aphasia	Tracheostomy

Treatments

Esophageal speech	Voice synthesizer	Voice prosthesis
Artificial larynx		

INTRODUCTION

Speech is the production of sounds with meaning. Speech is the result of a complex process involving the coordination of respiration, phonation (voice), and muscle movement for articulation. Voice quality and articulation are characteristics of the speech process.

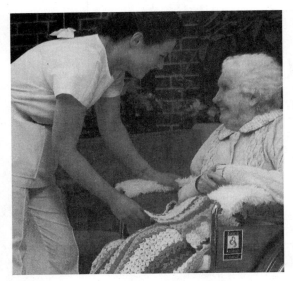

Figure 3–1   Words have meaning.

Language is the meaning of sound. Sounds make words; words have meaning (Figure 3–1). Specific words are spoken to indicate specific things and thoughts. Understanding the meaning of specific words and sounds is an important part of communication.

Audiology is the science of **hearing**. It relates to the perception of sound and the degree to which sounds are heard. Speech is a two-part process consisting of speaking and listening. Children learn to speak by first imitating the sounds they hear, then discovering that certain sounds mean certain things.

Audiologists determine if patients hear sound. Speech-language pathologists determine if patients understand the spoken word. Without the capacity to speak and hear, people cannot have ordinary conversations and usually cannot follow oral directions effectively. People who cannot speak, hear, or understand can be lonely and withdrawn. They may feel like they are not a part of the world around them. Both speech and hearing disorders can be caused by physical or emotional problems.

Patients may have been born with a speech or hearing problem or a physical disability with an accompanying communication disorder. Language disorders may occur as a result of an accident, illness, surgery, loud sounds, or medications. An accident can cause a traumatic brain injury that may result in **dysphonia**. A stroke might result in brain damage to the speech center and cause **aphasia**. Cancer of the larynx may result in the voice box being surgically removed, so the patient may need to learn to communicate by burping air through the mouth to make sounds called **esophageal speech**. Loud noise experienced at some rock concerts or on some job sites can result in damage to the middle ear and ultimately cause deafness. Some medications such as antibiotics can cause damage to the auditory nerve and result in deafness. Hearing loss can be acquired at any age.

GOALS
The goals of the communication disorders department are to identify and treat speech, language, and hearing problems, and provide counseling and guidance on social adjustment.

CAREER DESCRIPTIONS
Speech-language pathologists and audiologists work together closely on the rehabilitation team. Though both careers relate to communication, they differ in specialization, goals, job skills, diagnostic

CAREER HIERARCHY

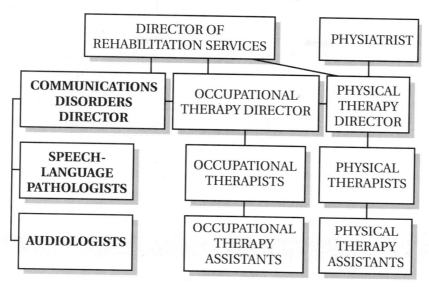

methods, and treatment techniques. Treatments depend on such factors as a client's age, medical diagnosis, physical or emotional problems, attention span, motivation, level of consciousness, and ability to cooperate. Speech-language pathologists and audiologists both work with people of all ages.

Career characteristics

Employment opportunities include hospitals, clinics, offices, school systems, speech and hearing centers, universities, research centers, and private practice. A doctoral degree is required to teach in most universities. Audiologists work to test, treat, and prevent hearing problems. Some work in government and industry in the specialty of dealing with noise pollution. They research the effects of environmental noise on hearing. The job market for both speech-language pathologists and audiologists is good but more limited than other health care professionals because fewer positions are available.

Work hours are usually during the day, from 9:00 A.M. to 5:00 P.M. Occasional evening or Saturday hours may be needed to meet with family members.

Career advancements include supervisory and director positions in large departments of language disorders, lateral moves to other institutions, or independent contracting services.

Job satisfaction comes from making a difference in peoples' lives. Both speech-language pathologists and audiologists know that their efforts improve the quality of their patients' lives. Gratification comes from being creative and using ingenuity. It also comes from observing improvements in patients' conditions and finding the variety of cases seen each day to be pleasantly challenging.

Career roles

Speech-language pathologists are often called speech pathologists. They help people who have disorders of voice, fluency, articulation, language, and swallowing. These problems can be the result of a **stroke**, degenerative disease (Parkinson's), cancer of the larynx, vocal nodules, abuse of the voice, accident or injury to the brain or the muscles of speech, or syndromes apparent at birth (cerebral palsy or Down syndrome.) A major portion of their work involves people who **stutter** or have a **cleft palate**, facial **paralysis**, or speech and language problems due to a stroke or autism.

Speech-language pathologists assess patients to identify problems with producing sounds and pronouncing, selecting, and understanding words. They assess by reviewing records, observing patients, talking with them, and examining the mouth. They determine the extent of disability and evaluate solutions. During the assessment, they look for answers to certain questions: Is the spoken word understood? Can thoughts be expressed in words? Are words spoken that are not intended? Are only sounds uttered, with no understandable words? Do tongue and facial muscles work properly?

Speech pathologists evaluate voice for quality, pitch, volume, and resonance. The quality of the voice may be hoarse or nasal, the pitch may be too high or too low, the volume may be too loud or too soft, and the resonance may be too nasal or not enough nasal resonance. The muscles used in speech may be too tense or too relaxed. Speech may be precise or slurred.

They develop treatment plans and confer with patients to set goals. They often work with family members to teach methods of treatment and counsel them on how to convey information when communication problems exist. They counsel patients who are lacking in self-esteem because of abnormal speech patterns. Speech-language pathologists work with the whole patient, not just the muscles that affect speech.

Speech-language pathologists work with methods of speech that involve communicating by instruments. **Voice synthesizers** are available for the person whose larynx has been removed. People who have had head injuries can use electronic devices that speak phrases to express ideas and requests. To activate this kind of apparatus, the patient pushes the appropriate button with a head control device and the computerized voice speaks such phrases as "I'm cold" and "I need some water." Research into the causes of speech problems and the development of electronic and computerized instruments continue.

Desirable personal characteristics include creativity and innovation. Since speech-language pathologists produce individual treatment plans that reflect the uniqueness of each patient and his or her special needs, they blend methods and treatments that have worked for others. They need to learn from their experiences and be considerate and honest with their patients.

Patience is another desirable attribute. Because change may come about slowly for patients, speech pathologists need to be pleased with appropriate increments of progress, even if they are necessarily small. Self-confidence, a sense of humor, and enjoyment of the work are other assets.

Audiologists assess patients to identify problems in hearing. They operate precise electronic instruments to detect hearing deficits and to evaluate the degree of **hearing loss**. They confer with physicians to determine treatment. They fit patients with electronic devices to improve hearing and offer instruction in the use and care of these devices. Hearing loss can be from such causes as a birth defect, disease, medication, brain injury, accident, or excessive noise.

Audiologists must pronounce test words accurately and present information clearly. They need to be aware of available electronic hearing devices (Figure 3–2) and, based on audiometric test findings, select the most effective device for the individual problem. Some patients benefit from several meetings for counseling on the social effects of hearing loss. Some situations require family interaction.

Desirable personal characteristics include the ability to work with precise instruments and painstakingly perform hearing tests. Audiologists need good problem-solving skills and motivation to keep up with current trends. They need insight into patients' feelings and the sensitivity to provide counseling and guidance.

JOB AVAILABILITY

The U.S. Department of Labor projects a good job outlook for speech-language pathologists and audiologists. Job growth is expected to increase faster than average to the year 2005. An increasing number of these professionals will go into private practice. Keep in mind that this is a relatively small group of practitioners.

SKILLS

To help patients gain or regain the communication skills of speech and hearing, speech-language pathologists and audiologists assess patients, review records, confer with physicians and other health team professionals, and develop treatment plans and goals mutually acceptable to the patient and health care worker. In speech pathology, skills and treatments center around oral function. In both speech pathology and audiology, motivation and selection of appropriate mechanical assistance are important factors in patient care.

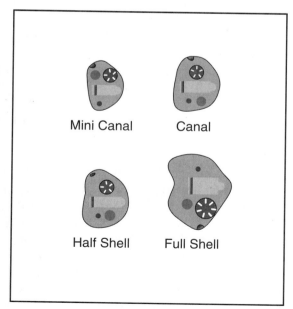

Figure 3–2 *Hearing aids amplify sound.*

EDUCATION AND CREDENTIALS

CAREER	YEARS OF EDUCATION AFTER HIGH SCHOOL	DEGREE OR DIPLOMA	TESTED BY; LICENSED BY
Speech-language pathologist (M.A., CCC-SLP) or (M.S., CCC-SLP) or (Ph.D. or D.Sc.)	6 years of school plus 9 months of clinical fellowship	Master's degree in speech-language pathology or Doctor's degree in speech-language pathology	Certification by ASHA; licensed by the state
Audiologist (M.A., CCC-A) or (M.S., CCC-A) or (Ph.D. or D.Sc.)	6 years of school plus 9 months of clinical fellowship	Master's degree in audiology or Doctor's degree in audiology	Certification by ASHA; licensed by the state

Key to abbreviations:

A—Audiology
ASHA—American Speech-Language-Hearing Association
CCC—Certificate of Clinical Competence
M.A.—Master of Arts

M.S.—Master of Science
SLP—Speech-Language Pathologist
Ph.D.—Doctor of Philosophy
D.Sc.—Doctor of Science

Exercise

Exercise of face, throat, and tongue muscles may increase functional ability and allow proper pronunciation of syllables, words, and sentences (Figure 3–3). Specific exercises develop muscle coordination to make speech clearer. Exercise of the tongue and mouth muscles is the basic treatment for patients with cleft lip and palate.

Overarticulation is an exercise to improve the speech of stroke victims. After a stroke, facial paralysis may cause drooping and lack of control of one side of the mouth. Overemphasizing mouth movements while reading phrases aloud hastens the return of controlled movement to muscles affected by the stroke. Patients are encouraged when they see drooping mouth muscles move more precisely. Their motivation increases and often carries over to exercising their weakened arm and leg. Facial muscles improve more rapidly than the muscles of the extremities.

Motivation

Motivation is a force from within that pushes a person to make an effort to act (Figure 3–4). It springs from a personal need or desire. It cannot be given to or forced on someone. It must come from within the person.

Motivation is the key to continuing the effort to improve speech. Because patients have to do the exercises for improvement, they must feel the need or desire to do them. Often, patients become discouraged because they do not see immediate improvement from their efforts. The speech pathologist tries to rekindle the fire of enthusiasm, the spirit

Figure 3–3 *Proper pronunciation is important.*

of wanting to continue to try, and the desire to improve. It is not an easy task.

The speech pathologist points out to patients each small increment of progress. Stroke patients want their smile to return immediately and become discouraged when it does not. The speech pathologist highlights small improvements that occur after exercise. Counting the number of teeth that show on each

Figure 3–4 *Motivation is a driving force.*

side of the mouth when trying for a full smile before exercise is one example. After exercise, the speech pathologist counts the teeth that show on each side of the mouth in a full smile. More teeth show on the droopy side after the exercise. Pointing out such progress encourages and motivates patients so they are more willing to cooperate with the exercise program. Motivation comes from seeing small differences, then struggling to make the next improvement.

Family members are encouraged to be a part of the rehabilitation team. They are with the patient in the home after the patient is discharged from the hospital. The family can continue the treatment plan. They are taught to encourage patients to do facial exercises before meals. That effort, in combination with the ac-

tion of chewing, increases the speed of recovery of the oral muscles.

Device selection

Selection of appropriate devices is a specialty of speech-language pathologists and audiologists. They recommend the best method of communication and provide appropriate training. One electronic device, for example, shows change in voice pitch. Changing the pitch of the voice may prevent polyp formation on the vocal cords. Compact amplifiers with attached microphones make sound louder if a patient does not have a hearing aid. A **voice prosthesis** can be surgically implanted to help speech production after a **laryngectomy**. An **artificial larynx** held against the neck can provide an external source of sound after a laryngectomy.

Biography

When I was a child, I lisped. It was an awful affliction. People either made fun of me or avoided talking to me because they did not want to embarrass me. I used to cry a lot because I wanted to talk but did not want to be ashamed. My mother finally took me to speech therapy. I practiced and practiced the exercises the therapist gave me. I vowed that if I was able to stop lisping, I would help others to overcome this affliction. My therapist encouraged me by telling me of all the public figures and TV stars who had the same problem and overcame it.

I practiced a lot, and my speech improved. Unfortunately, the lisp returned when I was nervous. To help prevent that, I joined the theater club at school and pushed myself to speak in front of others. Over time, I lost the lisp entirely.

After high school, I entered the speech pathology program in college. All through that program, I volunteered in a children's speech clinic while I held a paying job. I am especially aware of word pronunciation. I choose words that I can pronounce easily. Since I graduated, I have worked in the same speech clinic where I volunteered. I know I make a difference in the lives of my patients because I know how it feels to have a speech impediment. I love my work.

Career Search

To discover more about a career and the roles of members in a communication disorders department, contact the following organizations for online addresses, printed information, and videotapes.

American Speech-Language-Hearing
 Association
10801 Rockville Pike
Rockville, MD 20852
Phone: 301–897–5700
Toll-free phone: 800–638–8255
Fax: 301–571–0457

American Auditory Society
512 E. Canterbury Lane
Phoenix, AZ 85022
Phone: 602–789–0755
Fax: 602–942–1486

Range of Annual Incomes

Otolaryngologist	$120,000–$200,000
Audiologist	$ 32,000– $48,000
Speech-language pathologist	$ 33,000– $50,000

What's New

For people who are unable to say words or articulate understandably but can comprehend, computers will become a significant tool for communication. Programs are continually being developed and refined for use with laptop and handheld computers, as are other computer-driven devices, so people afflicted with expressive aphasia can be better understood.

A Passy Muir nerve valve may be implanted in the throat so that a person with a **tracheostomy** can speak. Speech therapists work with these patients to maximize the use of this tool.

Other devices are being developed for use by people who do not have a larynx. One such device is implanted in a denture and activated by an external button. Speech therapists work with these patients to gain correct articulation movements so words can be understood.

School to Work

Specific school-based learning that applies to skills in this department are listed here. Some of these skills may be learned in a high school laboratory, a mentorship or apprenticeship program, a shadowing experience, or a college career program.

Academic Studies	Workplace Skills
Arts	—Graph by month the number of patients seen last year. —Make a pie-shaped chart showing the age of patients seen last year.
Business Word Processing	—Write reports for the referring physician and chart.
Science Anatomy and Physiology	—Understand the structure and function of related body parts.
Pathophysiology	—Recognize the problem of the involved body part.
Pharmacology	—Understand the effects and side effects of certain medications.
Psychology	—Understand the relationship of stress and speech problems. —Encourage patients' efforts to repeat specific exercises. —Maintain patience with slow progress. —Understand the frustrations of people who have a hearing impairment. —Support strategies of independent living.

Review Questions

1. What are the goals of the communication disorders department?
2. What are the length of the programs to become a speech-language pathologist and an audiologist after high school?
3. What four personal characteristics are desirable in speech-language pathologists?
4. What four personal characteristics are desirable in audiologists?
5. Calculate the lowest hourly pay rate for a speech-language pathologist and the highest hourly rate for an audiologist.

DENTAL OFFICE

Objectives

After completing this chapter, you should be able to:

- ❏ Explain the goals of the dental office.
- ❏ Describe each career associated with dentistry.
- ❏ Identify the required education and credentials for each career.
- ❏ Describe the skills performed in this office.
- ❏ Recognize how academic subjects apply in the workplace.

Key Terms

Oral hygiene

Plaque	Tartar	Floss
Calculus		

Problems

Periodontitis	Gingivitis	Caries

Restorations

Bridge	Partial plate	Dentures
Crown	Filling	Inlay

INTRODUCTION

Dental offices provide tooth care, oral hygiene, diagnostic services, and preventive measures to people of all ages. Patients are instructed in the care of the mouth, teeth, and oral appliances. Details of potential and existing conditions are presented and discussed with pa-tients. Solutions to oral problems are re-viewed and agreed upon. Treatments are performed to preserve the natural teeth and maintain alignment or straighten teeth.

Dentistry has many areas of practice. Most dentists are general practitioners. Some dentists specialize in orthodontics, oral surgery, periodontics, or pedodontics. To be licensed as specialists, dentists must complete required educational programs and board exams. Areas of practice are clearly defined. Specialists do not perform procedures that general practitioners perform. General practitioners may perform special procedures if they have met specific educational requirements.

Goals

The goals of the dental office are to care for and preserve natural teeth and periodontium, provide prosthetics when necessary, and educate people about oral health and hygiene to prevent tooth decay and periodontal disease (Figure 4–1).

Career Descriptions

Though all careers in the dental field relate to the care of teeth and the maintenance of oral hygiene and health, areas of specialty and educational programs differ. Roles and responsibilities vary with the type of specialty and the position of the worker.

Career characteristics

Employment opportunities are many and varied. While the use of fluoride has

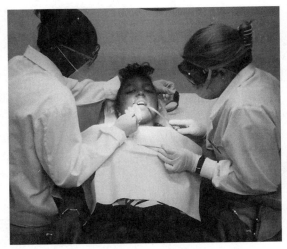

Figure 4–1 *The goal of dental office staff members is to care for and preserve teeth.*

reduced the number of dental caries, dental office visits have increased for prophylactic care.

Most dental professionals work in private practice offices. Others work in hospitals, clinics, health maintenance organizations, research laboratories, school systems, and public health agencies. Some dental professionals work in the military, correctional facilities, the Peace Corps, and with the World Health Organization. Some work as sales representatives for dental product manufacturers. Advanced training and education can lead to teaching in universities, clinics, and vocational schools.

Career Hierarchy

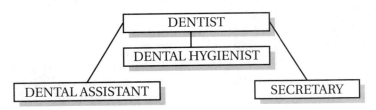

Work hours in an office setting are usually Monday through Friday with some hours on Saturday. Most offices have daytime hours, but some are open evenings. There are few emergencies in the dental field. Most people wait until a weekday morning to call the dentist, even when they have a toothache. A dentist may be contacted at any time patients have facial traumas that involve broken teeth or crushed jaw bones.

Career advancement occurs when duties are expanded, a dental assistant returns to school to become a dental hygienist, or a dental hygienist attends dental school. Otherwise careers in dentistry vary with job changes. The opportunity to advance to supervisor and administrator does not exist at most job sites.

Desired characteristics include a friendly manner, consideration of others, and communication skills. Since dentists and hygienists work inside the mouth and on accompanying delicate parts with fine instruments, good vision, manual dexterity, and coordination are helpful. Good grooming, meticulous personal hygiene, and the ability to maneuver well in small spaces are positive attributes. Attention to detail is particularly important when carrying out safety precautions with X-ray machines and following infection control and universal precaution procedures.

Job satisfaction comes from having a unique body of knowledge, performing procedures that are needed and appreciated by patients, relieving pain, and solving dental problems. It is rewarding to work with patients who care about their teeth and come to the office to maintain their oral health. Another source of job satisfaction is immediate feedback from a skilled performance. Patients often comment that they feel better after having their teeth cleaned. The congenial atmosphere of the office also adds to job enjoyment.

Special biomedical hazards that dental workers need to consider include possible exposure to viruses that causes AIDS and hepatitis. Since the emergence of AIDS, workers who come in contact with blood or saliva wear protective clothing to avoid becoming contaminated with disease-producing viruses. Most dentists and their assistants wear gloves; some wear goggles during procedures that involve drilling or preparing, extracting, and suctioning. Dental workers need to carefully handle instruments that have been in patients' mouths. Procedures for cleaning and sterilizing dental instruments need to be followed precisely. A hepatitis vaccine is available, but there is no vaccine against HIV, the virus that causes AIDS. Other hazards include exposure to mercury and radiation.

Career roles

Dentists graduate from dental school with the basic training that is required for all dental specialties. Though most dentists remain in general practice, some choose to enter special fields. General practice is geared to the care and cleaning of the natural teeth, hygiene of the mouth, and prevention of decay. Preservation methods include educating patients in techniques to minimize tooth decay and **plaque** formation and maximize the health of gum tissue. If the nerve in a tooth becomes infected, endodontists remove the infected nerve and pulpal tissue inside the tooth to prevent bone infection and tooth removal. If the natural teeth cannot be saved, oral surgeons remove them, and dentists fit artificial teeth into the mouth. These artificial teeth may be **bridges**, **partial plates**, or **dentures**. If teeth are broken, the remaining stubs are filed down and capped. When teeth become so decayed that only weakened shells remain, **crowns** may be made to fit over them.

Dentists assess the health of the mouth and teeth through inspection, X-ray review, and hands-on examination. **Fillings** and crowns are checked to be sure there is no decay underneath. Cavities are filled or restored, and restorations are replaced as needed. Bridges, partial plates, and dentures are inspected for cracks and loose parts. If these appliances need to be replaced or a crown needs to be made, an impression of the mouth is taken from which a plaster model is made and then sent to a dental laboratory. There, the dental technician uses the plaster model of the mouth to tailor the specific appliance or crown.

Dentists also solve the problems of toothaches and gum infections. They identify the cause and prescribe conservative treatment to save the tooth. If conservative therapy is not successful, a root canal or extraction may be necessary. Sometimes special treatment of the gums is necessary. Patients needing root canals and gum treatments are referred to specialists.

Orthodontists are dentists who specialize in straightening teeth. They assess patients by observation and extensive measurements and by taking panoramic radiographs and cephalometric radiographs. Impressions of the teeth and plaster models are made to study the articulation process. Some teeth may have to be extracted if there are too many or if they are too big for the mouth. Bands are placed on or around teeth and wires attached to shift them into the desired position. The whole correction process takes from two to three years. When teeth have been realigned, a retainer is made. It prevents teeth from shifting back to their previous positions after the braces have been removed.

Oral and maxillofacial surgeons are dentists who specialize in extracting teeth and correcting deformities of the face, mouth, jaw, and joints in the cranium. These surgeons diagnose and manage cysts and tumors. They correct deformities of the jaw bone, ear, eyelid, eye orbit, nose, forehead, palate, and lip. They correct damage resulting from trauma. Some procedures can be done in the office (Figure 4–2). If an extensive procedure is required, such as extracting all the teeth, it may be done at the hospital. The most common procedure done by oral surgeons is the extraction of wisdom teeth. They also remove extra teeth and some oversized teeth so that those remaining can be realigned.

Endodontists are dentists who specialize in performing root canals. They remove the infected nerve and pulpal tissue from the tooth's center to prevent bone infection and tooth loss. The dentist then restores the tooth.

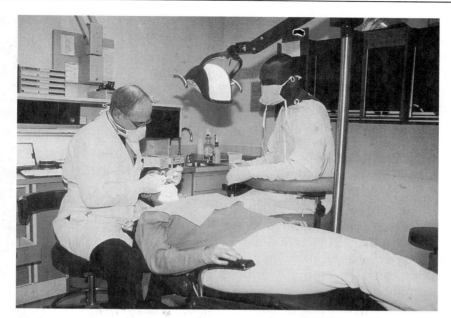

Figure 4–2 *Oral surgeon performing a procedure in the office setting.* (Courtesy of MetroHealth Medical Center of Cleveland, Ohio.)

Periodontists are dentists who specialize in treating gums and the supporting structure around teeth to prevent loss. The most common reason for the loss of teeth is periodontal disease, often caused by gum infection called **periodontitis**. Periodontists also treat gums that have receded from chronic irritation or inflammation (**gingivitis**), which is often caused by plaque and **tartar** buildup. As gums recede, teeth become loose. Wiggly teeth cannot be used to chew. If the gum treatment does not result in tightening the wiggly teeth, these teeth need to be extracted so they don't fall out during sleep and cause choking. Patient education about gum disorders and instruction in continuing **flossing** treatments at home is essential to prevent more gum erosion and tooth loss.

Pedodontists are dentists who specialize in the care and treatment of children's teeth. This includes education and measures to prevent caries and disease. Pedodontists care for baby teeth and permanent teeth. They work with patients from birth through adolescence. They are especially helpful with thumb-sucking children. They try to prevent the teeth shifting that often results from this activity.

Dental hygienists work under the direction of a dentist. They do all aspects of assessment and oral hygiene. They take patients' histories, asking about diseases and medications to determine possible effects on the condition of the mouth, teeth, and gums. They inspect the mouth for cavities, cracks in teeth, and loose fillings, bridges, or crowns. They look for gum disease, open sores, and cancerous tissue. They clean the teeth, removing plaque and **calculus** deposits from above and below the gum line. They x-ray teeth, then mount and scan the films for **caries** and potential decay. They teach patients proper oral care and diet for good oral health. They explain the effects of smoking on the oral cavity. They teach brushing and flossing techniques for plaque control. They may apply fluoride treatments and place temporary appliances and fillings in the mouth. They mix dental cements, prepare restoration materials, take impressions, and pour study models. They remove sutures, smooth and polish new amalgam fillings, and document findings and treatments.

Dental assistants work under the direction of dentists and dental hygienists. They position patients in dental chairs and prepare equipment for use. They take and develop X rays, mount films, and obtain records. They document the condition of teeth as instructed by the dentist or dental hygienist. They set up instrument trays and suction saliva and spray from the mouth while the dentist or hygienist is working on the teeth. They prepare restoration substances, dental cement, and material for impressions; take impressions; and trim models. They clean, sterilize, and maintain equipment and order supplies (Figure 4–3). They answer phones, make appointments, work with billing, and post accounts. In some offices, their duties are expanded to handle equipment and assist dentists and hygienists as they work with patients.

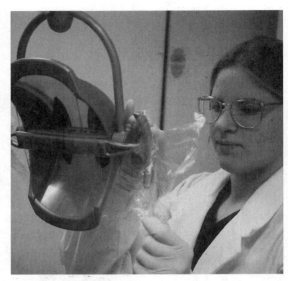

Figure 4–3 *Protective barriers, such as a plastic wrap or commercial covers, are placed on the handles and switches of the dental light.*

Dental laboratory technicians work in technical laboratories making appliances. They do not work directly with patients. They receive instructions, impressions, and study models from dentists. They make plaster models, bridges, partial plates, dentures, crowns, **inlays**, space maintainers, and orthodontic appliances. They work with a variety of materials and tools to make these appliances. Certification is offered in five specialty areas: crown and bridge, ceramics, partial dentures, complete dentures, and orthodontics.

JOB AVAILABILITY

The U.S. Department of Labor estimates that the job market will remain fairly good in the dental field. Since people live longer now, they require more dental

EDUCATION AND CREDENTIALS

CAREER	YEARS OF EDUCATION AFTER HIGH SCHOOL	DEGREE OR DIPLOMA	TESTED BY; LICENSED BY
Dentist (D.D.S. or D.M.D.)	4 years of college and 4 years of dental school	D.D.S. or D.D.M.	National board exam by Dental Commission during school plus regional boards by the Dental Examiner's Commission or state dental boards after graduation; State
Orthodontist (D.D.S.)	4 years of college, 4 years of dental school, and 2 years of postgraduate training	Same as dentist	Same as dentist plus regional boards in orthodontics; State
Oral surgeon (D.D.S.)	4 years of college, 4 years of dental school, and 3 years of postgraduate training	Same as dentist	Same as dentist plus regional boards in oral surgery; State
Endodontist (D.D.S.)	4 years of college, 4 years of dental school, and 2 years of postgraduate training	Same as dentist	Same as dentist plus regional boards in endodontics; State
Periodontist (D.D.S.)	4 years of college, 4 years of dental school, and 2 years of postgraduate training	Same as dentist	Same as dentist plus regional boards in periodontics; State
Pedodontist (D.D.S.)	4 years of college, 4 years of dental school, and 2 years of postgraduate training	Same as dentist	Same as dentist plus regional boards in pedodontics; State
Dental hygienist (LDH)	4 years or 2 years	B.S. or A.A.S.D. in dental hygiene	Written and practical national board exams by ADAJCNDE; State
Dental assistant (CDA)	1 year (4 quarters) or on-the-job training	A.A.S.D. in dental assisting certification	Certification exam by Dental Assisting National Board (optional)
Dental laboratory technician	2 years (7 quarters)	A.A.S.D. in dental laboratory technology	Certified exam by National Association of Dental Laboratories (optional)

Key to abbreviations:

A.A.S.D.—Associate of Applied Science Degree
ADAJCNDE—American Dental Association Joint Commission on National Dental Examinations
CDA—Certified Dental Assistant
D.D.S.—Doctor of Dental Science
D.M.D.—Doctor of Dental Medicine
LDH—Licensed Dental Hygienist

work. Job opportunities for dental hygienists will grow faster than average through the year 2005. Many dental hygienists hold more than one part-time job because dentists in private practice may need their services for only a few hours each week.

SKILLS

Most dental workers spend their time with patients. Dental technicians are the exception. Technicians work in a laboratory setting and do not have patient contact. Skills vary according to the education level of the worker and job responsibilities.

Job skills include visual inspection, diagnostic testing, cleaning, and tooth preparation for restoration procedures. Other activities include extracting, crowning, applying bridges or braces, doing root canal work, and working on gum restoration. Preparation of materials for diagnostic or therapeutic procedures, tissue and nerve injection to numb the work site, administration of general anesthetic agents, and monitoring vital signs are other tasks performed. Dental workers take mouth impressions, make study models, and prepare temporary appliances. Plaster models, dentures, crowns, bridges, and inlays are made in the dental laboratory.

Prophylaxis

Oral prophylaxis includes cleaning, scaling, and polishing skills with hand instruments, ultrasonic scaling equipment, and air-driven hand tools. Removing plaque and tartar from teeth, plus flossing, help to keep gums healthy and prevent tooth decay. Patient instruction in these techniques is important so that good oral hygiene is continued between dental visits. Applying topical fluoride gel to help reduce caries is another procedure used on children eighteen years of age and younger.

X rays

X-ray procedures vary with the type of specialty and purpose. Bitewing X rays are the small films that are placed in the mouth and held in place by the patient biting down on the cardboard film cover. A panoramic radiograph is a rectangular X ray showing a continuous view of the whole jaw and teeth structures. The patient's head is positioned in a stabilizing device and remains still throughout the procedure as the X-ray machine moves around the jaw to record the structures. Protective procedures to prevent exposure of other body parts to X rays are skills that ensure the safety of the patient and the worker.

Restoration

Restoration describes a group of procedures that includes drilling and scraping to prepare teeth for filling, capping, inlays, crowns, and root canal work. These procedures involve manual dexterity, coordination, and good vision. Knowledge of tooth structure and treatment options is essential. Evaluating drill-bit sizes and choosing equipment are pivotal to professional technique.

Structures

Placing and removing permanent and temporary dental structures are other skills used in the dental office. Applying bands and wires is a basic procedure for teeth straightening. After the orthodontic braces are removed, a retainer is made and placed into the mouth to maintain teeth alignment.

Prostheses

Making crowns, inlays, bridges, partial plates, and full dentures involves working with gold, porcelain, ceramics, acrylics, and metals. Crowns are made to cover and support teeth. Inlays are made to restore seriously decayed and weakened teeth. Bridges, partial plates, and full dentures are made to replace missing teeth. These parts and prostheses are made by dental technicians in laboratories. They are created from teeth and mouth impressions that have been taken by dentists and sent to the dental laboratories with written instructions.

Biography

When I came to this country, I spoke no English, only Spanish. I got a job in a dental clinic that had many Spanish-speaking clients. At first, I assisted in minor tasks. I cleaned the office and children's toys and boiled instruments. I was happy to have a job. I began to learn English by listening to the office staff. I decided that if I was to live in this country and be successful, I needed to learn the language as quickly as possible. As I became more fluent, I began to help the dentist and dental hygienists interpret information to Spanish-speaking adults and children.

As my knowledge of English increased, I was asked to spend more time in the dental rooms so I could interpret. Gradually, I started to assist the dentist and hygienists by obtaining instruments and preparing trays. This was the beginning of my training as a dental assistant. I learned on the job. I liked it so much that I decided to go to school for two years to become a certified dental assistant. I took most of my courses part time at the community college as I continued to work full time during the day. I had to do my clinical experience in the mornings, however, so I changed my job to part time. I worked in the afternoons, evenings, and Saturdays. It was hard to do, and I was on a tight budget, but I did it. I graduated. I am proud of my accomplishments. My co-workers are proud of me, too.

Career Search

To discover more about a career and the roles of members in a dental office, contact the following organizations for online addresses, printed information, and videotapes.

American Dental Association
211 East Chicago Avenue
Chicago, IL 60611
Phone: 312–440–2500
Fax: 312–440–7494

American Dental Hygienists
    Association
444 N. Michigan Avenue, Suite 3400
Chicago, IL 60611
Phone: 312–440–8929
Toll-free phone: 800–243–ADHA
Fax: 312–440–8929

American Dental Assistants
Association
203 N. LaSalle Street, Suite 1320
Chicago, IL 60601–1225
Phone: 312–541–1550
Fax: 312–541–1496

National Association of Dental
Laboratories
555 E. Braddock Road
Alexandria, VA 22314–2106
Phone: 703–683–5263
Toll-free phone: 800–950–1150

Range of Annual Incomes

Dentist	$120,000–$160,000
Orthodontist	$130,000–$180,000
Oral surgeon	$140,000–$200,000
Dental hygienist	$ 27,000– $40,000
Dental assistant	$ 12,000– $20,000
Dental laboratory technician	$ 12,000– $20,000

What's New

Dental whitening has increased in popularity for people whose teeth have become yellowed due to age, smoking, or drinking dark liquids such as coffee and red wine. For a specified period of time each day, the person wears thin trays over the upper and lower teeth that contain whitening gel. The dental assistant does all the preparation and makes the trays to fit over the entire tooth structure and edge of the gums. The trays are created with special moldable plastic from plaster models made from impressions. Care is taken to trim the edges of each tray to avoid irritating oral membranes.

An intraoral camera is a device that photographs teeth and the oral cavity. These pictures can be enlarged and stored in the patient's record. They are kept to show conditions before and after whitening, trauma damage repair, orthodontia, and cosmetic dentistry.

Dental implants are used to prevent bone loss after a tooth has been removed. Screws are positioned through the gum into the bone. Then restorative materials are placed over the top to create an artificial tooth. This procedure requires frequent visits to the dental office for care and treatment.

School to Work

This section demonstrates how school-based learning carries over to work-based learning. Some of these skills may be learned in a high school laboratory or in a mentorship or apprenticeship program.

Academic Subject	Workplace Skills
Arts	—Demonstrate brushing and flossing.
	—Take impressions and pour molds.
	—Make casts.
	—Make custom trays.
	—Mix dental cements and bases.
	—Prepare restoration materials.
	—Set up basic dental trays.
	—Fit an inlay.
	—Place a bridge.
	—Seat a cap.
	—Line a denture.
Business	
Time Management	—Work efficiently to keep appointments on schedule.
Communication	—Keep conversation pleasant as work is being done.
	—Give printed or written directions to the patient.
English	—Assess client history.
	—Write clearly and understandably in patient charts.
Computer Skills	—Use the dentist's computer program to its fullest.
	—Monitor the delivery of supplies to ensure order accuracy and completeness.
	—Use a modem.
Economics	—Bill the appropriate insurance plan for work done.
Bookkeeping Systems	—Collect overdue bills.
Filing Systems	—File patient charts with accompanying X rays.
Career and Guidance	
Career Exploration Activity	—Take a career interest inventory.
	—Shadow, volunteer, or work with a mentor.
	—View a video on dental careers.
	—Visit a community college or university on career day.
	—Obtain the catalogue of a college offering dental programs.
	—Write a paper discussing the duties of each dental career.
Education Levels	—Research the prerequisites for each dental career.
	—Describe the length and content of the education program for each dental career.
English and Communications	
Medical Terminology	—Chart the condition of the teeth.
	—Document work done as reported by the dentist.
Speech Class	—Express directions clearly and understandably.
	—Explain brushing and flossing.
	—Instruct patients in whitening techniques.
	—Explain the use of fluoride gel.

School to Work—continued

Academic Subject	Workplace Skills
Speech Class (cont'd)	—Teach patients to brush and floss their teeth.
	—Reinforce measures to avoid mouth infection.
Health Education and Safety	
Universal Precautions	—Use careful techniques to avoid infecting yourself and others.
	—Wash hands often according to the accepted technique.
	—Wear appropriate protective clothing.
	—Sterilize instruments accurately.
	—Clean stationary equipment as directed.
Mechanical Maintenance	—Keep dental chairs, chair lights, and tables in good order.
Mathematics	
Accounting	—Bill clients and dental insurance companies appropriately.
Addition, Subtraction	—Post insurance and client payments.
	—Prepare receipts.
	—Determine balances owed.
	—Prepare deposit slips.
	—Pay suppliers and dental labs.
Computer Skills	—Issue checks and pay suppliers electronically.
Division	—Order supplies.
	—Check that deliveries contain all supplies that were ordered.
	—Determine monthly payment plans for patients.
Science	
Anatomy and Physiology	—Identify structures, surfaces, and tissues of a tooth.
	—Identify individual teeth.
Biochemistry	—Use mouthwashes and dentifrices.
Microbiology	—Obtain and handle cultures.
	—Clean and sterilize instruments according to procedure.
	—Apply universal precautions techniques.
	—Clean stationary dental equipment for each patient.
Nutrition and Food Science	—Advise patients on the relationship of diet to tooth decay.
Pathophysiology	—Observe lesions in the mouth.
Pharmacology	—Prepare anesthetic syringes.
	—Advise patients on the use of whitening gel.
Radiology	—Take, develop, and mount bitewing X rays.
Social Sciences	
Culture	—Consider differences in ethnic practices when instructing patients.
Education	—Teach on a level that patients can understand.

Academic Subject	Workplace Skills
Ethics	—Maintain patient confidentiality.
	—Take care to clean instruments effectively.
	—Use quality products and compounds.
	—Do high quality work.
	—Bill only for the work done.
Group Dynamics	—Take time to be thoughtful of co-workers.
	—Maintain a positive atmosphere in the office.
Growth and Development	—Understand the differences in children's and adult's teeth.
Health Care	—Wear protective clothing to safeguard patients.
	—Wash hands often and appropriately.
Law	—Maintain complete and accurate documentation.
Mental and Social	—Understand that patients are under stress in the office.
Needs of Humans	—Protect patients from pain.
Psychology	—Encourage patients' efforts to use good dental hygiene.
	—Play soothing music in the office.
	—Maintain a quiet, relaxed, and pleasant atmosphere.
Religion	—Ensure that dental practices are in tune with your religious beliefs.
Teamwork	—Assist the dentist efficiently and effectively.
	—Understand the need for positive interaction in the office.

Review Questions

1. What is the length of each program to become a dentist, dental hygienist, dental lab technician, and dental assistant after high school?
2. List and define three dental specialties.
3. What is the difference between the role of a dental hygienist and that of a dental assistant?
4. Define *oral prophylaxis* and *restoration*.
5. What are two sources of job satisfaction in the dental field?

DIETARY DEPARTMENT

Objectives ——————————————————

After completing this chapter, you should be able to:

❏ Explain department goals.

❏ Explain how dietary needs are assessed.

❏ Describe each career in this department.

❏ Identify required education and credentials for each career.

❏ Describe the skills performed in this department.

❏ Recognize how academic subjects apply in the workplace.

Key Terms ——————————————————

Nutrients

Carbohydrate	Calorie	Fat
Protein		

INTRODUCTION

The principles of nutrition are the basis of dietetic plans for individuals, communities, and educational programs. Nourishment is essential to life and the healing process. Good eating habits promote healthy living (Figure 5–1). Well-balanced diets include a daily intake of the basic four food groups. Moderate-sized portions help to control weight.

When health problems occur, modifications in diet may need to be made. People with diabetes need to eliminate their intake of concentrated **carbohydrates** such as sugar. People with high blood pressure need to decrease their intake of sodium. People who have gastrointestinal surgery may need to eat different foods, in a different consistency, and in a different pattern than they did before their surgery.

Figure 5–1 *Good eating habits promote healthy living.*

Figure 5–2 *Serve attractive and nutritious food.*

Dietitians work with other health care professionals and community groups to provide nourishment, nutritional programs, and instructional presentations to benefit people of all ages with a variety of health conditions.

Food is digested in the gastrointestinal tract. The digestive system is the usual route for food to be ingested and processed by the body. When the system is diseased or affected by medical conditions, when certain organs are removed, or when the body cannot tolerate food because of symptoms, the body cannot ingest and process food as before. Other routes of ingestion and other forms of nourishment must be found to bring nutrition to the body to sustain life.

Because the scope of the dietary department has increased, it may be called the nutritional services department. The increased scope may include outpatient services, home care instruction, and home delivery of meals.

GOALS

The goals of the dietary department are to obtain, prepare, and serve flavorful, attractive, and nutritious food to patients (Figure 5–2), family members, and health care workers in a cost-conscious manner. Another goal is to educate patients and family members about diet and its effect on enhancing the healing process, maintaining health, and preventing illness or the recurrence of illness.

CAREER DESCRIPTIONS

In a health care facility, dietary needs are assessed and planned by registered dietitians. Meals and snacks are then pre-

CAREER HIERARCHY

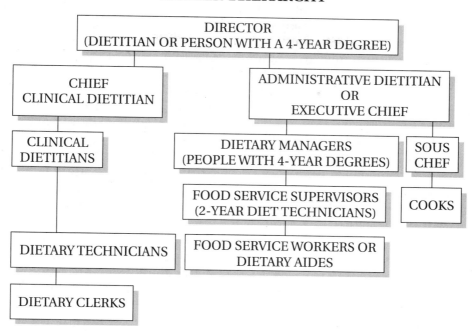

pared under the direction of an administrative dietitian, executive chef, or food service manager. Meal trays are served by dietary aides or service care assistants. Dietary technicians assist registered dietitians and may work as food service managers. Job responsibilities depend on the nature of the employing institution, department organization, and position of the worker.

Career characteristics

Employment opportunities include hospitals, skilled nursing facilities, long-term care and rehabilitation facilities, clinics, schools, universities, day care centers, retirement centers, assisted living residences, research centers, businesses and industrial facilities, the military, government agencies, international food organizations, and private practice. Hospitals are the largest employer of registered dietitians.

Work hours vary according to the facility. In hospitals, long-term care facilities, and assisted living residences, the dietary department functions 365 days a year with day and afternoon shifts. Usually, dietitians work the day shift, while dietetic technicians, food service workers, and dietary aides work day and afternoon shifts. In community, business, independent practice, and education settings, work hours are during the day, Monday through Friday.

Career advancements for dietitians include supervisory positions and directorships of departments in their chosen specialty. With a master's degree, dietitians can work in education, research, and public health agencies. The number of dietitians working as consultants in private practice is increasing.

Personal and professional qualities to be successful in this field include the ability to accomplish detailed tasks, understand science-related concepts, and develop nutritional care plans based on individual and group needs. Other characteristics include a keen interest in people as individuals and a desire to teach.

Job satisfaction comes from being respected members of the health care team and from contributing to the well-being of others. It comes from having a unique body of knowledge and meeting the challenge of planning and providing therapeutic nourishment. Professional fulfillment also comes from seeing the effects of teaching the principles of nutrition and the correlation of dietary intake with physical condition. Often, that teaching results in increased patient compliance with physicians' diet recommendations, which ultimately leads to greater comfort and a longer life.

Career roles

Registered or licensed dietitians may also be called nutritionists. They have studied biological sciences, food, how food elements are processed by the body, and the relationship between food elements and the body's needs. They are uniquely qualified to interpret the nutritional needs of various patients depending on age, gender, activity, and illness. Through education and planning, they promote health maintenance, prevention of illness, and treatment of disease. Dietitians choose a specialty area of professional practice. These career paths include clinical dietitian, community dietitian, administrative dietitian, business dietitian, educator dietitian, and consultant dietitian.

Clinical dietitians are a vital part of the health team in patient care settings such as hospitals, long-term care facilities, and clinics. They evaluate the relationship between nutrition and health status with patient and family interviews, medical record data, and lab reports. They develop individual plans to meet nutritional needs. These plans include diets, tube feedings, and education. Clinical dietitians provide individual and group educational programs for patients and family members about their nutrition and health, the importance of nourishment in the healing process, and the role of nutrition in preventing illness (Figure 5–3). Instructions may include the effects of **calorie**, **fat**, **protein**, and sugar intake; principles of well-balanced diets; details of special diets; and methods of food preparation. If prepared foods or medical nutritional supplements are to be used, information on the nutritional content of those items and where they may be purchased will be included. Details of the instruction will depend on the physician's orders and the patient's illness and ability to understand. Frequently, dietitians instruct family members who are responsible for preparing the patient's meals.

Figure 5–3 *Clinical dietitians teach classes about food and nutrition.*

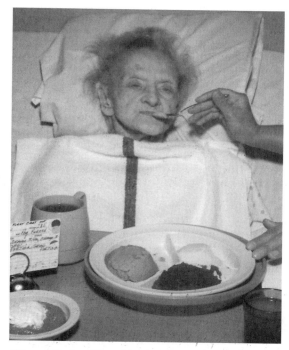

Figure 5–4 *The elderly is one of the groups that concern clinical dietitians.*

Clinical dietitians are concerned with the nutritional needs of people in all age groups (Figure 5–4)—from premature infants to the elderly—who are afflicted with a range of problems that affect their nutritional status. Often, when patients need nourishment to heal and regain health, other factors prevent eating. Some patients cannot chew or swallow, or have no appetite. Clinical dietitians plan ways to meet individual nutritional requirements by circumventing symptoms and illnesses. Clinical dietitians can specialize in certain areas such as nutrition support, cancer, diabetes, kidney disease, pediatrics, or gerontology. In addition to hospitals, they work in research labs and private practice.

Community dietitians work with wellness programs and international health organizations. They adapt food and nutrition education and information to lifestyles and geographic areas. They coordinate nutritional programs in prenatal clinics, public health agencies, daycare centers, health clubs, and recreational camps and resorts.

Administrative dietitians are also called management dietitians. They manage dietary departments in health care facilities, school food service programs, prisons, cafeterias, and restaurants. They oversee food preparation and service. They hire, train, direct, and supervise department employees. They develop systems for obtaining, preparing, and serving food. They are responsible for large-scale food planning and service (Figure 5–5).

Figure 5–5 *Dietitians manage food service systems, assess nutritional needs, and plan menus according to prescribed diets.*

Business dietitians serve as resource people for the media. They work as sales representatives for companies that make nutritional supplements and tube feedings. They work for food-manufacturing companies. They work as marketing specialists in corporate public relations.

Dietitian educators teach in colleges, universities, and hospitals. They teach courses on nutrition and food service management systems. They study food from the perspective of biological sciences. They demonstrate the effects of proper nourishment on health maintenance, disease prevention, and the treatment of illness.

Consultant dietitians work in private practice. They contract independently to provide nutrition services and educational programs to individuals, long-term care facilities, assisted living residences, acute care facilities, and industry.

Dietetic technicians work under the supervision of registered dietitians or managers (Figure 5–6). They are trained in writing regular and modified diets, nutritional screening, patient visitation, and food production and delivery. They supervise food production, visit hospitalized patients to obtain preferences, provide simple diet instructions, and work with dietitians to review menus and recipes. They need to be able to work well with others and follow directions accurately.

Responsibilities include ordering food items, processing orders to suppliers, and managing food storage. They can

Figure 5–6 *A registered dietician and dietetic technician.*

work in the dietary office, in the kitchen, and with patients.

Job opportunities include hospitals, nursing homes, universities, industrial food service, catering services, restaurant chains, day care centers, and community agencies. By continuing their education, they can become dietitians.

Dietary clerks work in the dietary department office. They enter data and record diet changes in the computer. They check menus against recent diet orders before trays are assembled. They are responsible for tracking financial data, such as the number of meals served. They provide communication between the patient care units and the rest of the dietary department. They are trained on the job.

Executive chefs plan and direct the production of food for patient service, retail (cafeteria) service, and catering. A certified executive chef is credentialed by the American Culinary Federation. A sous chef is an assistant chef.

Dietary managers are responsible for the direct management of a specific departmental function, such as retail (cafeteria), catering, or tray line. If an operation is large, it may have one or more dietary managers or food service supervisors to assist in directing the dietary workers. They are trained on the job.

Dietary workers prepare food and meal trays in the kitchen area (Figure 5–7). They work on the tray line, determining tray completeness and accuracy. They maintain the storage area for food supplies, practice sanitary procedures, and can identify food contamination situa-

Figure 5–7 *Dietary workers preparing food.*

tions. Dietary workers are trained on the job and can work in any commercial kitchen. Another name for this job is diet aide.

JOB AVAILABILITY

The U.S. Department of Labor projects limited job availability for dietary workers to the year 2005. The shrinking job market in nutritional careers is due to hospitals having fewer patients and the lack of insurance reimbursement for dietetic services. In addition, efforts are being made to reduce labor costs and cross-train other workers to accomplish basic dietary tasks. Some opportunities are available for basic-level jobs in residential facilities for the elderly. As contracting for food service with outside companies becomes more popular, more jobs will be available with those firms.

Jobs for dietitians will increase modestly. Their services include home care

EDUCATION AND CREDENTIALS

CAREER	YEARS OF EDUCATION AFTER HIGH SCHOOL	DEGREE OR DIPLOMA	TESTED BY; LICENSED BY
Registered licensed dietitian (RD, LD)	4 years plus 6 to 12-month internship or AP4 program: 4 years plus 900 hours of supervised practice	B.S. in food nutrition or master's degree in food and nutrition or institutional management	ADA; Registered by ADA; licensed by the state
Registered licensed dietetic technician (DTR)	2 years	A.A.S.D. in dietetic technology	Certified by ADA; licensed by the state
Certified chef (CEC or CWC)	2 years	A.D. in culinary arts or hospitality management	ACF
Cook (CC)	On-the-job training	—	Education and certification via ACF (optional)
Dietary Manager, Clerk, Worker, Aide	On-the-job training	—	—

Key to abbreviations:

A.D.—Associate Degree
A.A.S.D.—Associate of Applied Science Degree
ACF—American Culinary Federation
ADA—American Dietetic Association
ADCA—Associate Degree of Culinary Arts
AP4—Approved Practice for Dietitian Program
B.S.—Bachelor of Science Degree
CC—Certified Cook
CEC—Certified Executive Chef
CWC—Certified Working Chef
DTR—Dietary Technician Registered
LD—Licensed Dietitian
RD—Registered Dietitian

instruction and outpatient services such as dietary counseling and mobile meals.

SKILLS

Skills used by dietary workers in a hospital depend on job title and certification. Clinical dietitians assess and meet dietary needs according to physicians' orders, nursing requests, or directions from an interdisciplinary specialty team. Administrative dietitians manage the dietary department and develop methods to evaluate and improve food and cost-effective nutrition service systems. Dietetic technicians work with department employees and patients to record diet history, identify food habits, develop diet plans, and supervise food preparation and delivery. Dietary workers or aides prepare food and assemble meal trays. Diet clerks do clerical tasks related to menus and diet changes; and dietary aides or service care assistants deliver meal trays. Department skills center around management, food service, assessing and meeting nutritional needs, and patient education.

Department management

Administration of the dietary department involves identifying and accomplishing department goals, determining department policies and procedures, hiring and training workers, and scheduling work hours. Other tasks include planning and structuring studies to determine customer satisfaction and seeking ways to meet consumer needs more effectively. In addition, menus are simplified and more convenience items purchased in an effort to contain supply and labor costs.

Food service

Food service involves the purchasing of food according to planned menus for patients and workers. Amounts must be sufficient to feed the clients but not enough to spoil. Supplies such as plates, cups, napkins, and meal trays are ordered according to need and the type of equipment used in the food service system.

Food service includes preparing, assembling, transporting, serving, and collecting meal trays. Other responsibilities involve the delivery of between-meal nourishments and tube feedings. The quality of service and customer satisfaction is measured, and changes are made as necessary.

Meeting nutritional needs

Meeting nutritional needs entails the assessment of patients by registered or licensed dietitians to determine nutritional status and diet habits. Nutritional assessment begins with a medical record review for pertinent data, patient and family interviews, and calculation of calorie intake. It includes identifying how dietary intake affects the disease process and making a plan to encourage food intake to meet the needs of the body, promote or maintain health, and prevent illness recurrences. Accomplishing nutrition care plan goals involves educating and working with patients, family members, and other members of the health team (Figure 5–8). It also includes participation in meetings with patient-centered interdisciplinary teams, such as the stroke team or the oncology team. Dietary needs become evident in these meetings, and follow-up visits with patients are scheduled by dietitians.

Diet instruction

Instruction in nutrition and diet is done with individuals, in small groups, and in large classes. Topics include special diets for conditions or diseases and nutrition for various age groups. Classes in weight-reduction diets, diabetic diets, and gerontology nutritional needs may be offered. Diet instruction includes the rationale for the special diet, a listing of foods allowed or not allowed for the diet, and planning a day's menu. Appropriate teaching materials, such as brochures and videotapes developed by qualified dietitians, are used. Simple diet instruction may be done by qualified dietetic technicians. Complex diet instruction is done by qualified dietitians.

Figure 5–8 *Work with the family to make good nutrition a reality.*

Biography

When I was twelve years old, my father died and my mom returned to work. She worked long hours, from early morning to dinner time. So when I got home from school, I prepared dinner for both of us. She always praised my efforts, even though every dinner was not delicious. Over the years, I learned and became a better cook. I took over the grocery shopping and experimented with different spices and combinations of foods. My mother never complained, even when some of these combinations probably gave her a stomach ache.

I eventually decided that my favorite activity was cooking. When I was in high school, I got a job as a bus boy at a professional club. There, I worked my way up to being a beginning cook. Since I had so much experience at home, I was good at it. The club recognized my talents. After high school, I continued to work at the club. I began to contract to do private parties dur-

ing my off hours. I developed such a business that I quit my full-time job and started my own catering company. Business was great.

During that time I married and had two children. Soon I realized that I saw my family for only a short while each day. My work catering private parties took place during evening hours and all day on weekends. So I decided to look for a full-time job in a company where I could work Monday through Friday during the day. Being the chief cook at the hospital lets me do this. In addition, working at the hospital gives me other benefits, such as medical insurance and paid sick leave and vacation. Now I have the best job of all. I continue to cook and create menus. I learned that being self-employed in a successful catering business is a great financial opportunity. But at this time in my life, being with my family and having financial security is more important to me.

Career Search

To discover more about a career and the roles of members in the dietary department, contact the following organizations for online addresses, printed information, and videotapes.

American Dietetic Association
216 W. Jackson Boulevard, Suite 800
Chicago, IL 60606–6995
Phone: 312–899–0040
Fax: 312–899–1979

Society for Nutrition Education
2001 Killebrew Drive, Suite 340
Bloomington, MN 55425–1882
Phone: 612–854–0035
Fax: 612–854–7869

Range of Annual Incomes

Dietitian	$29,000–$48,000
Dietetic technician	$18,000–$31,000
Dietary clerk	$13,000–$22,000
Dietary worker or aide	$12,000–$18,000
Cook	$16,000–$25,000

What's New

Distribution of meal trays to hospital patients is one of the tasks taken over by service care associates from dietary workers. To help contain costs, basic-level workers stationed on the nursing units have been trained to perform tasks once done by workers in other departments.

A "kitchenless kitchen" system is another effort at cutting costs. In this system, prepared food already on plates is purchased and delivered to the nursing units by an outside company. The service care associate heats the appropriate plates and assembles meal trays in the unit pantry. This method bypasses the main kitchen and all dietary workers.

Reducing expenses and simplifying dietary activities are goals of the department. Simple menus are developed, more convenience food items are purchased, and the labor force is reduced to decrease costs.

School to Work

This section demonstrates how school-based learning carries over to work-based learning. Some of these skills may be learned in a high school laboratory or in a mentorship or apprenticeship program.

Academic Subject	Workplace Skills
Arts	—Create diet trays that are appealing to the eye. —Design menus with different colors of food on the main plate.

School to Work—continued

Academic Subject	Workplace Skills
Arts (cont'd)	—Print menus with large print and attractive designs.
Business	
Time Management	—Schedule appointments for dietitian visits.
	—Arrange for diet classes.
Communication	—Write a dietary newsletter.
English	—Assess patients' medical history.
	—Complete nutritional history completely and legibly.
	—Note the physician's diet instructions for the dietitian.
	—Send written diet instructions to the appropriate patient.
Computer Skills	—Enter diagnostic and diet data.
	—Note patients' food allergies, likes, and dislikes.
	—Change patients' room numbers as they are transferred.
	—Interpret incoming diet request data.
	—Arrange for late trays for delayed diets.
	—Schedule staff's working days and shift rotations.
	—Use a modem to download information for the dietitian.
Word Processing	—List daily menu selections for each diet.
Economics	—Order and bill for guest trays.
	—Enter patients' diet changes.
	—Enter discharge information promptly.
	—Order food in bulk.
	—Check the delivery of supplies for completeness and accuracy.
Bookkeeping Systems	—Enter supplies that have been ordered and received.
	—Approve a bill for payment when supplies have been received.
	—Transfer information to the accounts payable department.
Filing Systems	—Update data about patients' diets.
	—File paper dietary notices and reports appropriately.
English and Communications	
Medical Terminology	—Know the content of special diets.
	—Understand the significance of ordering the correct diet.
Medical Dictionary, Glossary	—Locate correct medical terms.
	—Spell terms in patients' nutritional history and diagnosis correctly.
Speech Class	—Help patients complete menus.
	—Honor diet requests when possible.
	—Express diet instructions clearly and understandably.

Academic Subject	Workplace Skills
Speech Class (cont'd)	—Reinforce instructions.
	—Determine the understanding of the listener.

Health Education and Safety

Universal Precautions	—Wash hands often according to the accepted technique.
	—Wear a hairnet and gloves when handling food.

Mathematics

Addition, Subtraction	—Post guest trays.
	—Pay suppliers or authorize payment by another department.
Division	—Order supplies.
	—Calculate costs.
	—Authorize payment when supplies are delivered.

Science

Microbiology	—Dispose of food that falls on the floor during preparation.
	—Avoid touching items in patients' rooms when passing trays.
Nutrition and Food Science	—Advise patients on the relationship of diet to disease.
	—Deliver the correct tray to the appropriate patient.
Pathophysiology	—Prepare tube feedings for patients who cannot swallow.
	—Serve between-meal snacks to those needing more caloric intake.
Pharmacology	—Understand the effects of medications on taste and digestion.

Social Sciences

Culture	—Consider ethnic differences in beliefs involving food.
Education	—Teach on a level that patients can understand.
Ethics	—Maintain patients' confidentiality.
Gerontology	—Serve soft diets to people who have no teeth.
	—Relate the effects of sodium on high blood pressure.
Group Dynamics	—Work with nursing staff for the patient's benefit.
	—Make a special effort to be cooperative on nursing units.
Growth and Development	—Provide different diets for patients of different ages.
	—Understand that certain foods appeal more to children.
Needs of Humans	—Realize that nourishment is essential to life.
Psychology	—Serve small portions to elderly patients.
Religion	—Respect religious practices related to food.

Review Questions

1. What is the goal of the dietary department?

2. After high school, how long are the programs to become a registered licensed dietitian, a registered licensed dietetic technician, and a certified chef?

3. What are seven areas of specialty available to registered licensed dietitians?

4. What are six employment opportunities for dietary workers?

5. What are the lowest and highest hourly wages for dietitians, dietetic technicians, and dietary workers?

Chapter 6

EMERGENCY DEPARTMENT

Objectives

After completing this chapter, you should be able to:

- ❑ Explain department goals.
- ❑ Identify the kinds of problems handled in an emergency department.
- ❑ Describe several careers in this department.
- ❑ Identify the required education and credentials for each career.
- ❑ Recognize how academic subjects apply in the workplace.

Key Terms

Cardiopulmonary resuscitation
Myocardial infarction
Asthma
Cardiac arrest
Cerebral vascular accident

Congestive heart failure
Fracture
Hemorrhage
Laceration

INTRODUCTION

Professionals who specialize in emergency care treat patients with traumatic injuries and sudden severe illnesses. They assess, diagnose, and treat the acutely ill patients who usually need immediate medical attention. Activities include **cardiopulmonary resuscitation**, stabilization of critically ill patients, and arranging the transfer of patients to the nursing unit or facility that will best meet their needs. Patients who have had **myocardial infarction** may be taken to the cardiac care unit. Patients who have been severely burned may need to be transported to a hospital with a burn unit. Those with minor ailments may be treated and released from the emergency

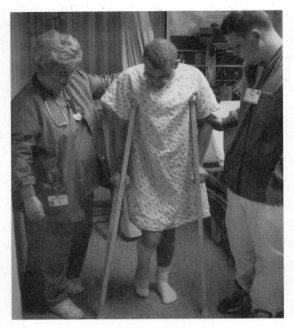

Figure 6–1 *Some patients are treated and released from the ER.*

Figure 6–2 *Help is on the way.*

care setting without being admitted to the hospital (Figure 6–1).

Other physical problems seen in an emergency room are **asthma**, **cardiac arrest**, **cerebral vascular accident**, **congestive heart failure**, **fracture**, **hemorrhage**, and **lacerations**. Each problem is treated according to the individual patient's diagnosis, immediate physical condition, age, expressed wishes, health history, and support system.

Patients come to an emergency care setting in a variety of ways. Some patients drive themselves to the emergency care setting, and some are transported by family, paramedics, or a flight crew. However they come, both patients and families are experiencing stress, especially if the illness is life-threatening (Figure 6–2).

GOALS

The goals of an emergency care setting are to assess, diagnose, treat, and stabilize acutely ill patients as quickly as possible in a friendly and comforting environment and to direct them to appropriate aftercare.

CAREER DESCRIPTIONS

Professional workers who specialize in emergency care need to be prepared to minister to patients of all ages with a variety of conditions—from minor injuries to major trauma, from mild symptoms to cardiac arrest. They care for patients with all types of illness and accidents, some of which are self-inflicted. Workers are often successful at saving lives; but sometimes

CAREER HIERARCHY

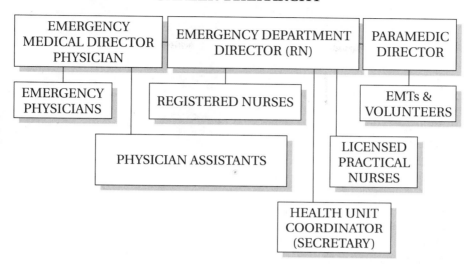

patients die. Some emergency care professionals work in hospitals or freestanding emergency centers; others work outside the institutional setting, administering prehospital emergency care and transporting the victim to the medical facility.

After completing their basic educational programs, physicians and nurses who work in emergency care usually have had specialized training in caring for acutely ill patients. A course in advanced cardiac life support and previous work experience in a surgical intensive care or coronary care unit may be required to work in emergency care settings and on the helicopter flight team. The entire emergency medical technician course is geared to first aid training for sudden acute illness.

Job responsibilities vary according to the education and position of the workers and the policies of the institution. In some hospitals, paramedics work in the emergency department when not responding to a rescue call. In some communities, they work out of the fire department and may also be firefighters.

Some workers are permanently assigned to the emergency department, while others come there when a critically ill patient arrives. Permanent workers include physicians with a specialty in emergency medicine, nurses, and health unit coordinators (secretaries). Medical centers may have a helicopter flight crew of doctors, nurses, respiratory therapists, and paramedics who work in the emergency care setting between rescue runs. Patient registration representatives help to obtain demographic information, initiate charts, maintain records, and arrange for hospital admission.

Workers who come to the emergency care setting when a critically ill patient arrives include an anesthesiologist, respiratory therapist, radiographer, medical laboratory technician, EKG technician, clergy, and social worker. Cardiologists, surgeons, and other specialists are called in as necessary.

Career characteristics

Employment opportunities include hospital emergency departments, freestanding emergency centers, critical care transport services, private ambulance services, government agencies, pharmaceutical and manufacturer sales positions, home care, and industrial clinics. Other options include working in the operating room, clinics, law offices, and insurance companies. With an advanced degree, teaching and research may be options. Experience in emergency patient care is background for positions on critical care nursing units, helicopter flight crews, and in surgery. Career opportunities for registered nurses, particularly those with critical care experience, are the broadest of all health careers. RNs are able to work with all age groups in all specialties. They can change their speciality and work in other cities, states, and nations.

Work hours vary according to the facility. Hospital emergency departments are usually open twenty-four hours every day of the year (Figure 6–3). Freestanding emergency centers may be open days and evenings seven days a week. Workers can often schedule flexible hours, depending on the needs of the facility. Eight-, ten-, and twelve-hour shifts may be available, as well as four-hour periods during busy times. Paramedics may work the same schedule as firefighters—on duty for twenty-four hours, off for forty-eight hours. Care givers in a twenty-four-

Figure 6–3   *Hospital emergency rooms never close.*

hour facility may need to rotate to evening and night shifts and work weekend hours and holidays. Positions in education and industry usually offer daytime work hours.

Career advancements include supervisory or department director positions. With further education, a worker with emergency care experience can move into other positions. A paramedic or practical nurse may become a registered nurse, perfusionist, or physician's or surgeon's assistant.

Desired personal characteristics include possessing a calm, kind demeanor; a friendly, reassuring manner; and a capacity for solving problems. Emergency care workers need to work well in stressful situations, be adaptable, give directions, take directions, and be prepared to help patients and family members cope with tragic situations. Other desirable qualities include dependability, skill in resuscitative measures, and an ability to communicate effectively both verbally and in writing (Figure 6–4).

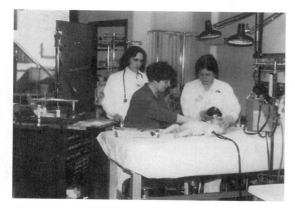

Figure 6–4 *Effective communication is never more necessary than in an ER situation.*

Nurses need confidence, leadership and teaching skills, the ability to make fast and responsible decisions, good interpersonal skills, and the ability to interact with many different types of people and personalities.

Paramedics need physical fitness—including the ability to lift about 150 pounds with the assistance of another person. Other attributes include the ability to communicate diplomatically with patients, family, and bystanders. Paramedics need a crisp appearance in a stain-free uniform. Both verbal skills and appearance are interpreted by patients and observers as indicative of the quality of care that will be given. Some paramedics keep a spare uniform at work in case the one being worn becomes spattered with blood or street soil. Leadership is another quality that is important in the field. Each paramedic needs to be able to take charge of the situation, make good decisions, go ahead with treatment of the victim, and prepare for transport. In a triage situation or when there are multiple victims, paramedics must lead or work alone.

Job satisfaction comes from feeling effective in easing suffering, calming fears, stopping a disfiguring process, stabilizing conditions, and saving lives. Making sound decisions under stress, good feelings that come from helping people who are severely ill and fearful, and variety in daily activities contribute to job gratification.

Personal safety is a concern for emergency care workers because of handling patients' blood and body fluids. Workers need to wear protective clothing in situations where they might contact body fluids.

Career roles

Emergency care physicians are doctors with special training in emergency medicine. They lead the emergency team and work with team members to diagnose and treat patients. Physicians assess patients, order diagnostic tests, interpret test results, identify illnesses, and develop treatment plans. Because patient conditions often are severe and unstable or life-threatening, these steps may need to be carried out in minutes. Physicians must recognize when to call in specialists, identify the need for hospitalization, and give discharge directions to those who do not need hospitalization. Physicians also determine the need to transfer a patient to another facility and the best mode of transportation—ambulance or helicopter. Physicians explain the diagnosis and treatment plan to patients and families. They may be employed by the facility or by an agency that contracts with the facility to provide physicians.

The registered nurse coordinates the patient care and personnel in the emergency department. In most cases, this is the first person to see the patient upon his or her arrival. The nurse must obtain a medical history from the patient or the family, including current medications and any drug allergies. In this setting, the nurse must do a fast and accurate initial assessment of the patient to determine the acuity level. If the nurse feels that the patient needs to be seen by the physician immediately, the nurse must seek out and notify the physician immediately of the patient's condition. In the event that the physician is unable to see the patient immediately, the nurse is responsible for initiating treatment. This may include starting intravenous fluids, drawing blood, applying oxygen, and anticipating any tests or treatments the physician may want to perform.

Nurses who work in the emergency department are responsible for coordinating all aspects of patient care (Figure 6–5). They not only carry out the physician's orders but must anticipate needs, make suggestions to the doctor, and intervene on the patient's behalf. The physician and nurse work together as a team.

Nurses monitor vital signs, provide physical comfort, administer medications, help patients to understand the diagnosis and treatment plan, instruct patients in aftercare, and work with physicians to identify other health team members who may be consulted. Nurses seek to identify unknown patients, locate

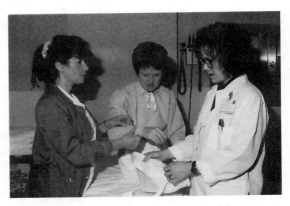

Figure 6–5 *Coordinating the health care team is one of the nurse's responsibilities.*

family members, and arrange for hospital admission or transport to another facility.

Emergency medical service (EMS) is the system of rescue workers. There are several levels of emergency medical service technicians based on the length and content of the education program: EMT—A, EMT—I or EMT—D, and EMT—P. Some programs are full-time and some are part-time. Programs vary from six hundred to fifteen hundred hours of instruction and experience. To complete the program, the student must have practice in certain emergency care situations. In addition, an EMT must have a good driving record. A conviction of driving while under the influence of alcohol or drugs is grounds for refusing to admit a student into an EMT program and for dismissing an EMT from the emergency squad.

The emergency medical technician— ambulance (EMT—A) has basic training in emergency care. These workers are qualified to drive an ambulance, do CPR, and assist paramedics in the field (Figure 6–6). Technicians are trained to

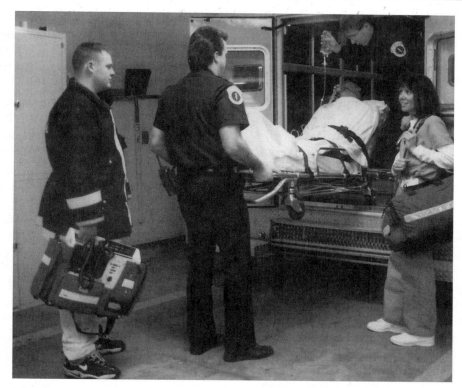

Figure 6–6 *EMTs and a firefighter arrive at the hospital and give a report to the ER nurse.*

provide first aid, administer oxygen, and apply mast trousers. They can work for a private ambulance company or a municipal government after passing a civil service examination. They transport stable patients from the hospital to a long-term care facility or from the hospital to diagnostic testing sites. In some geographic areas, this level is being phased out because more education is desirable.

In rural areas, volunteers assist an EMT—P on each call; these volunteers must be licensed EMT—As. When a call comes in, several volunteers and the EMT—P on call are notified. At least two volunteers respond. The EMT—P is in charge of the scene and communicates with a medical center by two-way radio. Depending on the emergency, the patient is either treated at the scene or transported to receive more advanced medical assistance.

The EMT—intermediate (EMT—I) or EMT—defibrillation (EMT—D) receives more in-depth training. These technicians work with more unstable patients, administer oxygen, apply mast trousers, and perform the more advanced procedures of starting intravenous fluids and administering defibrillation. They apply mast trousers to compress peripheral blood vessels of a patient in shock to reroute blood to the vital organs. They are employed by fire departments and municipal governments in rescue ambulances.

The EMT—paramedic (EMT—P) has the most education in this category. These technicians act as the eyes, ears, and hands of the physician in the field. They administer treatments for life-threatening emergencies—the same tasks as the emergency care physician would do. They administer oxygen, apply mast trousers, start intravenous fluids, defibrillate, plus administer medications. They have a thorough knowledge of first aid, quickly assess situations and extent of illness or injury, follow specific protocols to stabilize patients on the scene, treat conditions that need immediate attention, convey information and receive direction from the emergency care setting over a cellular phone or two-way radio, and transport patients to a medical facility. In some rural areas as well as cities in some states, EMT—Ps are allowed to treat patients within their homes or at the scene without transporting them to medical facilities. These paramedics are considered primary care givers.

Flight crew members include physicians, registered nurses, and EMT—Ps who travel by helicopter to airlift a patient to a designated location. They may have to rescue a patient from an automobile accident in a remote area not accessible to an ambulance or transport the patient from the scene of an accident to a distant hospital. Or a patient may need to be transferred from one hospital to another in the shortest possible time. Before the flight team is activated, both the medical crew and the pilots must approve the flight.

The medical crew members need to determine the feasibility of the rescue effort. To make that decision, they need an assessment of the situation and patient condition from the emergency workers on the scene. After the medical crew decides that the assignment is appropriate, the pilots are consulted. They are responsible for determining if weather conditions are safe for flight. If the pilots decide that flight is possible, the team is on the way (Figure 6–7).

Upon arrival, the medical team helps the on-site workers prepare the patient for flight. At an accident site, the patient is transported as quickly as possible with stabilization efforts conducted in flight (Figure 6–8). If the patient is in a hospital, the flight team helps the hospital workers stabilize the patient before preparing for transport. A physician or EMT—P, two nurses, and one respiratory therapist may all fly in the helicopter with one or two patients.

Figure 6–7 *Paramedics and flight crew en route to the scene.* (Courtesy of MetroHealth Medical Center of Cleveland, Ohio.)

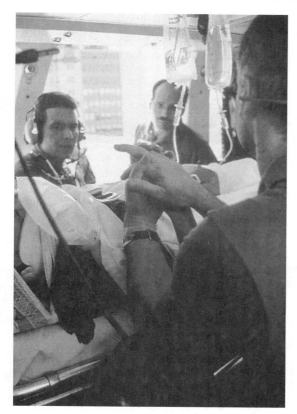

Figure 6–8 *Patient care is administered during the flight.* (Courtesy of MetroHealth Medical Center of Cleveland, Ohio.)

In addition to rescuing people from an accident scene and transporting critically ill patients from one site to another, flight crews are called upon to transport organs that have been harvested for transplant. Since the time organs can be without oxygen before they begin to degenerate is limited, their transport must be accomplished as quickly as possible. In some cases, the critically ill recipient is transported to the site of the dying donor. In others, both donor and recipient are transported to the medical center where the harvest and transplant will take place.

JOB AVAILABILITY

Job availability is good for paramedics, registered nurses, and licensed practical nurses through the year 2005. Competition for jobs will be keen in rescue squads and fire departments because of good pay, benefits, and job security. Turnover is high in rescue squads because the work is stressful and advancement opportunities are limited. In small cities, towns, and rural areas, there are no paid EMT jobs. Emergency workers in those areas are volunteers.

Job opportunities exist for registered nurses and paramedics in organ and tissue recovery. Jobs are in both local and regional organ donation centers. These jobs include teaching groups about organ and tissue donation, counseling family members about giving a loved one's organs, blood and tissue testing, matching donated organs with potential recipients, and contacting physicians to determine acceptance or rejection. Once the organ or tissue has been recovered, it is processed and transported as quickly as possible. Follow-up statistics and outcomes are tracked by computer. Families of donors are informed of the recipients' outcomes if they so request.

SKILLS

Workers need training in emergency skills before going to work in an emergency care setting. Assessing patients' conditions quickly, diagnosing the illness accurately, initiating a plan of action to stop the disease progression, stabilizing and treating conditions, and observing the beginnings of recovery are skills used by workers in this setting. The keys to this

EDUCATION AND CREDENTIALS

CAREER	YEARS OF EDUCATION AFTER HIGH SCHOOL	DEGREE OR DIPLOMA	TESTED BY; LICENSED BY
Physician (M.D. or D.O.)	4 years of college, 4 years of medical school, and 3 years of residency in emergency medicine	B.S. and M.D. or D.O.	National boards; 3 parts; Emergency medicine boards (written and oral); State registration ACLS; ATLS; PALS
Registered nurse (RN)	2 years 3 years 4 years	A.A.S.D. in nursing B.S.N.	State board of nursing; ACLS
Licensed practical nurse (LPN) (LVN)	1 year	Diploma	State board of nursing; BLS; pharmacology certification
Emergency medical technician—ambulance (EMT—A); volunteers	13 weeks	Certificate	Ambulance state certification; CPR required
Emergency medical technician—intermediate (EMT—I) or (EMT—D)	2 quarters plus EMT—A (9 months); same as EMT—I	Certificate or diploma if hospital program	State certification; written and practical administered by NREMT; and basic life support course required EMT—1 plus defibrillation
Emergency medical certification technician—paramedic (EMT—P)	9 months for paramedic plus EMT—P plus associate degree	A.A.S.D. in emergency medical technology	State administered by NREMT; and ACLS required

Key to abbreviations:

A.A.S.D.—Associate of Applied Science Degree
ACLS—Advanced Cardiac Life Support
ATLS—Advanced Trauma Life Support
BLS—Basic Life Support
B.S.—Bachelor of Science Degree
B.S.N.—Bachelor of Science in Nursing Degree
D.O.—Doctor of Osteopathy
EMT—Emergency Medical Technician
EMP—P—Emergency Medical Technician—Paramedic
LPN–Licensed Practical Nurse
LVN–Licensed Vocational Nurse
M.D.—Medical Doctor
NREMT—National Registry of Emergency Medical Technicians
PALS—Pediatric Advanced Life Support
RN—Registered Nurse

process are speed and accuracy, because lives often depend on swift intervention.

Emergency skills need to be practiced so that workers are ready to perform them effectively when a patient arrives. When paramedics are transporting a patient to the hospital, they may radio ahead regarding a patient's symptoms and traumatic injuries so workers can prepare to perform necessary skills. In a freestanding emergency care setting, workers may need to learn more skills than at a hospital, which has more disciplines.

Cardiopulmonary resuscitation

Cardiopulmonary resuscitation is the skill of providing oxygen and pumping blood when the heart and lungs are not functioning. Most patients who receive CPR after a witnessed cardiac or respiratory arrest survive with their mental capacities intact.

Defibrillating

Defibrillating is the procedure that "shocks" the heart with an electrical charge. It is done to change the heartbeat from an irregular rhythm to a regular rhythm.

Tending wounds

Cleansing and bandaging wounds, suturing lacerations, and casting fractured bones are other skills used in the emergency care setting. Physicians, paramedics, surgeons' assistants, and physicians' assistants suture wounds according to the policies of the facility.

Taking vital signs

Taking, interpreting, and documenting vital signs are essential skills in the emergency care setting (Figure 6–9). Temperature, pulse, respirations, and blood pressure readings indicate if patients' conditions are stable, improving, or deteriorating. Reporting changes in these signs may save lives.

Intravenous insertion

Inserting an intravenous needle is an essential skill needed to draw blood or administer fluid and medication directly into the bloodstream. In some patients, the procedure is difficult because of arte-

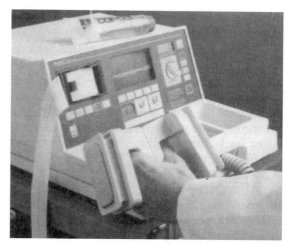

Figure 6–9 *Computers are used to monitor the heart and for defibrillation of abnormal heart patterns.* (Courtesy of Siemens Burdick, Inc.)

riosclerosis, small veins, or the collapse of venous circulation that may occur if the blood pressure is very low or absent. It is also difficult if the patient is unable to hold the arm still. This is often the situation with a baby, small child, or confused adult.

Patient safety

Planning for patient safety is a skill needed to protect the patient from events that could cause injury. The patient's identity is confirmed by the identification wristband applied on arrival. Side rails are used to prevent falling from the high, narrow treatment carts; signal cords are used to indicate that help is needed; and special procedures are followed to ensure administration of safe, compatible blood transfusions.

Triage

Triage, handling large numbers of patients in a community disaster, is a skill performed by workers in a hospital emergency department. If a plane crashes, a bus accident occurs, or an apartment building burns, large numbers of patients would be transported to the hospital for assessment and treatment. Each hospital has a disaster plan to handle such events. Though such disasters are rare, workers need to be thoroughly schooled in triage techniques. They need to practice sorting and directing "patients" to appropriate treatment areas so that real patients would be effectively and efficiently treated.

Communication
Communication skills for comforting, supporting, and educating patients and family members and informing other professionals are also necessary (Figure 6-10). Accurate and complete written communication is essential to providing adequate care and preventing error.

Confidentiality
Confidentiality is the skill that guarantees patients' privacy. Workers cannot talk

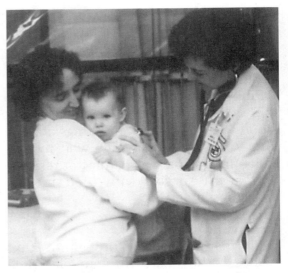

Figure 6–10   *Comforting care calms fears.*

about one patient to another or talk to friends or members of the media about patients' conditions or the facts surrounding an event. Workers cannot disclose the circumstances of an automobile accident or mention any information about injured victims.

Biography

I entered a high school medical career program thinking that I wanted to be a doctor. During this course, I discovered three things about myself. One, science classes are hard for me. Two, I didn't want to go to school for as many years as it takes to be a doctor. And three, I like excitement. I do not want to spend my life in an office.

When I began learning about careers associated with an emergency department, I realized that EMT would be the perfect career for me. So after high school, I entered the local community college and began my studies. Now I am a full fledged EMT—P. Because of the geology of my area, I have been specially trained in rappelling down cliffs and in underwater rescue. I love my work. I go to a scene not knowing what I will find. My partner and I do our best to stabilize the victim. If necessary, I communicate with the ER physician for further directions based on my observations. Then I transport the victim to the emergency center. The work is exciting and different every day.

Career Search

To discover more about a career and the roles of members in an emergency department, contact the following organizations for online addresses, printed information, and videotapes.

American College of Emergency
  Physicians
P.O. Box 619911
Dallas, TX 75261–9911
Phone: 214–550–0911
Fax: 214–580–2816

Emergency Nurses Association
216 Higgins Road
Park Ridge, IL 60668
Phone: 847–698–9400
Toll-free phone: 800–243–8362
Fax: 847–698–9406

National Association of Emergency
  Medical Technicians
102 W. Leake Street
Clinton, MS 39056
Phone: 601–924–7744
Toll-free phone: 800–34–NAEMT
Fax: 601–924–7325

American Academy of Physician
  Assistants
950 N. Washington Street
Alexandria, VA 22314
Phone: 703–836–2272
Fax: 703–684–1924

Range of Annual Incomes

Physician	$110,000–$190,000
Registered nurse	$ 33,000– $43,000
Licensed practical nurse	$ 20,000– $30,000
Paramedic	$ 22,000– $42,000
Physician assistant	$ 38,000– $56,000
Unit secretary	$ 16,000– $25,000

Paramedic pay is modest with private ambulance companies. On volunteer squads in rural areas, a minimum of three paramedics call in and report to the scene. Of those three, one must be a EMT—P who is being paid an "on call" fee (usually $1.50 per hour). At the scene, this EMT—P assumes the role of chief and is paid a minimum of four hours at the hourly rate established by the municipality.

What's New

Laptop computers will become part of the equipment in an ambulance. Paramedics will have immediate access to a patient's medical history, medication profile, and laboratory values. This will greatly increase information available to emergency workers on the scene and help them to make more knowledgeable patient care judgments.

Telemedicine is the ability to communicate by voice and video with a physician or hospital emergency department.

Necessary equipment includes a two-way camera and special high-speed telephone lines or a computer hooked up to the Internet. This voice and video transmission technology is especially valuable in rural areas where no hospital or physician may be available to treat patients. In that case, the rescuer is the primary care giver. Using a video phone with standard telephone lines is possible, but the picture is somewhat distorted.

The ER holding area is a nursing unit adjacent to the emergency department in which patients are kept up to twenty-four hours while their condition is evaluated.

The decision will be made to admit or discharge them during that time. This holding area has a staff separate from the emergency department and minimizes costs.

Cellular phones have replaced the two-way radio in large towns and cities. Emergency departments have dedicated lines for EMTs' cellular phones. In cities, radio communication is used only for backup communication. In rural areas, where funds are limited, the two-way radio remains the method of communication between EMTs and the ER.

School to Work

In addition to the general academic subjects and workplace skills contained in the "Job Skills" chapter, the following subjects and skills apply specifically to emergency department careers.

Academic Subject	Workplace Skills
Arts	—Graph results of emergency care.
	—Create a chart illustrating statistics about ER care.
	—Connect a video camera with a computer or special telephone lines.
Business	
Time Management	—Organize work to care for the sickest patient first.
Communication	—Justify supplies needed.
	—Request improvements in equipment.
English	—Review client history.
	—Write accurate, understandable messages and reports.
Computer Skills	—Obtain the patient's old medical records through the computer.
	—Retrieve the patient's recent history data.
	—Use a modem to connect with a poison control center.
	—Fax data to appropriate physicians and medical centers.
	—Connect with medical centers via computer.
Word Processing	—Write summary reports.
	—Use the spell checker.
	—Send messages to other departments and physician offices.

Academic Subject	Workplace Skills
Economics	—Transfer patients to the ER holding area or hospital unit, or arrange their discharge. —Understand insurance plans and managed health care. —Call insurance companies to request permission to admit or treat patients.
Bookkeeping Systems	—Enter insurance approval numbers. —Document charges of all disciplines treating the patient.
Filing Systems	—Enter the patient's data in the appropriate file. —Gain access to the patient's computer file with a security code.

English and Communications

Communication	—Remain calm in a stressful situation. —Speak clearly via phone or radio to EMTs in the field. —Contact appropriate personnel to meet the emergency squad on its arrival. —Relay information to EMTs accurately. —Give directions to staff to arrange for receiving the rescue squad's patient. —Listen to what patients and medical personnel say. —Do not give information over the phone or to the media. —Explain a delicate situation to the hospital public relations person. —Empathize with families.
Medical Terminology	—Use medical terms appropriate to ER personnel. —Interpret medical terms to the family.

Health Education and Safety

Universal Precautions	—Explain precautions to patients and families. —Wash carts and countertops with a bleach solution. —Clean up blood and body fluids using the appropriate technique. —Handle bloody clothing and instruments using the proper techniques.

Mathematics

Addition, Subtraction, and Multiplication	—Sign out controlled drugs according to policy. —Calculate medication doses according to patient age and body weight.
Division	—Set up an intravenous (IV) pump to prevent fluid over- or underdose. —Mix disinfectant solution according to the required percentage.

School to Work—continued

Academic Subject	Workplace Skills
Division (cont'd)	—Calculate IV drips per minute based on milliliters per hour.
Science	
Anatomy and Physiology	—Begin an IV solution if needed.
	—Apply a thermal blanket or mast trousers as appropriate.
	—Inject medication in the appropriate muscle or vein.
Biochemistry	—Determine the need for medication and a blood transfusion.
	—Replace specific elements in a patient with severe burns.
Microbiology	—Swab an infection source for a culture.
	—Wear protective clothing appropriate to the suspected infection.
Nutrition and Food Science	—Pump the stomach if food poison is the cause of illness.
	—Calculate nutritional needs in a patient with anorexia.
	—Estimate the need for diet instruction.
Pathophysiology	—Identify the lack of proper functioning of organs and systems.
	—Relate vital signs to the patient's overall body condition.
	—Restrict fluids with sodium if tissue edema is present.
Pharmacology	—Reverse an overdose of drugs with other drugs or dialysis.
	—Administer elements and medications to correct deficiencies.
Radiology	—Complete X-ray, scan, or ultrasound tests to identify problems.
	—Apply a cast to a fractured arm.
Physics	—Set up traction on the bed to align bones and decrease pain.
	—Apply Ted hose to support circulation and prevent leg edema.
Social Sciences	
Culture	—Interpret tests and treatments in the patient's native language if possible.
	—Offer to call a member of the clergy.
Education	—Explain tests and treatments as simply as possible.
Ethics	—Perform tests and treatments to the best of your ability.
	—Carry out patient's and family members' wishes.
Gerontology	—Consider the frailties of age when treating older adults.
Group Dynamics	—Work effectively and efficiently with all disciplines.
	—Assist other team members in an emergency situation.
	—Recognize the presence of stress and tension in emergencies.
	—Be supportive and understanding of team members.

Academic Subject	Workplace Skills
Growth and Development	—Encourage parents to remain with children when possible. —Recognize symptoms of child abuse. —Practice extra safety measures with dependent individuals.
Health Care	—Teach the patient as health care is administered. —Use antiseptic lotion after washing hands to prevent dry skin.
Human Relations	—Recognize that stress may result in frayed tempers. —Be supportive and understanding of patients, families, and staff. —Excuse negative comments made because of anxiety.
Law	—Maintain patient's confidentiality. —Return patient's valuables to the next of kin. —Notify a social worker if abuse is suspected. —Adhere to patients' living will requests. —Explain organ donation to the next of kin of terminal patients. —Gain proper signatures before confirming organ donations.
Mental and Social Needs of Humans	—Notify a social worker or clergy if this would be helpful. —Give nourishment and fluids where appropriate. —Inform family of eating facilities if their wait will be long. —Comfort the patient and family when possible.
Teamwork	—Help others to complete their work. —Offer assistance in the emergency situation.

Review Questions

1. What is the goal of an emergency care setting?
2. List three categories of professional workers in an emergency department and the length of education required after high school for each category.
3. What are the differences between the roles of the physician and the nurse in the ER setting?
4. What are the sources of job satisfaction in an ER setting?
5. List four academic subjects and two skills associated with each role in the ER.

MEDICAL LABORATORY DEPARTMENT

Objectives

After completing this chapter, you should be able to:

❑ Explain department goals.

❑ List common tests performed in the medical laboratory.

❑ Describe the specialties in this department.

❑ Identify required education and credentials for each career.

❑ Describe how academic subjects apply in the workplace.

Key Terms

Laboratory Sections

Blood bank	Hematology	Chemistry
Microbiology	Cytology	Histology
Immunology/Serology/Virology	Urinalysis	Pathology

INTRODUCTION

The medical laboratory provides vital information that guides physicians in making diagnoses, determining treatment, monitoring disease progress, identifying effectiveness of treatment, and establishing a health maintenance regime. The process that fosters accurate results in clinical studies includes careful preparation and examination of specimens, precise performance of clinical tests, and thorough study and interpretation of the condition of tissues and body fluids (Figure 7–1). The laboratory also issues compatible and safe blood and blood products for transfusion.

The laboratory is divided into sections. These divisions are determined according to specialty and the size of the hospital and laboratory. In every section,

Figure 7–1 *Specimens are examined carefully.*

specific tests are done by workers with special training. Some tests are done manually; others are done on specifically designed instruments that are maintained by laboratory personnel.

Tests ordered by physicians are conducted in clinical laboratories. Large institutions may have research laboratories as well.

GOALS

The goals of a medical laboratory are to report accurate test results of body substances and tissues, to issue compatible, safe blood and blood products for transfusion, and to determine a cause of death by tissue examination and autopsy.

CAREER DESCRIPTIONS

Medical technologists and technicians are essential workers on the health care team. Roles and responsibilities vary according to the size of the laboratory and the facility, types of tests performed, specimen collection techniques, complexity of testing instruments, availability and sophistication of computer programs, and method of reporting test results.

Responsibilities include the daily calibration of instruments, careful monitoring of test results, and quality control procedures to be sure each instrument is functioning accurately. Definite steps

CAREER HIERARCHY

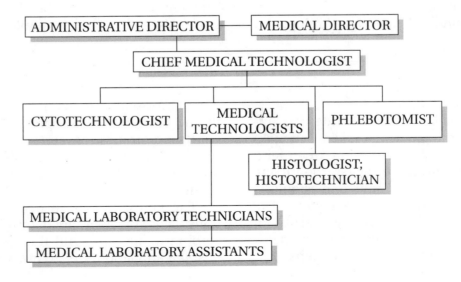

must be followed on each instrument before patient specimens are run. In large laboratories, tests are performed on automated, computer-driven instruments. In small laboratories, tests may be run manually. Chemistry, biochemistry, and microbiology are the basic courses in medical laboratory programs.

Laboratory personnel work more with specimens of body tissue, secretions, and excretions than they do with patients. Contact with patients includes drawing blood samples, receiving specimens from outpatients, and assisting physicians to obtain tissue specimens. Blood samples are usually drawn by phlebotomists, laboratory technologists, and laboratory technicians. Specimens of body secretions and excretions are usually obtained by nursing personnel. Tissue specimens are obtained by physicians. Laboratory personnel interact with health care professionals. Lab results are reported to physicians and nurses.

In small laboratories, medical technologists perform all tests. In large laboratories, technologists specialize in one or two sections. These sections may be **Blood Bank**, **Hematology**, **Chemistry**, **Microbiology**, **Cytology**, **Histology**, **Immunology/Serology/Virology**, **Urinalysis** and **Pathology**. Some small labs send specimens to large labs for out-of-the-ordinary tests.

Career characteristics

Employment opportunities for medical technologists include hospitals, clinics, physician offices, government agencies, research institutions, and pharmaceutical companies. Mobile laboratories take technologists into patients' homes. Other job sites include blood and organ donor banks, zoological settings, sperm banks, water treatment plants, government epidemiology labs, veterinary offices, and crime labs. Another area of employment opportunity is product development and marketing for companies that manufacture home testing kits and lab equipment.

Work hours vary with the institution and position. In a facility where acutely ill patients are treated, the laboratory operates twenty-four hours a day, 365 days a year. Full-time and part-time positions are available, sometimes on flexible schedules, depending on the needs of the facility and availability of personnel.

Career advancement includes section managers in large laboratories and supervisory positions in smaller facilities. An advanced degree in a biological science or education can lead to positions in teaching and research.

Desired characteristics include an aptitude for science, detail, and accurate and independent work. Other qualifications include the ability to operate complex equipment, calibrate instruments, run computers, and do scientific calculations. Also needed is the ability to strictly adhere to technical procedures and aseptic technique, work under pressure, and perform in emergency situations. Good vision and fine dexterity are needed to manipulate tissues, cells, and bacteria and to see minute gradations of color.

Job satisfaction comes from doing an essential job well. Professional fulfillment comes from knowing that the lab plays an important part in patient care and treatment. Through the precise work of laboratory professionals, disease-causing bacteria are isolated and identified, medication is recommended, medication treatment plans are evaluated, disease progress is monitored, and life-threatening levels of toxins, and abnormal cells are recognized.

Personal safety is a concern of laboratory workers because they work with body fluids and tissues that contain disease-producing bacteria and viruses. Careful technique is the key to handling contaminated materials without becoming infected (Figure 7–2).

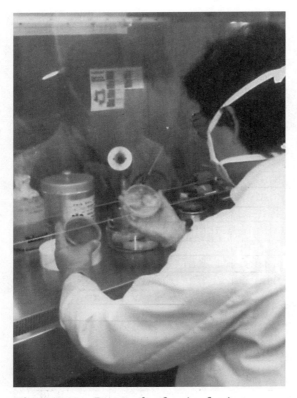

Figure 7–2 *Personal safety is of prime importance.*

Career roles

The administrative director can have a degree as a medical technologist and often has a doctor's or master's degree in a medical specialty. This person is responsible for the quality of specimen preparation, accuracy of test results, and correct reporting of those findings throughout the laboratory. He or she is also responsible for the business or financial aspect of laboratory operations.

A pathologist serves as the medical director of the laboratory. The pathologist is a medical or osteopathic physician who specializes in the study of the nature, cause, and development of diseases, and the structure and function of normal and abnormal body cells. This specialty includes detecting cellular misfunction, abnormal structure, and the extent of disease progress. This is a serious responsibility because a patient's treatment is often based on pathology findings. If a pathologist reports that malignant cells are present, a certain type of surgery and medical therapy may be carried out. If a pathologist reports that no malignant cells are present, a more conservative surgery and medical plan may be employed. Inaccurate cellular studies can result in a cancer growing and spreading. Pathologists need to be knowledgeable in both anatomical structures and clinical analysis of specimens.

Other responsibilities may include directing the clinical laboratory, monitoring quality-assurance studies, conducting research, analyzing statistical data, and advising on treatment strategies. Pathologists also perform autopsies to examine organs and tissues and establish a cause of death. Pathologists work in hospitals, medical schools, government, and private industry.

Medical technologists prepare and examine specimens of tissue, fluids, and cells. Under the supervision of a pathologist, technologists determine the presence of abnormalities and diseases. They perform complicated chemical microscopic and automated analyzer/computer tests. They know the clinical significance of tests results. Areas of specialization include microbiology, chemistry, blood bank, hematology, and immunology. The medical technologist is qualified to advance to a supervisory position.

Medical laboratory technicians work under the supervision of pathologists or medical technologists (Figure 7–3) and do the same tasks that are performed by medical technologists. They prepare tissue specimen slides for examination, perform cell counts, and run urinalysis. They draw blood samples from patients and perform tests in the hematology, serology, and bacteriology sections. They maintain supplies and equipment and keep up records.

Phlebotomists or venipuncture technicians are trained to draw venous blood samples (Figure 7–4). They process some blood samples and perform clerical duties.

Cytotechnologists work with pathologists in screening cells from tissue scrapings and body fluids for abnormalities, especially those changes that indicate cancer.

Histologists are classified as histologic technicians or histotechnologists. They prepare tissues for microscopic exam. The technician's findings are reviewed and confirmed by a pathologist. Before studying cellular changes, the technician may review the patient's medical record to learn about factors that affect changes

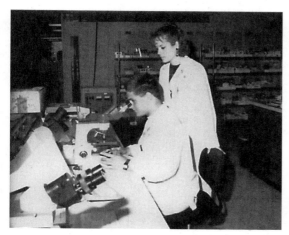

Figure 7–3 *A medical technologist supervises a lab technician.*

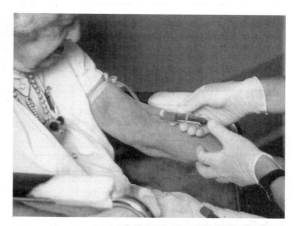

Figure 7–4 *Phlebotomists, medical technicians, and lab technicians learn to draw blood for testing.*

in body cells. Such factors sometimes alter cellular patterns and cause diseases. These factors include family medical history, personal medical history, and special information such as type of work; smoking, eating, and drinking habits; symptoms; and treatment program.

JOB AVAILABILITY

The U.S. Department of Labor estimates that job availability in the medical lab is expected to grow at an average rate through 2005. Jobs are most plentiful for lab technicians with an associate degree.

The growth in this field will be less than that of some other health care careers because of the increasing use of computer-driven automation in specimen preparation, test performance, and interpretation of results. In addition, fewer tests are being ordered as a result of increased patient monitoring. Another reason for this decline is that specific tests are now done for preoperative screening in place of the many standard tests once routinely ordered for all patients scheduled for surgery. In addition, the specialty testing of DNA and RNA and certain viral and bacterial studies are done only at major medical centers, not at the local hospital labs.

SKILLS

Tasks performed by medical technologists and technicians vary according to the section in which they work. They learn both manual and computer techniques during training (Figure 7–5). After training, they can specialize in certain sections depending on the size of the lab and job availability. Training is a continu-

Figure 7–5 *Computers have found their way into the lab.*

ous process because of scientific discoveries and advances in technology.

Many computer-driven automated analyzers are available in the marketplace. Laboratory workers learn to use instruments purchased by the facility (Figure 7–6). If instruments malfunction, technicians repair them, use backup equipment, or run the lab tests manually.

Blood bank

Blood bank (immunohematology) is the only section of the clinical laboratory that issues a product. All other sections prepare and test specimens and issue re-

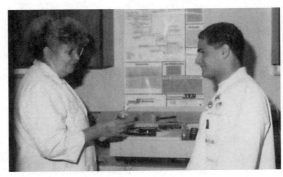

Figure 7–6 *On-the-job training in the lab.*

ports. Blood bank skills include identifying the patient, drawing the blood sample, determining the blood type, screening for antibodies, obtaining safe blood for transfusion, and ensuring compatibility by cross-matching donor and patient blood.

Another task is the drawing and storing of autologous donations, that is, obtaining blood from people who prefer to receive their own blood (if needed) when they undergo surgery. Another form of autologous transfusion is the salvaging of blood during surgery and returning those blood cells to the patient. This process can only be carried out in certain types of surgeries. The sterile solution that was suctioned from the operative site is taken to the lab and spun down (Figure 7–7) to remove excess liquid and concentrate the cells. It is then transfused into the patient's veins. Though some cells are damaged in the process, the danger of contracting a disease from an unknown donor is eliminated. This process may also be done with some postoperative wounds, usually knee and hip.

Figure 7–7 *Cell washer machine concentrates blood cells for transfusion.*

Preparing and permanently storing all records associated with transfusions administered in the facility is another task entrusted to the blood bank. These records include information about donors and recipients. If an illness later develops in a donor, transfusion recipients can be traced, informed, and treated.

Other tasks relate to prenatal work. An expectant mother's blood is typed to determine the Rh factor. When the baby is born, a blood sample is drawn from the umbilical cord and tested.

Hematology

In hematology, whole blood is tested to determine the number and quality of blood cells. Some blood cell counts are done with an electric counter. Another part of the blood cell identification is done by preparing glass slides of blood cells to view under a microscope. These tests indicate if the patient has enough blood or needs a transfusion. They also show infection, mononucleosis, leukemia, or anemia is present. An expectant mother's blood is routinely tested to avoid anemia. Computers may be used to identify different types of blood cells (Figure 7–8). Often, life-saving treatment is based on test results from this section.

Chemistry

In chemistry, the blood serum is tested to measure the levels of organic and inorganic components, enzymes, and electrolytes. Essential elements such as potassium can be life-threatening if too much or too little of one or more is present (Figure 7–9).

EDUCATION AND CREDENTIALS

CAREER	YEARS OF EDUCATION AFTER HIGH SCHOOL	DEGREE OR DIPLOMA	TESTED BY; LICENSED BY
Certified pathologist (M.D. orD.O.)	4 years of college, 4 years of medical school, 2 years of postgraduate residency, and 3–5 years of pathology training	M.D. or D.O.	American Board of Pathology; the state
Medical technologist (MT)	4 yers of college plus 1 year internship	B.S. in medical technology or chemistry, biology, or other science	National Certification Agency for Medical Laboratory Personnel; Licensure or registration required in some states
Blood bank technologist (MT, AABB)	Same as for MT plus 1 year of training in a certified program in the Specialty of Blood Bank (SBB)	B.S. plus certificate	AABB
Chemistry technologist (MT)	Same as for MT with specialty in chemistry	—	—
Hematology technologist (MT)	Same as for MT with specialty in hematology	—	—
Immunology technologist (MT)	Same as for MT with specialty in immunology	—	—
Medical laboratory technicial (MLT)	2 years of college and 1 year internship	A.A.S.D. in medical laboratory technology	ASCP; Licensure or certification required in some states
Cytotechnologist (CT, ASCP)	4 years of college plus 1 year internship	B.S. in biology or chemistry	ASCP
Histologic technician (HT, ASCP)	2 years	—	AASD/ASCP
Histotechnologist (HTL, ASCP)	4 years	B.S. degree	ASCP
Phlebotomist; venipuncture technician	10 weeks or 2 quarters of on-the-job training	—	APS

Key to abbreviations:

AABB—American Association of BLooiod Banks
A.A.S.D.—Associate of Applied Science Degree
ASCP—American Society of Clinical Pathology
B.S.—Bachelor of Science Degree
CT—Certified Technician
CMT—Certified Medical Technician
D.O.—Osteopathic Doctor
HOE—Health Occupations Education in high school

HT—Histology Technologist
IAPS—International Agency of Phlebotomy Science
M.D.—Medical Doctor
MT—Medical Technologist
NCAMLP—National Certification Agency for Medical Laboratory Personnel
SBB—Specialist in Blood Bank

Figure 7–8 *A hematology computer differentiates the types of blood cells.*

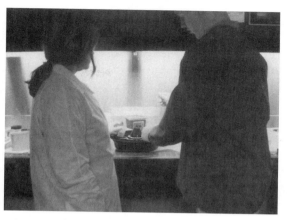

Figure 7–10 *Preparing a culture under a laminar flow hood.*

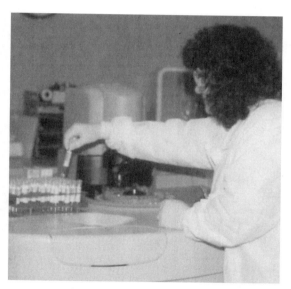

Figure 7–9 *Computers are used to perform blood chemistry tests.*

Microbiology

In microbiology, various body fluids are studied to determine the presence of disease-producing microorganisms. Specimens are inoculated on culture media on which microorganisms will grow in the incubator (Figure 7–10). Throat cultures are tested for strep, sputum specimens for tuberculosis and pneumonia, and urine cultures for bladder or kidney infections. Organisms are then isolated, identified, and tested to determine the most effective antibiotic medication.

Cytology

In cytology, tissue scrapings and liquid specimens are prepared to identify changes in cell structure, size, color, cytoplasm, and nuclei. Cancer is the most common type of abnormal cell detected. Cells from tissue scrapings, saliva, sputum, urine, and needle aspirations are all studied in this section. The Pap smear—cells from the uterine cervix—is the most common test done in this section. Specimen cells are smeared on glass slides and contrast stains sometimes added before the slide is viewed under the microscope.

Histology

In histology, tissue from a solid organ is cut, stained, mounted, and prepared for microscopic examination (Figure 7–11). If the tissue is obtained from a patient in the operating room, a "frozen section" is done for immediate analysis. This tissue is quickly frozen to make the slicing more accurate. Like other specimens in histology, the frozen tissue is placed in paraffin (wax) and sliced very thinly. These shavings are fixed on glass slides, stained with special dyes, and studied under the microscope by the pathologist. Other tasks include maintaining the paraffin, reagents, and other stains and solutions for tissue preparation. Tissues from fine-needle biopsies and autopsies are also studied in this section.

Immunology

Immunology/serology/virology is the section that identifies the ability of the body to resist pathogens by producing antibodies. In this section, tests are done to determine the body's response to viruses or allergy-causing agents. The efficiency of the patient's immune system is determined from the result.

Urinalysis

Urinalysis is the section that examines urine for cellular and chemical content (Figure 7–12).

Pathology

In pathology, body organs and tissues are studied, and autopsies are done by the pathologist.

Figure 7–11 *Solid tissue is prepared for microscopic examination in histology.*

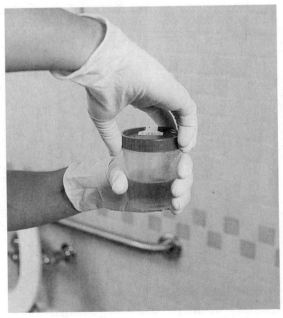

Figure 7–12 *Gloves are worn when handling specimens.*

Biography

During high school, I became ill with mononucleosis. Because I was absent a lot, I dropped out of school. I then left home, but had no means of support. I soon discovered how hard it is to get a good job without a high school diploma. After talking it over with my parents, I moved back in with them, studied, and passed the GED test. It was hard work, but I knew it was the right decision.

I got a job at the local hospital and learned to draw blood. With on-the-job training, I became a phlebotomist. I plan to return to school and work toward an associate's degree to become a medical lab technician. I am grateful to my parents for their support and for allowing me to live with them so I can work. I am a hard worker and believe I have a future in health care.

Career Search

To discover more about a career and the roles of members in a medical laboratory department, contact the following organizations for online addresses, printed information, and videotapes.

American Society of Clinical
  Pathologists
2100 W. Harrison Street
Chicago, IL 60612
Phone: 312–738–1336
Toll-free phone: 800–621–4142
Fax: 312–738–1619

American Society for Clinical
  Laboratory Science
7910 Woodmont Avenue, Suite 1301
Bethesda, MD 20814
Phone: 301–657–2768
Fax: 301–657–2909

American Medical Technologists
710 Higgins Road
Park Ridge, IL 60068
Phone: 708–823–5169
Toll-free phone: 800–275–1268
Fax: 708–823–0458

American Society for Microbiology
1325 Massachusetts Avenue N.W.
Washington, DC 20005–4171
Phone: 202–737–3600

American Society of Hematology
1200 19th Street N.W., Suite 300
Washington, DC 20036–2412
Phone: 202–857–1118
Fax: 202–857–1164

American Association of Blood Banks
8101 Glenbrook Road
Bethesda, MD 20814
Phone: 301–907–6077
Fax: 301–907–6895

American Association for Clinical
  Chemistry
2101 L Street N.W., Suite 202
Washington, DC 20037–1526
Phone: 202–857–0717
Toll-free phone: 800–892–1400
Fax: 202–887–5093

National Society for Histotechnology
4201 Northview Drive, Suite 502
Bowie, MD 20716–1073
Phone: 301–262–6221
Fax: 301–262–9188

National Phlebotomy Association
5615 Landover Road
Hyattsville, MD 20784
Phone: 301–699–3846
Fax: 301–699–5766

American Society of Cytopathology
400 W. 9th Street, Suite 201
Wilmington, DE 19801
Phone: 302–429–8802
Fax: 302–429–8807

American Association of
Immunologists
9650 Rockville Pike
Bethesda, MD 20814
Phone: 301–530–7178
Fax: 301–571–1816

Range of Annual Incomes

Certified pathologist	$155,000–$170,000
Medical technologist	$ 28,000– $40,000
Lab Section supervisor	$ 31,000– $48,000
Blood bank technologist	$ 22,000– $27,000
Chemistry technologist	$ 22,000– $27,000
Hematology technologist	$ 22,000– $27,000
Immunology technologist	$ 22,000– $27,000
Medical laboratory technician	$ 23,000– $31,000
Cytotechnologist	$ 29,000– $41,000
Histologist technician	$ 24,000– $36,000
Phlebotomist	$ 16,000– $26,000

What's New

Robotic systems have come into the lab in the form of self-contained, high-tech machines. For example, in the chemistry section, computer-driven equipment separates the serum part of the blood, pipettes it, dilutes it, and runs the tests. That is, it determines the amount of chemical elements within that sample, interprets whether the amount of each chemical is too high or too low, records in memory individual patient trends, stores the results in medical records, and prints out the results in the lab, on the specific nursing unit, and in the appropriate physician's office. In the hematology section, whole blood is pipetted into the tubing and passed along through the machine as the computer determines the number of red and white cells plus the amount of hemoglobin present in the sample. Another computer scans whole blood to analyze the different types of cells in the sample. In this program, cells that cannot be identified by the computer are flagged for human interpretation.

Lab findings are communicated through modems in desktop or laptop computers. This is especially helpful for instant reference when a patient is in a medical office, when a physician is called at home, and when a home care nurse is at a patient's house.

Methods of gene isolation, testing, and manipulation are being developed by biotechnology laboratories. Research results can be used by pharmaceutical companies to develop drugs to influence genes such as those of obesity and Alzheimer's disease.

School to Work

In addition to the general academic subjects and workplace skills contained in the "Job Skills" chapter, the following subjects and skills apply specifically to medical laboratory careers.

Academic Subject	Workplace Skills
Arts	—Design a pie chart to illustrate blood disease statistics. —Create bar charts to show lab usage.
Business Time Management	—Perform outpatient blood draws promptly. —Order supplies appropriately so tests are not delayed. —Assign lab tech work hours according to demand peaks.
Communication	—Greet patients pleasantly. —Explain procedures before performing them.
Computer Skills	—Enter the time specimens come into the lab. —Perform daily control studies on analytical computers. —Enter control studies data each day. —Refill diluent and chemicals in analyzers each day. —Order supplies with cost containment and quality in mind.
Health Education and Safety Universal Precautions	—Use careful techniques to avoid infecting yourself and others. —Wear a disposable gown or lab coat. —Wear gloves when handling specimens. —Wear a mask when working with tuberculosis bacteria. —Wipe counters with antiseptic solutions. —Work with specific microbes under a reverse airflow hood.
Mechanical Maintenance	—Run the control program on each analyzer each day. —Report equipment in need of repair. —Check the temperature of the refrigerator that contains units of blood.
Science Anatomy and Physiology	—Understand body chemistry and blood components. —Know the relationship between disease and lab values. —Comprehend what causes a blood transfusion reaction.

School to Work—continued

Academic Subject	Workplace Skills
Biochemistry	—Notify a nurse or physician of life-threatening element levels.
	—Identify high blood levels of alcohol, chemicals, and medications.
Microbiology	—Culture specimens.
	—Identify the name and dose of medication that fights the organism.
Nutrition and Food Science	—Determine if the blood levels of elements are related to diet.
Pathophysiology	—Assist the physician in determining diagnoses.
Pharmacology	—Understand the effects of medications on blood and body fluids.
	—Discuss with the pharmacist antidotes to neutralize overdoses.
Social Sciences	
Ethics	—Maintain patients' confidentiality regarding lab results.
	—Respect patients' right to privacy regarding diagnoses.
	—Think about gene isolation, testing, and manipulation.
Law	—Handle specimens in criminal labs according to procedure.
	—avoid talking to the media about lab results in criminal cases.

Review Questions

1. What are the goals of a medical laboratory?
2. Which lab worker is most in demand in the labor market?
3. What are the differences between the chemistry and the hematology sections of the lab?
4. Which lab career has the shortest training period? Which has the longest?
5. List three academic subjects and two skills associated with each as used in the medical lab.

MEDICAL OFFICE

Chapter

8

Objectives

After completing this chapter, you should be able to:

❏ Explain department goals.

❏ Recognize the various health professions that comprise a medical office.

❏ Describe several careers in this department.

❏ Identify required education and credentials for each career.

❏ Describe how academic subjects apply in the workplace.

Key Terms

Procedures

Electrocardiograph	Chemotherapy	Dialysis
Laser treatment	Lithotripsy	Radiation therapy

INTRODUCTION

A medical office, clinic, or hospital pread-mission testing department is a clean, pleasant place to work (Figure 8–1). Patients who come to this work site usu-ally are in more stable condition than those who are hospitalized. However, they do have concerns about their physi-cal condition and the implications of their illness. The atmosphere of the office depends on the people who work there and the nature of the care given.

Figure 8–1 *A medical office is a pleasant place to work.*

Generally, medical doctors have a practice of regular patients who return over years for checkups and medication regulation. After repeated office visits, staff befriend patients, develop ongoing relationships with them, show an interest in their progress, and help them develop coping skills. Patients with chronic illnesses may visit the office frequently during the course of those illnesses.

Working in a surgeon's office is different from working in a medical physician's office. Patients visit a surgeon's office, at a minimum, once before and once after surgery. After those two visits, the office staff might never see those patients again. Here, there may be a hurried feeling because the surgeon may be late coming from the hospital or be called away from the office for emergency surgery. Because of the nature of the work, a surgeon's schedule can be erratic at times. Surgeons need to be available to operate immediately on patients who need care without delay.

Tests and treatments that may be done in an office or clinic setting are **electrocardiograph**, **chemotherapy**, **dialysis**, **laser treatments**, **lithotripsy**, and **radiation therapy**.

GOAL

The goal of the medical office is to serve patients on an outpatient basis by facilitating the assessment, diagnosis, and treatment process and by meeting their educational, emotional, and psychosocial needs in a friendly, supportive, cost-effective, and professional manner.

CAREER DESCRIPTIONS

Careers in offices and clinics vary according to the type of medical specialty and the size of the work site. A large clinic will have more categories of professionals and more medical specialties than a small, one-physician office. Physicians often form partnerships and share their practices. In these group practices, physicians with the same specialty establish a business relationship. Though each maintains his or her own patients, the partner physicians try to meet all the patients. Partner physicians share office space and workers, take turns being on call during evening and weekend hours, and relieve each other for vacations. Some physicians have joined a managed care firm with hundreds of other physicians of all specialties.

CAREER HIERARCHY

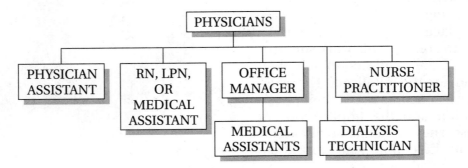

Whatever mode of practice is chosen, each physician remains responsible for practicing medicine ethically and for making a sincere effort to meet the needs of each patient. Physicians in a managed care practice work within certain guidelines developed by the corporations specifically to contain health care costs.

Office staff serve patients as well as physicians and try to make office visits as pleasant and expeditious as possible. Staff use universal precautions to maintain cleanliness, especially when handling blood and body fluids, because of the AIDS virus and other infectious agents (Figure 8–2).

Career characteristics

Employment opportunities depend on the career. Jobs are available in physician offices, clinics, hospital preadmission testing departments, and freestanding surgery or emergency care centers. Employability in office work is improved with keyboard skills and knowledge of medical insurance forms.

Work hours are usually daytime Monday through Friday, with some Saturday and evening hours. Offices may be open early morning to early evening, with fewer hours on Saturdays. Staff may work full or part time. In some offices, staff members may be assigned to work with certain physicians. Their work hours then coincide with those of the physicians. Wages in an office or clinic position may not be as high as in acute care settings because of the daytime hours, no rotation of shifts or holiday work, and stability of patients' conditions.

Career advancements are more lateral than upward. In a large clinic, moving into an administrative or teaching position may be an option.

Desired personal characteristics include being considerate, knowledgeable, personable, clean, well groomed, friendly, and eager to help others. Attributes include a positive attitude and the ability to be sympathetic, empathetic, patient, and tolerant. Even if patients come late to appointments, physicians are delayed, or it is past the usual quitting time, staff should never show irritation or speak sharply to patients.

Job satisfaction comes from being a part of a friendly and competent team that serves physicians and patients with cordial efficiency and sincere interest (Figure 8–3). It comes from mutual respect and the feeling of a job well done.

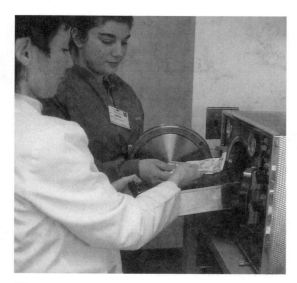

Figure 8–2 *Equipment sterilization is the office worker's responsibility.*

Figure 8–3 *Communication between professionals is essential for quality care.* (Courtesy of MetroHealth Medical Center of Cleveland, Ohio.)

Career roles

Physicians are either medical doctors (M.D.s) or doctors of osteopathy (D.O.s). Both M.D.s and D.O.s are called "Doctor," treat sick people, and teach good health practices. However, doctors of osteopathy stress the association between the muscles and bones of the body and the function of organs. When treating patients, they use manual manipulation and palpation techniques in addition to traditional medical techniques.

Physicians obtain health histories, perform physical examinations, order and interpret diagnostic tests, diagnose conditions, prescribe medications, provide health instruction, and refer to other physicians and specialists as appropriate. They treat persons who are ill and injured, and teach health maintenance and illness prevention.

Physicians specialize in one or two areas—internal medicine, family practice, general surgery, or other fields such as cardiology. They work in private practice, research, education, the military, veterans hospitals, public health and government agencies, school systems, private industry, and managed care groups.

Desirable personal characteristics include self-motivation, intelligence, clear thinking, and an aptitude for science. Physicians need to have good study skills, an interest in helping people, and the capacity to make good judgments under pressure.

Career advancement includes adding another specialty, learning more skills to serve patients, and becoming chief of the specialty or of the medical staff. Careers can expand to include teaching, scholarly writing, research, public speaking, and community projects.

Physician assistants work under the direction of physicians in clinics, offices, hospitals, and patients' homes. They do health screenings and physical exams, take patient histories, and may order laboratory tests. They identify initial diagnoses and initiate treatment plans according to guidelines. They confer with physicians and refer to specialists when appropriate. In rural areas, they may be the only health professional in the office or town. When questions arise, they contact the physician to whom they report for direction. If their educational program included surgical experience, they may do minor operations under local anesthesia and prescribe medication if allowed by state law and the state medical association.

Career advancement is more lateral than upward. Physician assistants can change offices or hospitals, move to a rural area or to a city, or work in clinics, nursing homes, or military service.

Nurse practitioners are registered nurses who specialize in a particular area of patient care, such as pediatrics or geriatrics. They care for more acutely ill patients and have more independence than do physician assistants. They assess patients, order laboratory tests, carry out treatment plans, and make independent judgments. In some states, they are licensed to order medications and treatments for specific illnesses and conditions. In some institutions, they are allowed to order certain medication and treatments according to accepted protocols of care. They contact physicians and refer to specialists when necessary. They are responsible for health teaching, and they counsel patients and family members about illness and coping mechanisms (Figure 8–4).

Desired personal characteristics include creativity, innovation, independent spirit, clear thinking, a willingness to accept responsibility, and good decision-making skills. As with physician assistants, career moves are lateral rather than upward.

Dialysis technicians are registered nurses, licensed practical or vocational nurses, or technicians who work with patients who have no kidney function and cannot make urine. Dialysis cleanses the blood of waste elements and excess fluid. This process is a life-saving treatment.

Dialysis technicians are trained to care for a patient on the hemodialysis machine, also known as an artificial kidney. This procedure involves monitoring vital signs and making sure that the patient's blood passes through the tubing on the machine and returns to the veins without mishap. Dialysis technicians monitor blood chemistry to determine if the treatment is effectively cleansing the blood of impurities and extra fluid (Figure 8–5). Dialysis treatments are usually done three times a week until a kidney becomes available for transplant or the patient dies.

Some dialysis technicians make home visits to teach patients how to perform dialysis there. Family members may be taught in case the patient becomes unable to perform the procedure. Some

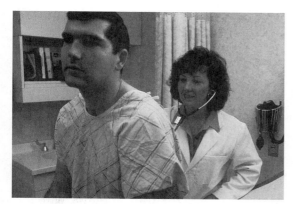

Figure 8–4 *A nurse practitioner assesses the physical condition of a patient.* (Courtesy of MetroHealth Medical Center of Cleveland, Ohio.)

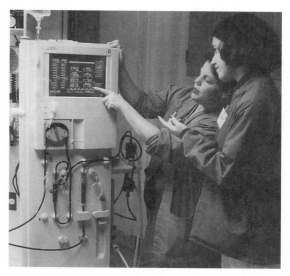

Figure 8–5 *The dialysis technician monitors calculations during treatment.*

patients may plug themselves into dialysis units at bedtime, allow the machine to run while they sleep, then unplug themselves, and go to work in the morning.

Career advancement is lateral in dialysis work. Job opportunities include hospitals, clinics, offices, and home care.

Medical assistants are trained to work with physicians, physician assistants, and nurses in an outpatient area. They answer phones and schedule appointments, hospital admissions, and surgeries. They greet patients and help them prepare for a physical exam. They obtain and record health histories, vital signs, weight, and height. They test vision, draw blood, perform some lab procedures, and assist with physical exams and minor surgeries (Figure 8–6). They take X rays, obtain vital capacities, and do electrocardiograms for physician interpretation. They change dressings and do some

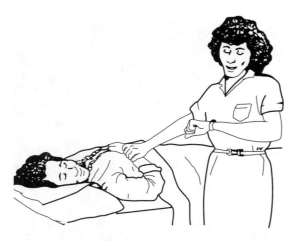

Figure 8–6 *A medical assistant takes vital signs and helps the physician with physical exams.*

treatments. They clean and sterilize instruments, straighten examining rooms, order supplies, and restock cabinets. They also work with the business aspect of office management. They handle correspondence, fax reports, process insurance forms, prepare bills, and post payments.

Job opportunities include offices, clinics, health maintenance organizations, and public health agencies.

Career advancements include becoming an office manager in a large office or clinic. Further advancement depends on obtaining a baccalaureate degree or a degree in another field.

JOB AVAILABILITY

The U.S. Department of Labor estimates that employment opportunities are excellent for nurse practitioners and physician assistants, especially in rural areas and inner-city clinics. Job availability will increase faster than average for medical assistants, medical secretaries, medical record technicians, receptionists, registered nurses, and licensed practical nurses. All jobs associated with medical offices and clinics are expected to grow faster than average through the year 2005 because of the emphasis on health maintenance and cost containment.

Job availability is especially good in family practice, where a medical physician acts as a primary care coordinator. This physician oversees and directs total patient care by referring patients to specialists only when absolutely necessary. This will result in less work for physician specialists, thus fewer available positions. Managed care insurance plans will pay only for consultations that have been ordered by the primary care physician.

EDUCATION AND CREDENTIALS

CAREER	YEARS OF EDUCATION AFTER HIGH SCHOOL	DEGREE OR DIPLOMA	TESTED BY; LICENSED BY
Physician (M.D.)	4 years of college, 4 years medical school, 1 year of internship, and 1 year of residency in specialty	M.D.	NBME and specialty organization (ECFMG exams are taken by graduates of foreign medical schools); State
Physician (D.O.)	3–4 years of college, 4 years of osteopathy school, 1 year of internship, and 1 year of residency in specialty	D.O.	Exams by specialty; State
Physician assistant (P.A.)	4-year college degree* plus 2-year associate degree or *5-year minimum (usually)	B.S. degree plus A.A.S.D. in physician assistant	NCCPA
Nurse practitioner (RN)	4 years registered nurse program plus 2 year practitioner program	R.N. plus B.S.N. plus M.S.N.; Certificate	State certification required in most states
Dialysis technician	Workshop on dialysis following RN or LPN program or OJT	Certificate	No specific licensure required beyond RN or LPN
Medical assistant (CMA or RMA)	2 years	A.A.S.D. in medical assisting	No licensure required; optional certification after exam by AAMA or AMT

*To be accepted by a physician assistant program, applicant must have a two-year associate degree in another health field and a minimum of one year significant health care work experience, in lieu of the four-year B.S. degree. Some programs have established a high school diploma as a minimum admission criterion.

Key to abbreviations:

AAMA—American Association of Medical Assistants
A.A.S.D.—Associate of Applied Science Degree
AMT—American Medical Technologists
B.S.N.—Bachelor of Science in Nursing
CMA—Certified Medical Assistant
D.O.—Doctor of Osteopathy
ECFMG—Educational Commission for Foreign Medical Graduates
LPN—Licensed Practical Nurse
M.D.—Medical Doctor
M.S.N.—Masters Degree in Nursing
NBME—National Board of Medical Examiners
NCCPA—National Commission on Certification of Physician Assistants
OJT—On-the-job training
P.A.—Physician Assistant
RMA—Registered Medical Assistant
RN—Registered Nurse

They also offer financial incentives to the primary physician to request fewer specialty consultations. These cost-containment measures will result in fewer referrals to specialty physicians.

SKILLS

Skills performed in an office or clinic are related to the physician's specialty. Electrocardiographs are done in a cardiologist's office; sutures are removed in a surgeon's office (Figure 8–7). Other factors that affect skill performance are job descriptions, formal education and certification, experience, office policy, and state laws. Some states require that certain tasks be performed by a specific worker category. They issue licenses to certify that practice as a way to protect the public against untrained persons administering care. Many tasks are done by more than one worker category.

Scheduling

Scheduling appointments is an important skill that requires organization and good verbal communication techniques

Figure 8–8 *Good telephone skills are an integral part of the medical office.*

(Figure 8–8). Scheduling includes office visits, diagnostic test appointments, and registration for surgery. This is an important service to patients and requires a certain knowledge base and an ability to negotiate. Patients may be too ill to wait for a long time to be seen by a physician or have a diagnostic test done. Understandably, patients may need to wait for a physician who is unexpectedly detained, but habitually poor scheduling may irritate patients and result in their seeking another physician.

Assessing

Assessment is a skill practiced by all those who have patient contact (Figure 8–9). Physician assistants, nurses, medical assistants, and physicians assess patients according to their ability and role. Staff members interview patients to obtain a health history, observe symptoms, notice physical appearance, take vital signs (Figure 8–10), and review lab

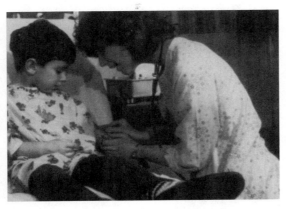

Figure 8–7 *Sutures are removed in the surgeon's office.*

Figure 8–9   *Assessment skills come into play.*

Figure 8–11   *Diagnostic tests are sometimes done in the office.*

work. Some staff members auscultate (listen), palpate (feel), document observations, arrange plans for treatment, and follow patients' progress.

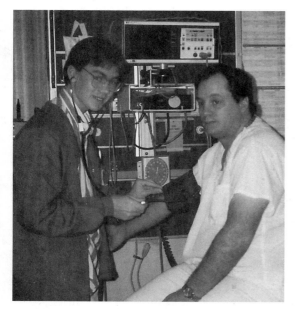

Figure 8–10   *Blood pressure is a vital sign.*

Diagnostic testing

Diagnostic tests are sometimes done in the office (Figure 8–11). For tests not done in the office, appointments need to be scheduled at the hospital or diagnostic center. Patients may need X rays, blood work, urinalysis, electrocardiographs, or pulmonary function and allergy tests in the office. The type of tests ordered will depend on patients' diagnoses and office specialty.

Treating

Treatments may be done in the office or clinic. Deep-heat treatments, removal of skin lesions, chemotherapy, allergy shots, suture removal, dressing changes, dialysis, and cast removal can all be done in an outpatient facility.

Providing equipment

Providing needed medical equipment is another service that may be done by the office or a medical supply store. The physician, office staff, patient, and family members determine the need for special devices and adaptive equipment and where they can be obtained. Contact lenses or glasses to improve vision may be dispensed by the office. Walkers, air mattresses, wheelchairs, and blood sugar testing instruments are usually dispensed by medical supply stores. Some equipment, such as artificial limbs, is made to order for patients. Other devices need to be fitted by specially trained salespeople or registered nurses and dispensed with extensive teaching and follow-up. These include a prosthesis after a mastectomy and collection bags for ostomy surgery.

Processing insurance

Processing insurance forms is a skill that is essential in every medical office today. Different insurance companies have different forms, rules, regulations, and reimbursement guidelines. It is almost impossible for many patients to understand how to apply for payment or reimbursement. In many offices, at least one worker is exclusively responsible for handling insurance forms. Other responsibilities may include preparing bills and posting payments.

Dialysis

Dialysis is the procedure that cleanses the blood of waste products and removes extra fluid from the body. The hemodialysis machine is called the "artificial kidney." Over a four- to six-hour period, blood is pumped through a semipermeable tubing that is immersed in a special saline-type solution. The chemical makeup of this solution determines how much of what electrolytes and waste products will be drawn out of the blood into the surrounding solution.

Biography

As a child, I had severe asthma. I couldn't take part in sports and lost a lot of time from school because I was sick. I knew just how debilitating and discouraging this disease could be, so I was determined to help others overcome it.

After graduating from high school, I went to nursing school. Then I married and had two children. Fortunately, my asthma improved as I grew into adulthood. But I never forgot how I suffered as a child. I was determined to work in the respiratory field.

Employment in a hospital meant I had rotating shifts. These irregular hours became too much for my health. I was often sick because I was unable to sleep in the daytime. So I applied for and got a job in the office of a pulmonologist. Now I am able to help a number of people of all ages with their respiratory concerns. I can empathize with the children and offer encouragement to adults. I am especially effective in patient education because I understand asthma from both the patient's and the professional's point of view. Though I make less money working in an office than I would have in the hospital, I am healthier and happier.

Career Search

To discover more about a career and the roles of members in a medical office, contact the following organizations for online addresses, printed information, and videotapes.

American Medical Association
515 N. State Street
Chicago, IL 60610
Phone: 312–464–5000
Fax: 312–464–4184

American College of Physicians
Independence Mall West
Sixth Street at Race
Philadelphia, PA 19106–1572
Phone: 215–351–2400
Toll-free phone: 800–523–1546
Fax: 215–351–2448

American Academy of Family
    Physicians
8880 Ward Parkway
Kansas City, MO 64114–2797
Phone: 816–333–9700
Toll-free phone: 800–274–2237
Fax: 816–822–0586

American Osteopathic Association
142 E. Ontario Street
Chicago, IL 60611
Phone: 312–280–5800
Toll-free phone: 800–621–1773
Fax: 312–280–3860

National Association of Managed
    Care Physicians
4435 Waterfront Drive
P.O. Box 4765
Glen Allen, VA 23058–4765
Phone: 804–527–1905
Toll-free phone: 800–722–0376
Fax: 804–747–5316

American Association of
    Occupational Health Nurses
50 Lenox Pointe
Atlanta, GA 30324
Phone: 404–262–1162
Fax: 404–262–1165

American Association of Medical
    Assistants
20 N. Wacker Drive, Suite 1575
Chicago, IL 60606–2903
Phone: 312–899–1500
Fax: 312–899–1259

American College of Occupational
    and Environmental Medicine
55 W. Seegers Road
Arlington Heights, IL 60005
Phone: 708–228–6850
Fax: 708–228–1856

National Alliance of Nurse
    Practitioners
325 Pennsylvania Avenue S.E.
Washington, DC 20003–1100
Phone: 202–675–6350

Range of Annual Incomes

Physician (depends on specialty)

Family practice	$120,000–$180,000
Cardiologist	$140,000–$300,000
Pediatrician	$ 90,000–$140,000
Internist	$110,000–$150,000
General surgeon	$140,000–$250,000
Obstetrician or gynecologist	$170,000–$230,000
Physician assistant	$ 25,000–$ 56,000
Nurse practitioner	$ 38,000–$ 60,000
Licensed practical nurse	$ 19,000–$ 25,000
Dialysis technician	$ 25,000–$ 35,000
Medical assistant	$ 15,000–$ 21,000

What's New

Computerized medical records at the hospital are now accessible from the physician's office. Lab results, pathology reports, surgical procedure data, EKG readings, and consultants' summaries are available from the hospital's main-frame computer. For security reasons, physicians are able to retrieve information on their patients only.

Direct dictation regarding patient progress information to the hospital medical records transcription department can be done from the physician's office or through a cellular phone.

Interactive electronic medical education programs for physicians will be available through the Internet. These programs will provide professional education and relate new medications and treatments. Physicians will work through each program at their own pace. When they are finished, the completion of the program will be logged in the physicians' record for state medical license renewal.

CD-ROMs will contain the contents of journals and other information. These will be updated monthly.

Computer-assisted diagnosis will help the physician, nurse practitioner, and physician assistant narrow the possibilities of diagnosis. Symptoms and history will be entered, and the program will identify possible problems. Through the process of elimination, a definite diagnosis will be reached.

Patient education via the Internet will be done in the office or on a home personal computer. Much health information will be available on both the Internet and CD-ROMs.

Video patient examinations will be conducted using a special camera and the telephone lines between the patient's home and the physician's office. Such exams may be health screenings or treatment follow-ups. This procedure may be used in rural areas where the physician's office is far from the patient's home.

School to Work

In addition to the general academic subjects and workplace skills contained in the "Job Skills" chapter, the following subjects and skills apply specifically to medical office careers.

Academic Subject	Workplace Skills
Arts	—Design booklets, cards, and flyers about health information. —Arrange a display of what's new in health. —Develop instruction sheets about test preparation. —Develop checklists to summarize changes and monitor care. —Create an appointment card to remind patients of their next visit.
Business	
Time Management	—Respect patient's time when scheduling appointments. —Allow a reasonable time for the visit when scheduling.
Communication	—Phone patients to delay a visit if the physician is behind schedule. —Answer the phone pleasantly; include your name and greeting.
English	—Explain instructions so patients can understand them. —Locate a translator if the patient does not speak English. —Document clearly and understandably.
Computer Skills	—Enter data according to physician requests for each visit. —Obtain test data from the hospital computer to give to the physician.
Economics, Accounting	—Bill the appropriate insurance company for care administered. —Code treatments according to billing procedures. —Track amounts owed to the lab for patient tests from office specimens.
Bookkeeping Systems	—Respond to insurance company questions regarding billing. —Review bills not covered by insurance companies. —Review accounts periodically to identify accounts receivable.
Filing Systems	—Organize department files for hard chart copies. —File charts and reports appropriately. —Determine if the physician wants hard copies of lab data.

School to Work—continued

Academic Subject	Workplace Skills
Mathematics	
Addition, Subtraction	—Post insurance and client payments.
	—Determine the patient's portion of balances owed.
	—Prepare deposit slips and receipts.
	—Track what is owed to labs and amounts paid.
	—Pay lab for tests run from specimens obtained in the office.
Division	—Order supplies.
	—Count supplies to verify that all were delivered.
	—Pay suppliers.
English and Communication	—Learn a second language to speak with patients who do not speak English.
	—Interpret reports and manuals.
Speech Class	—Instruct patients in preparing for specific tests.
	—Give directions through a translator or family member if necessary.
	—Speak loudly enough that patients who are hard of hearing can understand.
	—Request feedback to determine patients' understanding.
	—Inform patients of when to return to the physician's office.
Science	
Anatomy and Physiology	—Identify problems with body structures.
Biochemistry	—Identify abnormal lab tests.
Microbiology	—Obtain specimens for culture and analysis.
	—Sterilize instruments.
Nutrition and Food Science	—Instruct patients on special diets.
	—Teach the principles of weight loss.
Pathophysiology	—Determine signs and symptoms of diseases.
	—Observe improvements in symptoms over time.
	—Record an EKG.
	—Perform vision and hearing screening tests.
Pharmacology	—Identify the effectiveness of medications.
	—Change medications to improve the patient's condition.
	—Instruct the patient in the desired effects of medications.
	—Inform the patient of the side effects of medications.
Radiology	—Determine when radiological studies are needed.
Social Studies	
Culture	—Determine if the patient will comply with the medical regimen.
	—Encourage family members to help the patient to comply.
	—Order home care for the patient.
Gerontology	—Arrange transportation to office and home with senior centers.

Review Questions

1. What four careers, other than physician, might be found in a medical office? Give the length of education and anticipated range of annual income for each career.

2. What are three advantages and three disadvantages of working in a medical office?

3. What is the role of the dialysis technician?

4. What are three differences between the physician assistant and the nurse practitioner?

5. List four academic subjects and two skills associated with each career in the medical office.

MEDICAL RECORDS DEPARTMENT

Objectives

After completing this chapter, you should be able to:

❏ Explain the goals of a medical records department.

❏ Describe each career in this department.

❏ Identify required education and credentials for each career.

❏ Describe the skills and activities performed in this department.

❏ Recognize how academic subjects apply in the workplace.

Key Terms

Terms

Confidentiality	Chart analysis	Microfiche
Reimbursement	Abstracting	Coding

Abbreviations

DRG	JCAHO	TD filing

INTRODUCTION

The medical records department plays an important role in health care. Department activities include the coordination of all written information about every patient treated at the facility. Responsibilities include completing, sorting, compiling, analyzing, storing, and retrieving patients' records (Figure 9–1). Other activities involve coding information for in-surance company or government reimbursement and assembling statistics about illnesses and treatments.

Each time a patient is treated at a medical facility or physician's office, that care is recorded (Figure 9–2). This documentation includes diagnosis of the illness, care and treatment administered, medication prescribed, and health maintenance instruction. All information

129

Figure 9–1 *Retrieving a patient's record.*

must be documented before the record is permanently filed. The completed record is then stored according to a specific universal system so it can be retrieved when needed. Implementation of the storage and retrieval system is a major activity in the medical records department.

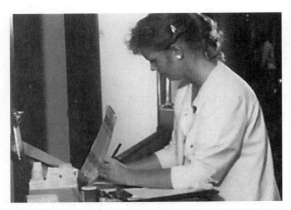

Figure 9–2 *Recording care given to a patient.*

Other activities performed by workers in the medical records department include assigning a unique number to each new patient, copying chart forms for legal correspondence, and analyzing charts. Transcription, managing health information, biostatistics, system analysis, and classifying information are other department activities.

GOALS

The goals of the medical records department are to manage information, identify optimum reimbursement for patient care, and maintain confidentiality of patient data.

CAREER DESCRIPTIONS

Medical records personnel work more closely with information than with patients. The roles and responsibilities of medical records workers are determined by education and experience. Two educa-

CAREER HIERARCHY

```
          MEDICAL RECORDS ADMINISTRATOR
         ┌──────────────┼──────────────┐
    MEDICAL         ACCREDITED         TUMOR
TRANSCRIPTIONISTS     RECORD        REGISTRATION
                   TECHNICIANS      COORDINATOR
```

tional programs are available: registered record administrator and accredited record technician. In small departments or physician offices, technicians will be expected to perform all duties related to the completion, storage, and retrieval of a record (Figure 9–3), as well as coding and indexing of diagnoses and treatments. In large departments, technicians specialize.

Career characteristics

Working hours vary according to the facility. In a hospital where acutely ill patients are treated, medical records are retrievable twenty-four hours a day, 365 days a year. Full- and part-time positions are available during the day and evening shifts. Some night-shift positions are available in large facilities. In a physician's office, registered record technicians work when the office is open—usually the day shift, Monday through Saturday. Technicians who work for insurance companies can negotiate their working hours according to mutual need.

Employment opportunities include hospitals, clinics, physician offices, research centers, nursing homes, and government agencies. Other opportunities include health maintenance organizations, home health agencies, long-term care facilities, law firms, and insurance companies.

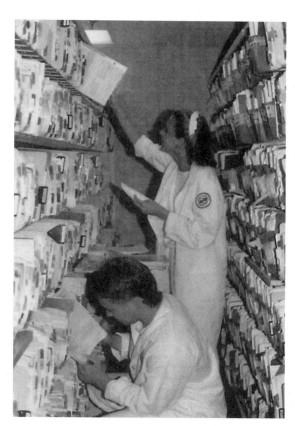

Figure 9–3 *Retrieving patient records, adding forms, and refiling.*

Career advancement depends on education and availability of positions. Few director positions are available. A change in facility or type of work may be necessary for a career advance.

Desired personal characteristics include sharp organizational skills, precision with paperwork tasks, ability to function independently, good verbal and written communication skills, and accuracy with detailed work. Recognizing the importance of the medical record and taking pride in being a part of the information management system are other characteristics.

Job satisfaction comes from doing the work well; serving patients, physicians, and the facility; being a part of the health care team; and gaining the respect of peers and other professionals. Medical records personnel interact with physicians, nurses, attorneys, insurance people, administrators, and other professionals.

Career roles

The registered record administrator is responsible for all functions of the medical records department. These functions include planning and implementing the system for completing, analyzing, storing, and retrieving patients' charts. Functions also include providing statistical data to plan future patient care, support research, and plan services. The director facilitates timely billing for reimbursement, reviews bed utilization, and monitors quality of care. Directors ensure the **confidentiality** of patient information. Other areas of responsibility include supervising medical transcription services, microfilming of patient records, obtaining and coding the final diagnoses for all inpatient and outpatient visits, and securing maximum reimbursement.

The registered record administrator needs to manage effectively and work well with people. The ability to make de-cisions quickly and with good judgment is important. Other characteristics needed are organizational skills and the ability to complete large volumes of work, delegate duties effectively, determine priorities, and work under pressure.

Accredited record technicians carry out all skills in the department according to facility guidelines. They maintain patient confidentiality. Though they can complete all tasks in the department, they usually specialize in certain skills, depending on the size of the department. Skills include coding diseases and surgeries on the medical record according to the ICD–9–CM (International Clinical Classification of Diseases–9th revision-Clinical Modifications) classification system and UHDDS (Uniform Hospital Discharge Data Set) definitions, and assigning a Diagnostic Related Groups (**DRG**) code through computer data entry. Obtaining proper reimbursement for the facility is ensured by identifying the correct DRG assignment. Technicians help physicians to interpret guidelines of regulatory agencies and participate in the utilization review process and quality assurance analysis.

Registered record technicians need to have a high degree of accuracy, attention to detail, initiative, judgment, discretion, and understanding of the confidential nature of their work. Good organizational skills and the ability to complete a large volume of work with little supervision are important qualities. The ability to work effectively with the medical staff, members of other departments, and medical records co-workers is another vital characteristic. It is also helpful to type well enough to work with a computer.

Figure 9–4 *Medical transcription of a doctor's notes.*

Figure 9–5 *Coding is an important part of the reimbursement process.*

Medical transcriptionists type data that has been dictated on an audiotape recorder system by physicians (Figure 9–4). This data consists of history and physical exam summaries, surgery reports, consultation findings, pathology studies, radiology reports, progress reports, and discharge summaries. Medical transcriptionists need to concentrate for extended periods at a word processor, listen and interpret recorded reports with accuracy, spell medical terms accurately, and produce a perfectly typed report with reasonable speed. A word processor is used to facilitate the typing process. In a hospital, the data is entered into the facility's mainframe computer.

Medical record coding personnel code the names of diseases and surgeries identified on medical records according to the ICD–9–CM classification system and UHDDS definitions. This procedure is done upon admission, concurrently as requested, and upon discharge. Coders assign DRGs through computer data entry

to the maximum reimbursement justified, based on services received by the patient (Figure 9–5). Another coding system used is CPT (Current Procedural Terminology). This is required by some third-party payers for ambulatory surgery procedures. As with DRGs, a fixed amount of reimbursement is assigned to these payment groups.

Tumor registration coordinators report all cancer cases according to the guidelines of the American College of Surgeons' Commission on Cancer. Other responsibilities include entering statistical data so that reports can be developed to compare regional and national cancer statistics. Participating in quality assurance studies is another form of reporting cancer data.

JOB AVAILABILITY

The U.S. Department of Labor estimates that job availability for medical records technicians is good. Because of technological advances and requests for patient information, the job market will grow faster than average to the year 2005.

SKILLS

Workers in the medical records department learn skills that will help them to organize, store, retrieve data and examine documents for completeness and accuracy. They identify trends in the health care institution through statistical data and obtain insurance reimbursement for health care rendered.

Chart analysis

Chart analysis is the process of reviewing a medical record to be sure that all information, reports, and signatures are present and conform to the standards of the Joint Commission on Accreditation of Healthcare Organizations (**JCAHO**). The record is arranged in a specific order, missing information (deficiencies) identified, and problems or unusual cases reported to the department director. Completed records are stored; incomplete records are filed in a specific area and appropriate persons are notified to document deficiencies. Charts must be completed within a specified time from the date of patient treatment. If charts are not completed within that time, the facility can lose its license to treat patients.

EDUCATION AND CREDENTIALS

CAREER	YEARS OF EDUCATION AFTER HIGH SCHOOL	DEGREE OR DIPLOMA	TESTED BY; LICENSED BY
Registered record administrator RRA	4 years	B.S.	AMRA
Accredited record technician ART	2 years	A.A.S.D. in medical record technology	AMRA
Medical transcriptionist AMT	9 months	Competency award	Certified by AMT (optional)
Tumor registration coordinator ART	2 years	A.A.S.D. in medical record technology	Licensed by AMRA and can be certified by ACS
Certified coding specialist (CCS)	Within ART program or independent study program from AMRA	Certificate	AMRA

Key to abbreviations:

B.S.—Bachelor of Science Degree
A.A.S.D.—Associate of Applied Science Degree
ACS—American College of Surgeons
AMRA—American Medical Records Association
AMT—American Medical Transcriptionist
ART—Accredited Record Technician
CCS—Certified Coding Specialist
RRA—Registered Record Administrator

Statistics gleaned from the analysis process include data on deaths and types of surgical cases.

Transcription

Transcription is the process that transforms the spoken word into typewritten copy. Usually, physicians have access to a recording system throughout a facility by dialing a certain number on the telephone. Information, such as a summary of illness or the details of surgery, can be dictated onto the system. A transcriptionist receives the audiotaped information through a headset, types it, then erases the audiotape. This typed report is placed in the medical record, and a copy is sent to the physician's office.

Figure 9–6 *Completed records are sometimes stored on microfiche.*

Tracking

Chart tracking is the system used to locate a medical record that was stored using the **TD filing** system. Whenever a patient is treated in the health care system, a written record is generated, completed, and filed. That record is forever accessible. When a patient again becomes ill, all previous records can be retrieved and used as reference by the treating physician. Chart tracking occupies much of a worker's time. Because hospital stays tend to be short, a large volume of documents must be completed, stored, and retrieved.

Records are stored for approximately five years in hard copy (on paper), then transferred into **microfiche**, a photographing process (Figure 9–6). Each page of the medical record is photographed on tiny film. The resulting strips of film are stored in plastic holders, like pages in a photo album. This microfiche is stored forever, and the paper copy is destroyed.

Reimbursement

Another function important to both the patient and the institution is the **reimbursement** process for services rendered. Every health care consumer hopes that the fees for services rendered by the physician and hospital will be paid for or covered by a health insurance policy. This is not an automatic process. It is a complicated process, conducted by the medical records department. The system consists of precertification, **abstracting**, and **coding**, followed by submission to third-party payers.

Precertification. Some surgical procedures must be preapproved by insurance companies before they are performed. This ensures that insurance carriers will cover the cost. This process is called preprocedure certification. The medical records department assumes the responsibility of contacting some carriers, particularly Medicare, to ensure coverage. Many insurance carriers require the patient to get permission before the procedure is performed, particularly if hospitalization is required.

Abstracting is the process of reviewing medical records to gather data related to the hospital and to collect facts for physicians. This information is entered into the central register. From this central register, data is gathered for statistical purposes. Some examples of the reports written from this data are: the number of patients admitted to the hospital with a stroke during the previous year; the number of patients between twenty and thirty years of age who had their gallbladder removed during a particular year; and the most common cause of death of persons between certain ages.

Coding is the process used by the technician to identify the primary diagnosis and the principal procedure performed on the patient in the treatment of illness. The names of the diagnosis and procedure must be verified by the attending physician. The medical records technician locates the DRG from a book listing all groups, then enters that DRG into the computer. The computer then codes the information based on the data entry. In other words, each diagnosis is assigned to a group of similar diagnoses and each of these groups is assigned a code according to the ICD–9–CM guidelines. Each code is assigned a sum of money. That is the amount of money sent to the facility as payment for the care of the patient. The medical records technician works with the data to obtain optimal

reimbursement for the hospital. The agencies that use the coding system to determine reimbursement are the federal government (Medicare and Medicaid), Blue Cross Blue Shield, and other private insurance companies. Coding is a vital function of the medical records department. It is the determining source of income for the facility. If maximum reimbursement is not obtained, a hospital might not have sufficient operating money and would have to close.

Correspondence

Correspondence is another important responsibility of the medical records department (Figure 9–7). Hundreds of requests for data come into the department each month from such sources as insurance companies, attorneys, physicians, other hospitals, and employers. Requests also come from insurance carriers for disability verification and liability claims.

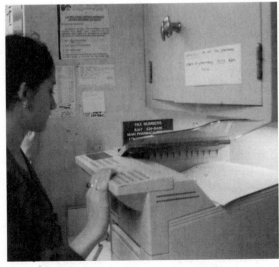

Figure 9–7 *Correspondence may be done on paper, by modem, and by fax.*

Clarifying the legitimacy of each request, gaining patients' permission for the release of information, and processing each request are painstaking tasks. Care is always taken to protect the confidentiality of each medical record.

Often, information is needed from the medical records department for worker's compensation and disability cases. Persons who claim injury are responsible for proving the extent of injury by verification through medical records. Because of patient confidentiality, the medical records department follows strict guidelines before releasing any records.

Quality assurance

Quality assurance is the process of studying the delivery of health care as it relates to patient satisfaction, safety, comfort, and successful outcome. It is an important part of a care-giving institution. Through statistical analysis of illnesses, accidents, and occurrences, patient care and safety can be improved. The medical records department is an important source of statistical data for that review. Ultimately, the delivery of health care improves because of these studies and resulting corrective actions.

Consultation

Consultative services are offered to physicians for their information and their committee reports. This data can be helpful for many reasons. For example, data can show that new equipment is needed to improve medical practice. It also can illustrate health trends in the community. The department helps physicians interpret guidelines of new docu-

mentation requirements that are periodically revised by institutional accrediting and regulatory agencies. Certain documentation can only be provided by the physicians.

Standards of documentation dictated by institutional accrediting and regulatory agencies are strictly adhered to by the medical records department. These agencies include the Joint Commission on Accreditation of Healthcare Organizations; the U.S. Department of Health and Human Services; state health departments. New standards from these agencies are reviewed, and the system is modified to meet them. A health care facility must be accredited by agencies designated by the U.S. government to receive Medicare and Medicaid reimbursements. Accreditation is based on the ability of a facility to meet guidelines for patient care. This care must be documented on the medical record to be verified. Though verification of documentation is time-consuming, it is the only way to show that care was delivered. The system was established to protect the public from substandard and unsafe facilities.

Tumor registry

Tumor registry is a central data bank that collects information about cancer in specific geographical areas. All cancer cases are reported to this central data bank. Treatments and follow-up survival rates are also entered. Comparative analysis can be done related to city, state, and national data. The tumor registry is approved by the American College of Surgeons' Commission on Cancer and serves as a source of statistical data.

Biography

As a high school student, I loved business, word processing, and computer classes. Even then, I recognized that I did not want to be in a service business. I liked researching data, managing information, and creating spreadsheets. I liked creating computerized charts and graphs. I did not like to have to depend on others to get the job done. I liked to work independently.

When I graduated, I went to work in an accounting department of a business. I was assigned my own computer and entered figures most of the day. I tired of that rather quickly. I was not interested in the math aspect of that job. Since my mother worked as a nursing assistant at the local community hospital, she suggested I try the medical records department.

I made an appointment for an interview there and liked what I saw. I learned that to qualify for a job in that department, I needed to take the medical records technician program at a community college. So that became my goal. I continued with my job at the accounting department but began night classes. This program was totally different than high school. I was responsible for studying and completing assignments on my own. I learned so much! Medical terminology, coding, abstracting, and chart analysis were some of the topics we covered. It has taken me longer than two years to complete my associate's degree because I am attending part time, but I am nearing graduation and have the job I wanted at the hospital. I am proud of my achievements and enjoy my new job.

Career Search

To discover more about a career and the roles of members in a medical records department, contact the following organizations for online addresses, printed information, and videotapes.

American Health Information
    Management Association
919 N. Michigan Avenue, Suite 1400
Chicago, IL 60611–1683
Phone: 312–787–2672
Fax: 312–787–9793

American Association for Medical
    Transcription
P.O. Box 576187
Modesto, CA 95357–6187
Phone: 209–551–0883
Toll-free phone: 800–982–2182
Fax: 209–551–9397

Range of Incomes

Medical records director	$42,000–$70,000
Medical records technician	$24,000–$40,000
Medical records clerk	$14,000–$23,000
Medical transcriptionist	$17,000–$27,000

What's New

Medical records are entered into a hospital's mainframe computer from the lab, radiology, biometrics, surgery, and physician dictation. In some facilities, health care workers input patient care directly into the computer. Nurses, nursing assistants, and speech, physical and occupational therapists can enter data. Care givers in the home may use laptop computers that can connect directly to the hospital's mainframe or be entered on disk for later input.

Direct dictation of patient progress can be done by a physician from the office, home, or cellular phone. Lab results, pathology reports, EKG readings, and consultants' summaries can be accessed. For security reasons, physicians can retrieve information about their patients only.

The Positive Patient Identity System uses a patient's thumbprint for access to legal records. In some areas, it is being used as the exclusive way to access a patient's medical record. This method prevents unauthorized access by insurance companies, employers, and others.

School to Work

In addition to the general academic subjects and workplace skills contained in the "Job Skills" chapter, the following subjects and skills apply specifically to careers in the medical records department.

Academic Subject	Worplace Skills
Arts	—Create a chart that shows the types of diagnoses in the hospital.
	—Print a graph that shows bed usage at the hospital.
	—Illustrate the length of hospitalization in the current year compared to other years.
	—Detail the kinds of surgeries performed at the facility.
	—Microfiche old paper charts.
Business	
Time Management	—Employ transcriptionists to complete reports in a timely manner.
	—Determine an alternate plan in case facility computers go down.
Communication	—Notify physicians if documentation is not complete.
Computer Skills	—Assign secret entry codes to the appropriate individuals.
	—Transcribe dictated reports.

School to Work—continued

Academic Subject	**Worplace Skills**
Computer Skills (cont'd)	—Download reports to the mainframe computer at the appointed hour. —Track specific information for periodic reports. —Determine the length of stay for various diagnoses. —Enter codes in the computer for reimbursement.
Word Processing Economics	—Enter physician dictation. —Consolidate patient billing for all physicians' services. —Code the principle diagnosis for hospital reimbursement. —Understand insurance and managed health care plans.
Filing Systems	—Assign a permanent number to each new patient. —Place paper chart forms in order. —File microfiche. —Shred charts after making microfiches. —File and refile charts and reports accurately. —Retrieve old charts when a patient is in ER or readmitted.
English and Communication	—Notify physicians if you are behind in completing dictation and documentation. —Analyze charts to be sure all information is complete. —Tag sections that need to be completed. —Read and interpret medical documentation. —Understand which diagnosis to code as primary.
Medical Terminology Medical Dictionary, Glossary	—Code the diagnosis for reimbursement. —Locate correct terms to accomplish coding. —Locate code numbers in the directory according to the diagnosis.
Mathematics Biostatistics	—Analyze the frequency of admissions per diagnosis. —Show bed usage for various diagnoses. —Glean data about the types of surgeries performed. —Identify the ages of patients seen in the ER. —Demonstrate the types of tumors detected in pathology. —Summarize the kinds of bacteria grown in the microbiology lab. —Summarize the types of radiology procedures performed each year.
Law	—Testify in court in worker's compensation cases. —Copy certain chart forms for legal correspondence. —Guard patients' confidentiality. —Transport charts and reports so they are not read by others. —Manage the thumbprint scanner if one is used to identify patients.

Review Questions

1. What are the goals of the medical records department?
2. What career requires the most education in this department? What career requires the least? How long is the education program for each of these careers?
3. List three desirable characteristics of workers in this department.
4. What are the sources of job satisfaction in this department?
5. Identify three academic subjects and two ways each is implemented in this department.

MENTAL HEALTH DEPARTMENT

Chapter

10

Objectives

After completing this chapter, you should be able to:

- ❐ Explain the goals of the mental health department.
- ❐ Recognize the difference between normal and dysfunctional feelings.
- ❐ Describe each career in this department.
- ❐ Identify the required education and credentials for each career.
- ❐ Recognize how academic subjects apply in the workplace.

Key Terms

Classification of disorders

Anxiety	Mood	Psychosis
Personality	Addictive	

INTRODUCTION

Mental health and mental illness are states of mind that are influenced by several factors. These factors relate to feelings of well-being and the ability to control behavior, maintain emotional balance, cope with problems, and function in society. Mental health is jeopardized when one of these factors becomes a negative influence on the state of mind.

A state of mind can change because of a physical condition, illness, emotional stress, environmental factors, food and chemical intake, and mental disorders. Each disorder has a range of mental states that extends from normal to extremely dysfunctional (Figure 10–1). Some conditions that fall within this range are **anxiety** disorders, **mood** disorders, **psychosis**, **personality** disorders, and **addictive** disorders.

People with normal states of mind commonly experience mild symptoms of distress or imbalance sometime in their

NORMAL FEELINGS	EXTREMELY DYSFUNCTIONAL CONDITIONS
• Anxiety before tests or before a job interview	• A fear that so immobilizes the person that he or she does not leave home
• Grief and sadness	• Severe depression with a suicide attempt
• Ability to distinguish reality from fantasy	• Hearing voices or seeing objects that are not really there
• Personality idiosyncrasies, such as shyness	• Sociopathic behavior
• Compulsions with no negative consequences	• Addictive problems with major or even life-threatening consequences

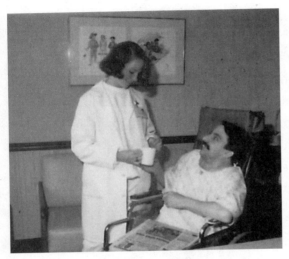

Figure 10–1 *The range of states of mind is wide.*

lives. But they cope with those periods, keep their symptoms under control, and continue with their lives.

In the extreme, these disorders can cause people to become dysfunctional. People with these extreme states of mind cannot cope with their lives or manage their behavior. With some disorders, individuals may be unsafe to themselves or to others. In this case, hospitalization may be necessary for a time.

Addictive behavior is conduct that is carried out compulsively despite the neg-ative consequences that result. When one family member is addicted, all family members experience the effects. They alter their ways of thinking, feeling, and behaving to cope with the stress caused by the addiction. Being hooked on alcohol or drugs is a common addiction, but there are many others. Workaholism, sexual addictions, and gambling are examples. Each addiction involves a loss of control over the chemical or behavior and a progressive deterioration of the health of the addict and those close to him or her.

People with behavior or personality disorders live in the community and appear relatively normal. But they are troublesome to themselves, to their family members, and society.

A wide range of treatments is available for personality or behavior disorders: self-help books, support groups, walk-in clinics, psychotherapy, hot lines, emergency centers, and hospitalization. Medication may be prescribed by physicians to relieve stress, elevate mood, level out mood swings, or regain control of aggressively hostile behavior.

It is normal for people to seek counseling to improve the quality of their lives and relationships and to lessen stress. Some patients seek counseling when

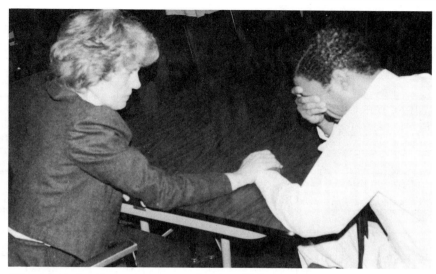

Figure 10–2 *Stress is a normal part of life.*

they or their family members recognize that their behavior is not manageable. This recognition frequently comes when the symptoms of the problem—extreme fears, hostile actions, or threats of suicide, for example—intensify.

Mental health workers often counsel healthy people who have stress-related problems and personal tragedies, (Figure 10–2). Loss of a job, death of a loved one, end of a romance, or the process of divorce are normal stresses in life. Individual, family, and group counseling on coping with these problems is conducted by mental health professionals.

Behavior disorders and mental illness can become evident in young children. Attention is increasingly being given to behavior disorders of youth in schools and in communities.

GOAL

The goal of the mental health department is to provide a safe, therapeutic, interactive environment; intensive counseling; and participatory activities for patients who have mental, emotional, and psychosocial problems.

CAREER DESCRIPTIONS

Many careers are associated with mental health. While some careers involve years of schooling, the study of psychology, and practice in patient counseling, a few involve only on-the-job training.

Mental health professionals interact with people of all ages, degrees of illness, self-awareness, and stress levels. Some patients may be members of the same family: battered children, abusive parents, and depressed elderly may all need counseling simultaneously. Patients' conditions vary in acuteness. Some patients are functional, live at home, and work full-time. Some patients are severely ill and repeatedly require therapy and hospitalization. Others experience severe stress that leads them to need

CAREER HIERARCHY

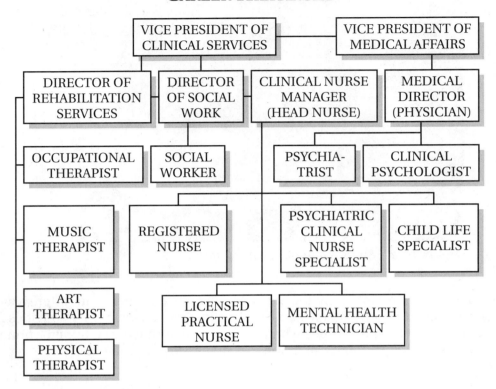

assistance only once in their lifetime. Recovery can require only minimal intervention (a few visits to a counselor) or ongoing help over many years. Mental health professionals help patients regain contact with reality, manage their behavior by developing healthy coping skills, recapture feelings of well-being, and interact positively with their environment.

Career characteristics
Employment opportunities include hospitals; outpatient clinics; home care; school systems; government agencies; mental retardation centers; child, adolescent, and family mental health centers; business and industry; chemical abuse clinics; correctional institutions such as jails; social service organizations; and private practice. Some mental health professionals work in research where they deal more with animal than human studies.

Career specialties vary with the type of facility and the education of the worker. Some mental health workers specialize in specific areas, such as acutely ill hospitalized patients, counseling in homeless shelters, suicide hot lines, rape crisis centers, substance abuse, eating disorders, behavior modification, and sexual abuse. Others specialize in counseling of school children, community education, and prevention of mental illness. Workers can change their specialty area without difficulty.

Work hours depend on the type of facility and job responsibilities. Many facilities are staffed twenty-four hours a day, every day of the year. Personnel can work full time, part time, or a few hours per month. Shifts vary from a few to twelve hours a day. Some mental health professionals establish their own counseling practice and set their own working hours.

Career advancement depends on the education of the worker and the area of interest. Promotion to a management position in a patient care facility, community setting, or national organization is possible with an advanced degree. Entrepreneurship is fostered in the mental health field both on the job as well as with independent projects.

Job satisfaction comes from helping needy people and from making a difference in their lives, from determining effective treatment methods and evaluating results. Gratification comes from helping clients solve problems so they can straighten out difficult situations. It also comes from guiding patients to make sound decisions about their lives and relationships. Other sources of satisfaction are providing a safe, therapeutic environment and using innovative and problem-solving techniques to help patients help themselves. Mental health workers are challenged by the variety of situations that occur every day.

Desired personal characteristics include inner strength. Mental health professionals see many deplorable situations. They see pain and hardship that must be faced and dealt with realistically. To be successful, they must have the patience to counsel rather than direct, sensitivity and empathy, and insight into thought processes.

The safety of the patients, families, and staff is always at the forefront of concern for the mental health workers. Professionals remain alert for hazards and opportunities for accidents and injuries.

Career roles

Psychiatrists are physicians. They graduate from medical school, then specialize in the diagnosis and treatment of mental illness. Psychiatrists direct patient care. They diagnose patient illness, prescribe medications, interact with family members, and administer treatment.

Several forms of treatment are possible. The two most common are prescribing medication for the psychiatric symptoms and providing psychotherapy, that is, meeting regularly with patients to talk about symptoms and concerns, determining the cause, and identifying coping mechanisms. Another form of treatment is electroshock therapy, which involves passing an electrical charge through the brain. Another is psychoanalysis, an in-depth study of thoughts, feelings, and behavior.

Most psychiatrists are in private practice, counseling patients in an office setting. Some work in research, industry, government, or school systems.

Clinical psychologists have studied psychology. They work with patients to help them understand their needs and how those needs can be met. They help patients to identify their strengths and abilities. They help patients to set goals. They guide patients to channel their energies into productive, acceptable, goal-directed behaviors. Their guidance helps decrease patients' stress levels and increase their coping mechanisms. They interact with patients and families to increase communication and improve relationships. They cannot prescribe medication or admit patients to hospitals. If these measures are necessary, the patient must be referred to a psychiatrist.

Some psychologists work in market research to discover motivational factors that influence human behavior. Some work in clinical research to investigate the effects of physical, emotional, and social factors on human behavior. Some develop and administer aptitude and intelligence tests. Some work in laboratories to perform controlled experiments. Some work in industry, and some counsel in private practice.

Social workers consult with individuals and families to identify concerns that relate to interaction with family members and the community. These include homelessness, lack of income, and abuse. Social workers often contact community agencies to help find solutions. Social workers help people of all ages, from newborns to the aged adult (Figure 10–3). (See Chapter 11 for more information.)

Occupational therapists work with patients to increase their independence by helping them perform activities of daily living. They structure therapy to raise confidence and skills. Some activities relieve anger, frustration, and antisocial behavior; some change compulsive behavior.

Figure 10–3 *Social workers help people of all ages.*

Psychiatric clinical nurse specialists are registered nurses who have a master's degree in psychiatric care. They work with patients, family members, and nursing staff to develop the most effective treatment plans to help patients resume responsibility for themselves. They teach other workers about crisis intervention techniques and have expertise in handling difficult patients. They teach programs, such as on stress reduction, in the community to encourage mental health. They serve as consultants within a clinical facility to patients, families, and professionals outside the psychiatric unit (Figure 10–4).

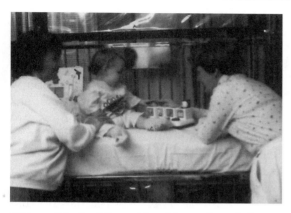

Figure 10–4 *Mental health workers help family members to improve interaction.*

Registered nurses work in a variety of settings in the mental health field. In a hospital, they spend the most time with patients and their family members. When patients are admitted, nurses initiate care plans for them based on assessment and the medical diagnosis. The goals of these plans are mutually set with the patients. The plans are carried out during the day, evening, and night shifts. Patients expect a safe environment, understanding, and consistent guidance throughout their hospital stay and course of therapy. These are provided primarily by nurses, who are with the patients twenty-four hours a day. Nurses listen to patients' concerns and discuss options for behaviors and thoughts. They work with patients to identify factors that trigger unmanageable thoughts and behaviors. Nurses structure social activities, group therapy, and interactions on the unit; they also supervise activities of daily living and work to maintain a calm and safe environment. They document patients' progress and response to therapy and administer medications ordered by physicians.

Licensed practical nurses assist registered nurses in carrying out patient care plans. They supervise patients during the activities of daily living, talk with them, and help them communicate their feelings and thoughts. They document progress and response to therapy and administer medications ordered by physicians.

Most practical nurses work in hospitals and long-term care facilities. Some work in private homes, clinics, and offices.

Mental health technicians work directly with patients under the direction of the registered nurse. Technicians carry out the care plans, listen to patients, and help to clarify their thoughts and feelings, (Figure 10–5). They confer with other professionals on the mental health care team.

Mental health technicians are employed in hospitals, mental health clinics, mental retardation facilities, long-term

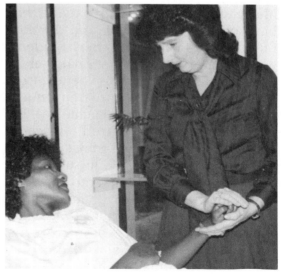

Figure 10–5 *Above all, therapists listen!*

care facilities, and day-care centers. Some work in private homes.

Psychiatric aides work as assistants to the nurses or mental health technicians. They help with physical care and feeding tasks. They sit with patients who may be frightened of being alone. They escort patients during "off unit" excursions approved by physicians.

They are employed in hospitals, clinics, and chronic care facilities.

Art therapists work with patients of all ages to help them express feelings and emotions through a variety of visual projects. Patients express themselves through color choices and the type of art project selected. Art therapy is especially effective with children. Often they can draw pictures depicting their feelings more easily than they can express those feelings in words. Art therapy is also effective for adults whose traumatic experiences may be too painful to relate in words.

Music therapists work with patients who have physical, emotional, and developmental handicaps. Generally, patients who benefit from occupational therapy and psychiatric therapy also benefit from music therapy. In music therapy, music helps promote therapeutic changes. For example, language-delayed preschool children or brain-injured adults may sing and vocalize but not talk. In such cases, music therapy is a precursor to language. Physically handicapped patients might learn to play an instrument to increase strength in a broken arm or improve finger dexterity. This type of work draws on knowledge of music, psychology, and physiology.

Child life specialists help children in health care facilities adjust to whatever is happening to them. These specialists talk to children about going to surgery, explain what to expect, and accompany them there. They listen to children's ideas and fears, then talk about these ideas and fears with the children. Play therapy is used to allow children to act out their fears under the guidance of the child life worker. Play therapy reduces stress and helps children accept the pains and discomforts of illness and the separation from family during hospitalization.

Chemical dependency counselors assess people for alcohol and other chemical dependencies, intervene in crisis situations, develop therapeutic plans, facilitate group therapy, conduct relapse prevention programs, and refer patients to community resources and other professionals as appropriate. Counseling of family members and significant others; discussion of cause, effect, and recovery issues; and knowledge of treatment centers, aftercare, and outreach programs are other areas of expertise.

Certified recreational therapists evaluate patients through interviews, leisure activities, and group functions to determine their ability to care for themselves and interact with others. They confer with other professionals to evaluate patient needs and provide therapy. They work with family members to implement plans to increase patients' interaction and ability to care for themselves. They monitor progress and suggest new methods to broaden therapeutic strategies.

JOB AVAILABILITY

The U.S. Department of Labor estimates that the demand for mental health workers will increase to the year 2005. Jobs for psychologists, registered nurses, licensed practical nurses, occupational therapists, and social workers will be concentrated in mental health clinics, home care, and drug and alcohol counseling settings. Jobs for mental health technicians and psychiatric aides will be concentrated in hospitals.

SKILLS

Tasks in psychiatry involve communication skills, observation skills, quick thinking and good judgment, problem solving, assessing postdischarge needs, and evaluating the capabilities of the elderly and disabled.

Communication

Communication skills involve the ability to listen and hear what is being said. This is especially important in psychiatry because how something is said is often as important as what is said. Sometimes what is said is not what is meant. Comprehending this involves insight by the listener. Also, what is said may mean more than what the words convey. Communication also involves body language, facial expression, and tone of voice. Refusal to speak is also significant.

Evaluation of the written word is another facet. Patients sometimes write about feelings more truthfully than they talk about them. They may write threatening letters to someone or express bizarre ideas in writing.

Staff is responsible for documenting treatment sessions and the progress or regression of behaviors and thoughts. It is important to report suicidal thoughts and actions to appropriate staff members so protective measures can be taken.

As in all health care, confidentiality is important (Figure 10–6). No information about patients in a psychiatric setting is to be told to anyone other than staff working directly with those patients.

Observation

Good observational skills are also important. Behavior observed by the worker is often as important as what patients say. If an unanimated patient who is slouched in a corner and facing the wall responds "Fine" to the question "How are you?", it can be assumed that the response is not a

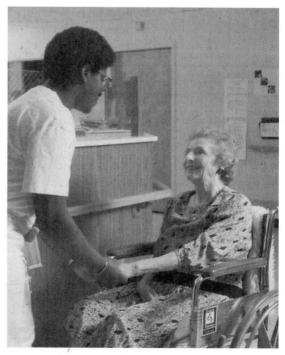

Figure 10–6 *Confidentiality is always important.*

EDUCATION AND CREDENTIALS

CAREER	YEARS OF EDUCATION AFTER HIGH SCHOOL	DEGREE OR DIPLOMA	TESTED BY; LICENSED BY
Psychiatrist (M.D. or D.O.)	4 years of college, 4 years of medical school, 1 year of internship, and 3 years of residency	M.D. or D.O.	Board exams by ABPN; State
Clinical psychologist (Ph.D.)	4 years; 2 years; 2–3 years	B.A. degree; Masters degree; Ph.D. in clinical psychology	Board exams by ABPP; State
Occupational therapist (O.T.R.)	4 years plus 6–9 months of internship or 5 years plus 6–9 months of internship	B.S. in occupational therapy or B.S. in another field plus master's degree in occupational therapy	AOTA national exam; State registration
Psychiatric clinical nurse specialist (RN)	4 years plus 2 years	B.S. degree in nursing plus Master's degree in psychiatric nursing	State board of nursing; State
Registered nurse (RN)	2 years or 3 years or 4 years	A.A.S.D. in nursing; Diploma in nursing; B.S. in nursing	State board of nursing; State
Licensed practical nurse (LPN)	1 year	Diploma in practical nursing	State board of nursing; State
Mental health technician	2 years	Associate of arts degree	State
Psychiatric aide	On-the-job training or brief course in vocational school	Certificate	—
Art therapist	5 years of college plus 1 year of clinical training	B.F.A.	Board certification examination
Music therapist	4 years of school plus 6 months of internship	B.M. in music therapy	Board certification available from AAMT and NAMT (both grant registration)
Recreational therapist	4 years	B.A. in recreational therapy	Board certification examination
Child life specialist	6 years	B.A. in early child development or psychology and M.S. in child life specialist	Certificate from child life certifying commission (optional)
Certified chemical dependency counselor (CCDC)	2 years with work experience*; plus 2 years (4,000 hours) precepted counseling experience	Certificate	CDCCB (oral and written exams); State certification by CDCCB

*Applicants may substitute years of education and training for qualifying work experience, but not for the precepted experience.

EDUCATION AND CREDENTIALS (continued)

Key to abbreviations:

AAMT—American Association for Music Therapy
ABPP—American Board of Professional Psychology
ABPN—American Board of Psychiatry and Neurology
ACSW—Academy of Certified Social Workers
AOTA—American Occupational Therapy Association
B.A.—Bachelor of Arts
B.F.A.—Bachelor of Fine Arts
B.M.—Bachelor of Music
B.S.—Bachelor of Science Degree
CDCCB—Chemical Dependency Counselors Credentialing Board, Inc. (state)
D.O.—Doctor of Osteopathy
LPN—Licensed Practical Nurse
LISW—Licensed Independent Social Worker
LSW—Licensed Social Worker
M.D.—Medical Doctor
M.S.—Master of Science
NAMT—National Association for Music Therapy
NASW—National Association of Social Workers
Ph.D.—Doctor of Philosophy
RN—Registered Nurse

true picture of how this patient feels about him or herself. Observations can reveal how patients feel about themselves. Meaningful observations include body language, quality of interaction with others (Figure 10–7), choice of activities, and talking with imaginary people.

Judgment

Quick thinking and good judgment are needed in psychiatry. Workers must anticipate patients' responses, thoughts, and actions. This involves understanding how a patient is thinking. Workers need to be alert to potentially hazardous behavior. They must make good decisions about measures to protect themselves, patients, and other workers in case a patient's behavior escalates out of control.

Problem solving

Problem solving is constantly used in the field of mental health. Workers know when they can handle a situation and when

Figure 10–7 *Physical contact fulfills a human need.*

to request help. Patient safety and a calm, therapeutic environment are of foremost importance in mental health care.

Assessment

Assessment of postdischarge needs is an important service rendered by social service workers and other professionals. Placement in an appropriate facility after being discharged from the hospital may be a necessary step in a patient's rehabilitation.

Evaluation

Evaluation of an elderly person's functional status is done by nurses, social service workers, and other professionals on the geriatric team (Figure 10–8). The purpose of this assessment is to determine the patient's ability to carry out activities of daily living safely. This will help to identify the mental status of the patient and what living accommodations will be in the patient's best interest.

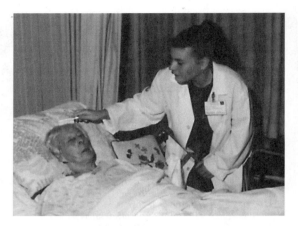

Figure 10–8   *Evaluation of ADL needs.*

Counseling

Counseling is a skill that can be done with individuals, family members, and groups. Types of counseling are in-depth, cognitive, and eclectic. In-depth counseling is insight-oriented. The past is reviewed and studied to determine the connection between past events and current behavior. Cognitive counseling fo-

Biography

I am the youngest in a family of six children. When I was three, I was sent to an orphanage after my mother was hospitalized with schizophrenia. My father could not both work and take care of us six kids. The orphanage had ten homes in which kids were housed with surrogate parents. Each home had twelve children grouped according to age. Someimes I was lonely for family, but there usually was someone ready to play.

My father stopped visiting me when I was eight years old. I realized that I was on my own in this world. My parents were not available to help me. I'm glad that I came to understand that at an early age. I felt sorry for those around me who got into trouble and resisted learning. I knew that if I was to make something of my life, I would have to study hard and get good grades. I did this because I wanted to win a scholarship to nursing school. Even as a child, I knew that I wanted to help others.

After graduating from high school, I had to leave the orphanage. I enrolled in a school of practical nursing and rented a room from a family. By baby-sitting and helping with housework, I earned my room and board. Soon after graduating from nursing school, I was employed in the psychiatric unit of the community hospital and got married.

cuses on current ways of thinking and be-having. The present is reviewed, problems identified, and coping strategies developed to modify behavior. Eclectic counseling is a combination of in-depth and cognitive. Some past events are reviewed, goals are set, and behavior is changed.

Career Search

To discover more about a career and the roles of members in a mental health department, contact the following organizations for online addresses, printed information, and videotapes.

American Psychiatric Association
1400 K Street N.W.
Washington, DC 20005
Phone: 202–682–6000
Fax: 202–682–6114

American Psychiatric Nurses
  Association
c/o Carolyn Freeland
1200 19th Street N.W., Suite 300
Washington, DC 20036
Phone: 202–857–1133
Fax: 202–223–4579

National Association of Social Workers
750 First Street N.E., Suite 700
Washington, DC 2002–4241
Phone: 202–408–8600
Toll-free phone: 800–638–8799
Fax: 202–336–8312

American Therapeutic Recreation
  Association
P.O. Box 15215
Hattiesburg, MS 39404
Phone: 601–264–3413
Toll-free phone: 800–553–0304
Fax: 601–264–3337

(Continued)

Biography (continued)

The marriage was a mistake. I wanted the home and loving relationships that I never had. But my husband turned out to be cruel and abusive. We had three children while I continued to work and went on to school part time to become an RN. When I graduated with a bachelor's of science in nursing, I took the children and left my husband.

I first worked in public health. As my children grew, and took on more responsibility at home, I was able to return to school. Eventually, I earned a Ph.D. in nursing and became the director of health care services for the homeless in my city. In time, I de-veloped four new clinics to meet the needs of this population. Besides my administrative duties, I counsel the homeless in one of the clinics two evenings a week and hold a group therapy session for abused children one afternoon a week. I feel that I am helping those that cannot help themselves just as someone helped me when I was little and couldn't help myself.

My children and I volunteer at a soup kitchen each week. I want them to realize how fortunate we are and that there are others less fortunate in our community who need our help.

National Association for Music
  Therapy
8455 Colesville Road, Suite 930
Silver Spring, MD 20910
Phone: 301–589–3300
Fax: 301–589–5175

American Psychological Association
750 First Street N.E.
Washington, DC 20002–4242
Phone: 202–336–5500

American Association of Psychiatric
  Technicians
P.O. Box 14014
Phoenix, AZ 85063
Phone: 602–873–1890
Toll-free phone: 800–391–7589

National Association of School
  Psychologists
4340 East-West Highway, Suite 402
Bethesda, MD 20814–4411
Phone: 301–657–0270
Fax: 301–657–0275

American Art Therapy Association
1202 Allanson Road
Mundelein, IL 60060
Phone: 708–949–6064
Fax: 708–566–4580

Association for Play Therapy
c/o Kevin O'Connor, Ph.D.
California School of Professional
  Psychology
1350 M Street
Fresno, CA 93721
Phone: 209–486–0851
Fax: 209–486–0734

Range of Annual Incomes

Psychiatrist	$100,000–$160,000
Psychologist	$ 30,000– $80,000
Clinical nurse specialist	$ 34,000– $48,000
Registered nurse	$ 33,000– $44,000
Social worker	$ 30,000– $46,000
Licensed practical nurse	$ 20,000– $30,000
Mental health technician	$ 16,000– $25,000
Psychiatric aide	$ 14,000– $22,000
Occupational therapist	$ 32,000– $55,000
Art therapist	$ 29,000– $38,000
Music therapist	$ 29,000– $38,000
Child life specialist	$ 29,000– $38,000
Chemical abuse counselor	$ 27,000– $39,000

What's New

Outpatient treatment is becoming more common than hospitalization. Unless patients are a danger to themelves or others, they receive treatment as outpatients. The same is true for people who have alcohol or drug dependencies. Because of the cost of hospitalization, patients are being treated while living outside the medical facility.

Counseling by independent practitioners has increased. These professionals are clinical nurse specialists, social workers, and psychologists. In many states, these counselors work under the supervision of a psychiatrist with whom they periodically review patient progress. Patient visits are reimbursed by insurance. This system is effective and helps to contain costs.

School to Work

In addition to the general academic subjects and workplace skills contained in the "Job Skills" chapter, the following subjects and skills apply specifically to careers in the mental health department.

Academic Subject	Workplace Skills
Arts	—Interpret drawings representing patient's thoughts and feelings. —Administer the Rorschach inkblot test. —Participate in art and music therapy. —Select music to play in the nursing unit.
Business	
Time Management	—Schedule individual and group therapy sessions. —Arrange group activities for inpatients. —Determine therapeutic activity schedules for individual patients. —Assign staff to attend patients who are on a suicide watch.
Communication	—Confirm payment for hospitalization with insurance companies. —Arrange with a court for a patient's commitment hearing.
English	—Write an application to a court for a commitment hearing. —Document significant events during a patient's hospitalization. —Write accurate, understandable notes on patient activities.

School to Work—continued

Academic Subject	Workplace Skills
Computer Skills	—Print out a list of medications.
	—Enter a plan of care and estimated hospitalization period.
	—Notify an insurance company of a patient's hospitalization.
Economics	—Arrange home care or group therapy for a patient who is being discharged.
	—Advise a patient of insurance coverage options.
English and Communication	—Review patient history.
	—Identify the need for other disciplines to be involved in the treatment.
Speech Class	—Assist the patient in identifying concerns.
	—Include the patient in planning the goals and course of therapy.
	—Incorporate the family in planning after-hospital care.
Health Education and Safety	
Mechanical Maintenance	—Ensure the safety of the shock therapy machine.
	—Be sure the emergency call system is working properly.
	—Avoid allowing patients to have matches.
	—Place glass and razor blades out of patients' reach.
Body Mechanics	—Call for assistance if a patient is out of control.
Science	
Biochemistry	—Check that blood chemistry elements are in normal limits.
Nutrition and Food Science	—Counsel a patient who has an eating disorder.
Pharmacology	—Monitor the levels of psychotropic medications.
	—Document the effects of drugs.
Social Sciences	
Culture	—Understand the effects of different ethnic practices on mental health.
Ethics	—Guard every patient's confidentiality with the family and the public.
Gerontology	—Know that depression is a common problem among the elderly.
	—Evaluate patients for symptoms of Alzheimer's disease.
	—Seek information to determine if a patient is safe living alone.
Group Dynamics	—Coordinate group therapy sessions.
	—Direct staff meetings on patient progress.
	—Meet with psychiatrists and staff to determine patient therapy.
Growth and Development	—Work with the art therapist in treating children.
	—Approach abused children using established protocols.
	—Notify social service workers if abuse is suspected.

Academic Subject	Workplace Skills
Health Care	—Avoid physical altercations with patients who are acting out.
	—Call security if assistance is needed to avoid injury.
	—Apply medications as ordered to patient's self-inflicted wounds.
Law	—Adhere to the guidelines of the court's commitment order.
	—Protect the patient's safety by restraining when necessary.
	—Document the need for restraints.
	—Rotate restraints according to policy.
	—Assign personnel to attend a suicidal patient according to policy.
	—Report injuries and write an incident report after an event.
Needs of Humans	—Support the patient's physical and emotional needs.
	—Encourage patients to express their views.
	—Allow patients to plan for their future.
	—Give positive reinforcement where appropriate.
Psychology	—Keep patients focused on reality.
	—Maintain a calm attitude.
	—Encourage patients' efforts to change their lives and views.

Review Questions

1. What are the goals of the mental health department?
2. What are the differences between a psychiatrist, a clinical psychologist, and a psychiatric clinical nurse specialist?
3. What are the employment opportunities in this field?
4. What are the sources of job satisfaction in mental health care?
5. List three academic subjects and two ways each is used in the mental health workplace.

NURSING DEPARTMENT

Objectives

After completing this chapter, you should be able to:

- ❏ Explain department goals.
- ❏ Relate the numerous roles of the nurse and social worker.
- ❏ Describe each career in this department.
- ❏ Identify the required education and credentials for each career.
- ❏ Recognize how academic subjects apply in the workplace.

Key Terms

Nursing process

Counseling skills

Utilization review

Case management

INTRODUCTION

Nursing is a caregiving profession that serves every aspect of human need. The process of nursing includes assessing patients' conditions through interpersonal communication, observing, conducting the physical exam and obtaining the health history, and identifying patients' needs using problem-solving techniques based on scientific knowledge. Once a plan to meet identified needs is developed, the nursing process concludes with implementing, evaluating, and adjusting those measures to provide comfort, care, and education to help patients realize their full potential (Figure 11–1).

Nurses interact with patients, family members, and other professionals;

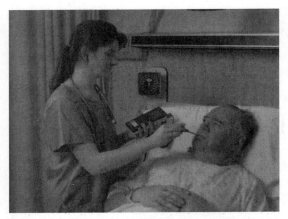

Figure 11–1 *A nurse helps patients realize their full potential.*

coordinate patient care; and help move patients through the maze of the health care system. Nursing represents the interests of patients and seeks the best and most effective care for them.

Nursing is a large and versatile career. Employment is available to those with a current state license and acceptable skill performance. Nursing professionals, as in some other health careers, take continuing education classes to renew their state license. Nursing positions are available in every state and every country in the world.

EDUCATIONAL PROGRAMS

The career of nursing offers several educational programs consisting of academic and clinical experience. After the introductory courses, patient care is integrated with the academic courses.

Nursing programs may be full or part time. Some offer flexible day, evening, and weekend classes; some require an internship.

Aides and assistants

Nursing assistant, nurse's aide, and home health aide programs are offered in high schools, vocational schools, technical schools, and long-term care facilities, as well as by the Red Cross. They consist of a 75-to-120-hour training course over approximately four months and include supervised clinical experience in a hospital or long-term care facility. Certificates are awarded for successful course completion (Figure 11–2). Passing a practical and written exam is required to become certified in the state.

Practical nurse

Practical nurse programs are offered by hospitals, technical schools, city school systems, and community colleges. Technical schools and hospital- and college-based full-time programs are one year long. City school- and college-based programs may be taken in one year full time or in two years part time. Graduates are awarded a certificate. Though programs

Figure 11–2 *A nursing assistant certificate program class in session.*

EDUCATIONAL LADDER

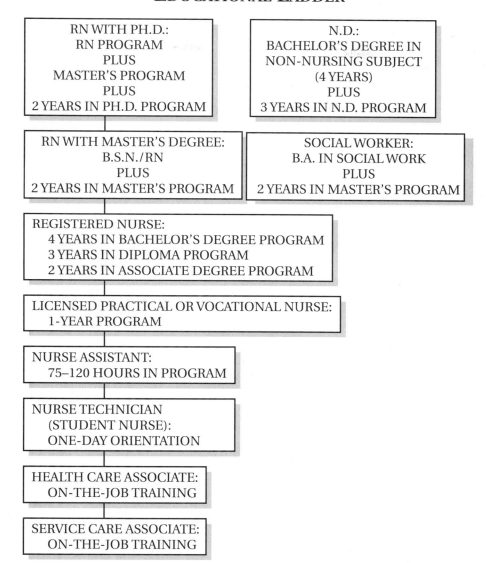

RN WITH PH.D.:
RN PROGRAM
PLUS
MASTER'S PROGRAM
PLUS
2 YEARS IN PH.D. PROGRAM

N.D.:
BACHELOR'S DEGREE IN
NON-NURSING SUBJECT
(4 YEARS)
PLUS
3 YEARS IN N.D. PROGRAM

RN WITH MASTER'S DEGREE:
B.S.N./RN
PLUS
2 YEARS IN MASTER'S PROGRAM

SOCIAL WORKER:
B.A. IN SOCIAL WORK
PLUS
2 YEARS IN MASTER'S PROGRAM

REGISTERED NURSE:
4 YEARS IN BACHELOR'S DEGREE PROGRAM
3 YEARS IN DIPLOMA PROGRAM
2 YEARS IN ASSOCIATE DEGREE PROGRAM

LICENSED PRACTICAL OR VOCATIONAL NURSE:
1-YEAR PROGRAM

NURSE ASSISTANT:
75–120 HOURS IN PROGRAM

NURSE TECHNICIAN
(STUDENT NURSE):
ONE-DAY ORIENTATION

HEALTH CARE ASSOCIATE:
ON-THE-JOB TRAINING

SERVICE CARE ASSOCIATE:
ON-THE-JOB TRAINING

differ, all graduates of approved practical nurse programs are qualified to take the written state board of nursing examination to practice as a licensed practical nurse (LPN) or a licensed vocational nurse (LVN).

Registered nurse

Professional nursing programs may be two, three, or four years long when taken full time. They are based in a variety of settings, such as colleges and universities, community colleges, hospitals, and technical schools. The amount of college credit awarded to graduates varies among programs. All graduates of accredited schools are eligible to take the same written state board of nursing examination to obtain state license and practice as a registered nurse.

Significant differences between the LPN and the RN programs and between the two-, three-, and four-year RN programs are depth of knowledge; amount, depth, and expectations of clinical practice; and professional responsibility. Nurses with a B.S.N. degree have the highest undergraduate academic degree. They usually advance more rapidly on the career ladder and have more career options.

Degrees and diplomas

Associate degree programs are usually two years long with full-time attendance. They are based in a community college, university, or hospital. The academic courses can be taken part or full time. Clinical rotations may take place in several hospitals. At the conclusion of the program, graduates are awarded an associate degree in nursing (A.D.N. or A.A.S.N.) and have earned two years of college credit.

Diploma programs are three years long when taken full time and are usually based in hospitals. The first year generally consists of academic courses at a community college or university that can be taken full or part time. The second and third years include clinical courses and patient care rotations in the "home hospital," if all services are available. At the conclusion, graduates are awarded a diploma and have earned more than one year of college credit.

These kind of diploma programs no longer exist in some states. Instead, programs have been developed in conjunction with a community college's or university's two-year associate degree program; graduates of these programs are awarded an associate degree (A.D.N.) and a diploma from the hospital. These graduates have more clinical experience than the two-year associate degree graduates but have earned only two years of college credit after the three-year program.

A bachelor of science in nursing (B.S.N.) is obtained through a four-year degree program that is college- or university-based. After the initial courses, patient care experience is integrated with the academic courses. This program may have a "home hospital" that is associated with the university or affiliations with several hospitals. The four-year, full-time program is ideal because of the academic approach, consolidation of courses, sequencing of courses, and amount of college credit granted.

Some schools have a two-plus-two program. In this program, a registered nurse with an associate of applied science degree in nursing (A.D.N.) can obtain a bachelor's degree in nursing (B.S.N.) with two additional years of full-time schooling.

Graduates of traditional two- and three-year programs may return to college to obtain a bachelor's degree, often spending more than two years in the process. Time, money, study habits, and other responsibilities in life influence the decision of program selection. Some hospitals offer scholarships to students who agree to work at them after graduation.

Advanced degrees

Advanced study in nursing leads to graduate degrees: master's of science in nursing (M.S.N.), doctor of philosophy in nursing (Ph.D.), and doctor of nursing (N.D.). These degrees require a bachelor's degree, but it need not be in nursing.

A master's degree in nursing usually takes two years in graduate school, going full time. Candidates select a specialty and earn a degree in that area. For example, graduates may be awarded an M.S.N. in gerontology mental health, administration, oncology, or maternal or child health. They may become a nurse practitioner.

A doctor of philosophy degree in nursing requires a two-year program beyond a master's degree in nursing. Graduates of this program are awarded a Ph.D. in nursing and participate in research or teach nursing in colleges or universities.

A doctor of nursing program is three years long. This program accepts candidates with a bachelor's degree in a field other than in nursing. The goal of the graduates of this program is to work in administrative and community planning positions. For example, they work with federal or state government agencies, the Veterans Administration, school systems, or community health planning commissions. Graduates of this program are awarded an N.D.

Health unit coordinator

Health unit coordinator programs (unit secretary programs) consist of on-the-job training (Figure 11–3). Participants in these programs are high school gradu-

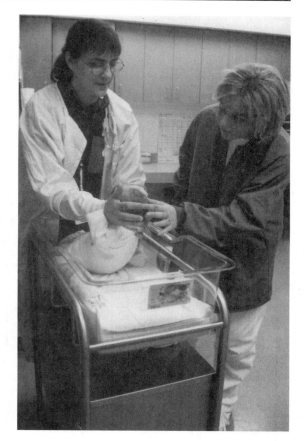

Figure 11–3 *Examining an infant's skull is a nursing skill.*

ates who have completed at least one course in medical terminology. Keyboard or typing skills are helpful, but not required.

GOALS

The goals of the nursing department are to plan and administer safe, comprehensive care to those in need of assistance and to help them achieve maximum potential and manage their illness. Other goals include health education, counseling, and disease prevention.

Career Hierarchy

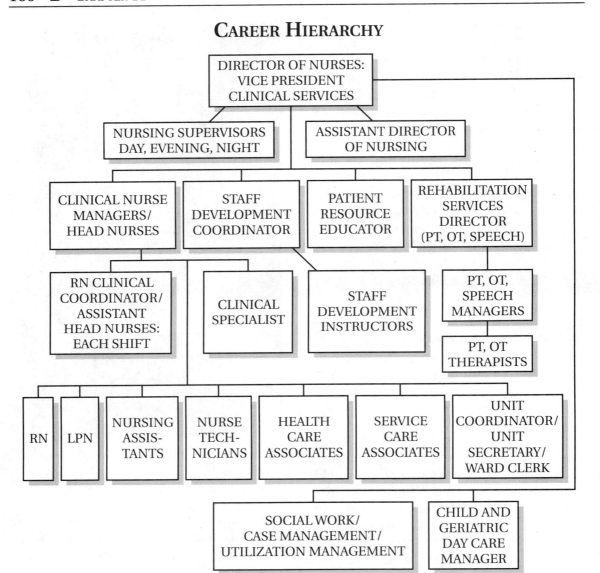

Career Descriptions

Nurses plan and provide direct patient care. They give care to those who are unable to help themselves, and they show patients how to carry out the activities of daily living by themselves. For example, nurses feed, bathe, dress, and move pa-

tients into comfortable positions. They help patients stand, walk, and move from bed to chair. They administer treatments and medications to help them feel better and heal faster.

Nurses plan with patients, family members, and social workers to determine where patients should go when it is time for them to leave the hospital, extended care center, or rehabilitation facility. They help patients face sad diagnoses and make hard choices; they rejoice with them when their health returns. Nurses realize that not all patients will be cured and return home. They work toward helping patients reach their maximum potential and live with residual conditions. They give compassionate care to those who will not recover and try to make their last days as comfortable as possible. They recognize death as a fact of life and know that a caring person at the bedside can provide solace at the end of life.

Nurses care for all aspects of those who come for assistance—including mental, physical, and emotional. They recognize needs best served by others and refer those to appropriate members of the health care team.

Career characteristics

Employment opportunities include many specialty areas of practice, such as medical, surgical, pediatrics, maternity, psychiatry, geriatrics, intensive care, cardiac care, emergency room, or operating room in a hospital facility (Figure 11–4). They work on helicopter rescue teams and in freestanding emergency centers; in clinics and physician offices; in law firms and insurance, medical equipment and pharmaceutical companies; in homes, public health agencies, schools, and rehabilitation centers. They work in shopping malls, on ocean liners, and at summer camps, ski resorts, racetracks, drug detoxification centers, and jails. They work for the military, the World Health

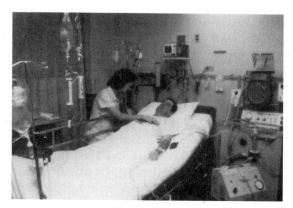

Figure 11–4 *Nurses assess and care for critically ill patients.*

Organization, the Peace Corps, Vista, and the Red Cross. They work in broadcast media and for magazines and newspapers. They teach, write, and develop health maintenance programs.

Nurse practitioners work alongside physicians within a family or specialty practice. They work alone in clinics or rural areas and contact physicians when necessary.

Some nurses are employed by a facility or agency; some practice independently and contract for services. Nurses work in every country in the world with people of all ages, from those in the womb to the very old.

Work hours depend on the job site and type of work. In hospitals, skilled care facilities, inpatient rehabilitation facilities, and long-term care facilities, nursing staff are present twenty-four hours a day, every day of the year. Offices and clinics are open during the day shift, five or six days a week, with some evening and Saturday hours. Home care hours are usually during the day on weekdays with rotation to weekends. Some patients need twenty-four-hour care every day in the home.

Nurses may work full time, part time, or a few hours a week. They can work day, evening, or night shifts any day of the year. They can work four days of ten-hour shifts (and have three days off a week). Or they can work a few hours in the morning or evening during peak patient care periods. Some nurses are self-employed, working out of their homes and determining their own working hours.

Career advancement depends on education, credentials, and experience. Career advancement for registered nurses can be in the fields of administration, clinical practice, and education. In administration, advancement leads to a position of clinical nurse manager of a unit, supervisor, manager of a department, director of nurses, or director of the agency. In clinical practice with education beyond the B.S.N. degree, advancement leads to such positions as clinical specialist, nurse practitioner, midwife, nurse anesthetist, dialysis technician, flight nurse, organ donor team nurse, and enterostomal therapist. Advancement in education requires graduate degrees. It can result in moving from staff instructor to senior instructor or to director of the section, department, or school. Educators work in staff development departments, nursing schools, and community and government agencies such as high schools and vocational schools.

Career advancement for LPNs includes positions as coordinators and supervisors in long-term care facilities and facilities for the mentally retarded. LPNs may make a variety of lateral moves to change facilities or areas of practice, but substantial career advancement depends on obtaining the education to become a registered nurse.

All nurses are capable of giving physical care to patients. With more education, the nurse's knowledge deepens so that more job responsibility can be assumed and more job opportunities become available.

Career advancement for nursing assistants depends on additional education to become licensed practical nurses, registered professional nurses, or members of other medical careers.

Desirable personal characteristics include sensitivity to the needs of others, good verbal and written communication skills, clear thinking, sound decision-making skills, and reliable judgment. Nursing staff need to perform calmly in stressful situations. Other characteristics include patience, friendly demeanor, and a sense of humor. They should speak kindly to people who may be irritable and short-tempered. They take pride in their work and their profession.

Job satisfaction comes from caring for people who cannot care for themselves and showing others how to help themselves (Figure 11–5). It comes from making a difference in the lives of patients, family members, and co-workers. Other sources of satisfaction include the challenge of using problem-solving techniques and professional skills developed over years of study and professional practice. It comes from observing sick people regain their health, realizing the effectiveness of instruction, and seeing patients develop adaptive skills to cope

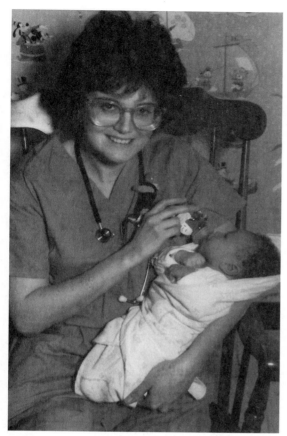

Figure 11–5 *This nurse evidently enjoys her work.*

Nursing roles

Registered nurses use the **nursing process** and nursing skills to meet patient needs. They assess patient status, observe strengths, identify problems, determine possible solutions, implement the best solution, evaluate the effectiveness of the solution, and change the action plan if another solution would be more effective. Much of the problem solving and planning is done with patients, family members, and other professional staff.

Once a basic RN program is completed, additional education can lead to even more job opportunities. Some post-RN programs grant certificates; some grant college degrees. Positions that require education beyond the two-, three-, or four-year basic professional nurse programs are administrator of a health agency, director of nurses, instructor in a nursing school, staff development instructor, nurse practitioner, organ donor team nurse, enterostomal nurse, dialysis technician, flight nurse, nurse anesthetist, midwife, and clinical specialist (Figure 11–6).

with the constraints of illness. Fulfillment comes from the sensitive, caring investment of self in the well-being of others, from the feeling of doing a worthwhile job well, and from the respect of peers.

Personal safety is an issue in health care today. Nursing is considered a high-risk career because patients have diseases that may be contagious or infectious. To protect themselves and patients, nurses use body substance precautions and other protective measures.

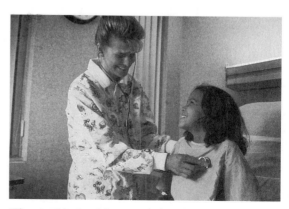

Figure 11–6 *Nurses with advanced practice skills have more job opportunities.*

Both RNs and LPNs are required to complete a certain number of educational hours to renew their state licenses in most states. Generally, twenty-four hours of classes must be attended every two years.

Licensed practical nurses use the nursing process and identify and minister to patient needs. They give physical care, take vital signs, give medications, and hang and regulate tube feedings. In some states, with special training and in certain circumstances, they are permitted to hang premixed intravenous fluids, regulate flow, and discontinue this therapy with a physician's order. LPNs assess patients, carry out sterile procedures, and administer more complex treatments such as irrigations, suctioning, tracheostomy care, inspecting the neurological status, and hot and cold applications. They write clear and descriptive notes regarding care and observations.

Nurse technicians are student nurses who help nurses assess, plan, carry out, and document patient care. Their role includes providing nourishment, hygiene, comfort and evacuation measures, and treatment needs. Though nurse technicians administer direct patient care, they are not required to be certified.

Nursing assistants are certified by the state to care for patients' basic needs. They attend to patients' hygiene, comfort, nourishment, and social needs. They take vital signs, measure intake and output, perform some procedures and treatments, change bed linen, help with ambulation and positioning, and transport patients to other departments (Figure 11–7).

They monitor patients' well-being, observe physical and mental changes, and report those to the charge nurse.

Health care associates are "unlicensed assistive personnel" (UAPs) who administer direct patient care. They are trained on the job to help with a patient's bath, comfort measures, position, vital signs, and transport. They provide a safe, comfortable environment; they obtain and deliver specimens and equipment. They may be trained to draw blood and perform sterile procedures. They keep pa-

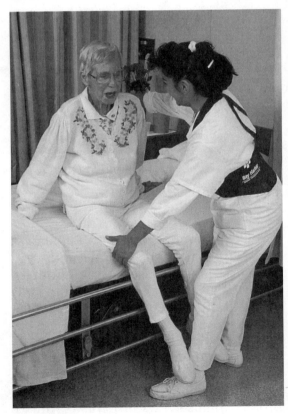

Figure 11–7 *Assisting patients in and out of bed is part of a day's work.*

tient rooms tidy, straighten up the utility rooms, and clean and exchange equipment. A formal educational program does not exist for this role, and certification is not required. UAPs may be cross-trained to perform the duties of a service care associate.

Service care associates are UAPs who provide indirect patient care or environmental services. They are trained on the job to help keep the nursing units neat, clean, and functional. They clean the patient rooms, bathrooms, shower rooms, utility rooms, nursing station, and community rooms. They change lightbulbs and fix simple malfunctioning equipment. They heat food in the microwave and distribute meal trays. They keep track of patients' dietary intake (Figure 11–8). They help the patients complete their menus. They clean and replace equipment. They deliver specimens to the lab. This role does not require a formal education program or certification. Service care associates may be cross-trained to perform the duties of a health care associate. This position replaces the housekeeper and entry-level dietary and maintenance workers.

Figure 11–8 *Unlicensed workers feed patients who are unable to help themselves.*

Social worker

Social workers work independently and with other professionals to counsel individuals and family members. They work as case managers to follow hospitalized patients from admission to discharge. They assist the patient and family members in deciding issues of after-hospital placement. They make recommendations about after-hospital placement according to patient needs, rehabilitation potential, and insurance criteria. That is, they determine if individual patients qualify for insurance-covered skilled care or rehabilitative care and counsel patients and family members accordingly. They monitor the use of hospital beds.

They help people of all ages, from newborns to aged adults. They find foster homes for abused and abandoned children and advise families about long-term care facilities for the confused and agitated elderly. They conduct group therapy sessions with cancer and rape victims. They work with individuals, groups, and government agencies to prevent and manage the social problem of homelessness. They help plan and develop health and recreation services. They counsel people on housing, welfare, pregnancy, abuse, abortion, and coping with death and dying. They locate agencies to help people who have specific needs, such as for housing and clothing after a house fire.

Employment opportunities include hospitals, skilled care facilities, long-term care facilities, inpatient rehabilitation facilities, social agencies, hospices, home care agencies, government agencies, correctional institutions such as jails, human resources departments, religious organizations, and research organizations.

Some are in private practice or contract with agencies for services.

Work hours depend on the job site and type of work. In hospitals, social agencies, and all inpatient facilities, social workers are present during the day, Monday through Friday, plus some Saturdays. In addition, a social worker is on call, available to come to the premises in case of need. In private practice, social workers work Monday through Friday with some Saturday and evening hours. Being available to take a turn on call is also necessary if the social worker is in a group practice.

Social workers may work full time, part time, or a few hours a week. Some facilities offer ten hour days, four days per week as a full-time option.

Career advancement depends on education and experience. With a bachelor's degree, opportunities are limited to positions where supervision is available. With a master's degree, hospital work, clinical counseling, administrative, government and teaching positions are accessible. With a Ph.D. in social service, research, government, teaching, and administrative positions are available.

Desirable personal characteristics include patience, a caring, helpful attitude, sensitivity to the needs of others, and a strong desire to help others. The social worker needs to develop insight into situations, determine psychological states quickly, think clearly under pressure, and make objective decisions. Other characteristics include being kind, friendly, and able to clearly explain a plan of placement or why it is necessary to proceed in a particular manner. The ability to speak another language is helpful, especially the language spoken by the largest immigrant community in the area. People under stress may relate best in their native language.

Job satisfaction comes from helping those in need and making a difference in the lives of patients, family members, and co-workers. It comes from resolving problems, making practical decisions, encouraging patients to help themselves, and protecting those who are unable to help themselves.

Health unit coordinator

Health unit coordinators (unit secretaries or ward clerks) perform secretarial tasks on the nursing unit. They synchronize activities at the nurses' station, serve as a resource to the nursing staff, schedule patient appointments, transcribe physicians' orders, obtain necessary equipment, manage incoming telephone calls, and communicate messages. Most tasks are performed to ensure that physicians' orders are carried out so that patient care will be prompt and accurate. Coordinators communicate with other departments to request tests, treatments, nourishments, and medications for patient comfort and rehabilitation. Using a computer, they enter data and order tests. In emergency situations, they call for appropriate assistance and facilitate patient transfer to an acute care setting. They greet patients and visitors, answer questions, and provide directions. They assemble charts for new patients, file reports, replenish forms, and graph vital signs on the medical record.

Employment opportunities are most available in hospital patient care areas on medical, surgical, intensive care, obstetric, pediatric, psychiatric, and emergency care nursing units, as well as in the medical records department (Figure 11–9). Other opportunities may be in patient service areas in the radiology, biometrics, respiratory, occupational therapy, and physical therapy departments. Other job sites include skilled nursing, rehabilitation and long-term care facilities, outpatient clinics, physician offices, pharmaceutical companies, and research institutes.

Work hours depend on the facility and department. In patient care areas in a hospital, coordinators work day and evening shifts, seven days per week, including holidays. Few positions are available on night shift, but some rotation to day and evening shifts may be necessary. Part- and full-time jobs are often available. In an office setting, work hours are Monday through Friday, with some evening and Saturday hours.

Career advancement may include teaching and supervising health unit coordinators within a department or facility. However, most moves are lateral. With additional education, a coordinator may become a health care professional, assume more responsibility, and give direct patient care.

Desired personal characteristics include a pleasant disposition, a positive attitude, an aptitude for detail work, and the ability to concentrate and work accurately in the midst of interruptions, noise, and distractions. Other qualities include good communication skills, pride in

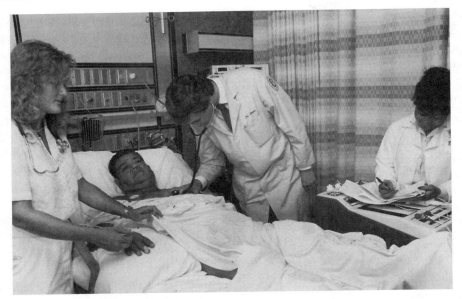

Figure 11–9   *Employment opportunities are available in many areas.*

doing good work, versatility, and ability to maintain a calm, friendly environment at the nurses' station.

Organization is especially necessary. The health unit coordinator needs to set priorities, rank tasks, and complete the most important first. Accuracy, conscientious effort, and acceptance of responsibility are other desirable attributes.

Job satisfaction comes from smoothly managing the nurses' station; completing detailed work accurately and promptly; serving professionals, patients, and families in a positive, helpful way; and knowing that your work is greatly appreciated.

JOB AVAILABILITY

Job opportunities are especially good for registered nurses in advance practice and in rural areas through the year 2005. Fewer jobs will be available for registered nurses in hospitals than in home care, outpatient facilities, same-day surgeries, rehabilitation centers, and chemotherapy clinics. Jobs for licensed practical nurses will increase in long-term care facilities, home care, health maintenance organization offices, emergency centers, and ambulatory surgical centers. Jobs for unskilled, unlicensed care givers and nursing assistants will increase through the year 2005 as part of medical cost-containment efforts.

Job availability will increase for social workers in hospitals because of the focus on early patient discharge. Also, more attention will be focused on increased counseling of the mentally ill, efforts to decrease crime and juvenile delinquency, and families in crisis.

EDUCATION AND CREDENTIALS

CAREER	YEARS OF EDUCATION AFTER HIGH SCHOOL	DEGREE OR DIPLOMA	TESTED BY; LICENSED BY
Registered nurse (RN)	2 years, 3 years, or 4 years	A.A.S.D. in nursing* Diploma; A.A.S.D. in nursing (few programs)* B.S.N. required	Written exam by state board of nursing; State registration renewed every two years with CNE
Clinical nurse specialist (RN)	4 years plus 2 years	B.S.N.; M.S.N.	Same as for RN plus certification in area of specialization (required in some states)
Nurse practitioner (CRNP)	4 years plus 2 years	B.S.N.; M.S.N.	Same as for RN plus National certification exam
Licensed practical nurse (LPN)	1 year	Certificate	Written exam by state board of nursing; State license renewed every two years with CNE
Nursing assistant or home health aide (CNA)	75–120 hours (4 months)	Certificate	Written and practical exam; State
Nurse technician (NT)	A student nurse in second year of diploma program or third year of bachelor's degree program	—	—
"Unlicensed assistive personnel" (UAPs)	On-the-job training	—	—
Nurse anesthetist (CRNA)	4 years college plus 1 year critical care experience plus 2–3 years anesthesia program	B.S.N. degree plus M.S.N. in anesthesia	Same as for RN plus exam for certification by AANA Council; Certification and state license
Social worker (ACSW) (LISW or LSW)	6 years or 8 years	Master's degree in social service; Ph.D. in social service	ACSW is national accreditation; exam given by NASW; state licensure required in some states. LISW granted with M.S. and two years clinical experience; LSW granted with M.S.; indicates less than two years clinical; supervision required

Education and Credentials—continued

EDUCATION AND CREDENTIALS (continued)

CAREER	YEARS OF EDUCATION AFTER HIGH SCHOOL	DEGREE OR DIPLOMA	TESTED BY; LICENSED BY
Case manager (RN or ACSW)	4–6 years: RN or Social Worker	B.S.N. or Master's degree in social work	State board for RN; licensed in state (voluntary) exam for social worker
Child life specialist	(See Chapter 10)		
Enterostomal therapy nurse (CETN)	8-week program (must be RN)	Certificate	National boards exam by IAET; State certification
Midwife (M.S.N., CNM)	2 years (must be RN to qualify for program)	M.S.N. in midwifery	National boards exam by ACNM to attain state certification
Health unit coordinator (unit secretary or ward clerk)	1 course in medical terminology (one quarter or semester); keyboard keyboard knowledge is helpful	High school diploma (usually required)	—

*Some universities offer graduates a one-year "bridge program" to obtain a B.S.N.

Key to abbreviations:

A.A.S.D.—Associate of Applied Science Degree
ACNM—American College of Nurse Midwifes
ACSW—Academy of Certified Social Workers
B.S.N.—Bachelor of Science in Nursing
CETN—Certified Enterostomal Therapy Nurse
CNA—Certified Nurse Assistant
CNE—Continuing Nursing Education
CRNA—Certified Registered Nurse Anesthetist
CNM—Certified Registered Nurse Midwife
CRNP—Certified Registered Nurse Practitioner
IAET—International Association of Enterostomal Therapists
LISW—Licensed Independent Social Worker
LPN—Licensed Practical Nurse
LSW—Licensed Social Worker
M.S.N.—Master of Science in Nursing
NT—Nurse Technician
RN—Registered Nurse

SKILLS

Nurses learn patient care skills during their basic nursing program. Although most nurses work directly with patients, some have no patient contact. Basic nursing skills include, but are not limited to, the nursing process. Nurses develop skills to care for the physical, emotional, cognitional, and social needs of their patients.

Nursing

The nursing process is a procedure that involves the skills of assessment, observation, communication, clear thinking, problem solving, decision making, therapeutic action, and revision of action plans. Nurses work with patients and family members to identify problems that can be helped by the efforts of the health care team.

The next step is to decide what to do about those problems. A problem may be physical, such as a sudden decrease in a patients' blood pressure, or social, such as bulimia. With a decreased blood pressure problem, nurses determine the actions and then act. They give medication or intravenous fluid to solve the problem. With bulimia, the patient must decide the actions and then act. Nurses may counsel, identify possible actions, or make a referral to another professional, but the patient must decide the actions and follow through to resolve the problem.

Sometimes the chosen action does not achieve the established goal, so other actions are tried. This is the process of nursing.

Physical care includes all the actions necessary to attend to the body's needs— bathing, toileting, feeding, changing dressings, inserting tubes, using medical and surgical aseptic techniques, and doing treatments (Figure 11–10). While nurses are doing these tasks, they are assessing, observing, and teaching.

Physical care is only one nursing skill that nurses carry out to meet patients' needs of comfort and cleanliness (Figure 11–11). Bathing and bed making are actions that patients and family members see and associate with nursing. But much of what nurses do involves thinking, solving problems, teaching, and communicating with patients and other professionals. In addition to physical care, nurses attend to the emotional, cognitional, and social needs of their patients.

Figure 11–10 *Gloves are worn when obtaining a blood sample for a glucose level test.*

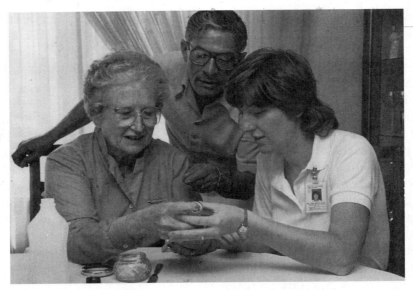

Figure 11–11 *Physical care is not the only skill practiced by the nurse.*

Emotional care relates to feelings. Nurses provide the opportunity for patients to express their feelings and give them emotional support during that process. Though nurses may not be able to solve every problem that worries patients, nurses often help put worries into perspective. Patients may have worries related to their illnesses and treatments. For example, there might be anger or sadness associated with a diagnosis of cancer, fear of the prognosis, and hate for the fate that befell them. Though nurses cannot change the diagnosis or prognosis, they can listen to patients vent their feelings. They can encourage them to talk, offer alternative ways of thinking, and suggest ways that may help them accept the facts.

Cognitional care relates to patients' need to know about their illness—what it means to their life, how to help them-

selves, and when they can expect to feel better. Patients who are newly diagnosed with diabetes may experience an emotional shock. Before they can intellectualize, they will need to deal with their emotions and accept the disease. Then, they will want to know exactly how the disease works, what it will mean in their life, how it will affect their diet, how to test their blood sugar level, what the effect of exercise is, and how to inject insulin. Nurses teach diabetic patients and families about all facets of the disease, along with how to maintain health and prevent complications.

Social care involves patients' need to be cared about and accepted by family members, friends, and health care workers. Some patients may have trouble accepting their need for care. In the hospital, for example, patients may not signal for medication to relieve pain when they are uncomfortable because they don't want to bother the nurses. Nurses work closely with patients before and after surgical procedures that change body image. Otherwise, patients may have problems adjusting after mastectomy, limb amputation, or colostomy surgery because of the change in physical appearance. Another problem may be fear relating to social acceptance because they feel different.

Teamwork is important in hospital nursing (Figure 11–12). Two or three different shifts of nurses work every day with every patient. A change-of-shift report informs nurses starting a shift about patients and their needs so they can be continuously addressed. This is one way the nursing team works together to carry out the nursing process.

Social work

Social workers learn patient **counseling skills** during their basic social work education program. Although most social workers work directly with patients (or clients), some have no direct contact.

Basic skills include, but are not limited to, assessing mental and emotional states, the quality and impact of relationships, environmental hazards, the ability of a client to live successfully in a situation, and the choices available to correct unsatisfactory situations. Social workers are experienced in counseling and guiding clients about social situations and personal habits. They work with people of all ages and in all situations.

Counseling may be done on the scene in the emergency department or on a routine basis in an office setting. It is often done with the patient and family members in the hospital to determine after-hospital placement. It may be done over the phone on a rape hot line or in person at a rape crisis center.

Placement alternatives are well known to social workers. People who are physically, mentally, or emotionally at risk for serious problems may be placed in different environments for protection and further evaluation. Social workers make arrangements with the individual or responsible family member to house the at-risk person in an institution or foster home.

Utilization review is the process for monitoring the use of hospital beds to ensure the medical necessity of hospitalization. The system was developed to contain health care costs while maintaining quality care. When **utilization review** began, studies were done to determine the average number of days patients were hospitalized with each illness or diagnosis. Insurance carriers then averaged those days and assigned that average number of days to each diagnosis. Usually, that is the number of days for which an insurance carrier will pay when a patient is

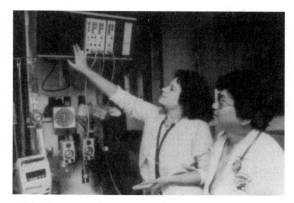

Figure 11–12 *Team work is important.*

hospitalized. Depending on the facility, patients may be responsible for paying for days that exceed that number. If patients have more than one illness, additional days of hospitalization may be covered by insurance.

The system of utilization review that requires daily monitoring of the use of hospital beds is called a concurrent utilization review. In this system, statistical data is recorded on the number of days all current patients with specific diagnoses spend in the hospital. To do this, a nurse or social worker follows the progress of each patient from day of admission. This nurse or social worker is called a case manager. The case manager keeps track of each patient's hospitalization, rehabilitation, or skilled nursing needs. **Case management** is an effective cost-cutting system.

The facts accumulated by the case manager are compared with the number of days allowed or covered by insurance carriers. When the number of days is near the insurance maximum, the physician is notified. The physician then decides if the diagnosis has changed during hospitalization and thus would allow for more paid hospital days, if application for an extension of hospitalization should be made to the insurer, or if it is time to discharge the patient.

To ensure accuracy and honesty in data reporting, representatives from Medicare and other insurance providers regularly visit hospitals to review charts. This is called retrospective utilization review of medical records because the patients have already left the hospital.

Valuable information and statistical data are gleaned from the process of utilization review. Some of the data is shared with the state's peer review organization.

Health unit coordinator

Health unit coordinators work under the direction of registered nurses and perform skills in the categories of communication, transcription of physicians' orders, maintaining medical records, handling supplies, and organization.

Communication is interpersonal and by telephone and computer. Interpersonal communication is reflected in attitude, facial expression, body language, and the tone and content of speech. The health unit coordinator influences the atmosphere of the nursing station. A receptive and pleasant atmosphere is the goal.

Unit coordinators are in telephone communication with many departments and offices. They answer incoming calls almost constantly. They beep physicians and personnel on the silent pager, then deliver messages to the responder. Accurately taking and delivering telephone messages and responding to pages for busy staff are essential services. Maintaining a positive attitude and responding cordially to negative or angry callers are challenges of the job, achievements to be mastered, and skills required in this position.

The use of computers and fax machines in health care is becoming standard. Information is sent and received from nursing units to other departments, offices, and hospitals. Health unit coordinators enter data from physicians' orders into the computer terminal in their department. These messages are instantly transported to the terminal of the receiving department. With some computer programs, a nurse checks the accuracy of the unit coordinator's work before the computer sends entries. This procedure ensures that the nurse is informed of the new order and serves as a safety check to prevent errors that may be costly in patient comfort and dollars. Lab results, pathology reports, and consult reports may be faxed to nursing units and to physicians' offices. When information is received by the computer terminal on the unit, it is printed out, reviewed by the nurse, and posted in the medical record.

Transcription of physicians' orders is the most important function of the health unit coordinator's role. This skill must be done accurately (Figure 11–13). If errors are made, procedures may be performed on the wrong patient, test results attributed to the wrong patient, medications ordered for the wrong patient, or departments not notified about tests to be performed. Orders that must be carried out immediately take precedence over other activities. In addition to notifying departments of new treatments and medications ordered for patients, the coordinator follows up to see that the orders were carried out.

Coordinating the order and completion of each patient's chart is part of the health unit coordinator's role. Medical records are permanent legal documents that serve as an account of patient care, treatment, and progress. The health unit coordinator collates a new chart for each newly admitted patient. Forms are stamped with an identification nameplate, organized into sections, and replenished as needed. The coordinator graphs temperatures on the chart and inserts reports from the laboratory, radiology, and surgery, along with consultation summaries. When the chart becomes too large to handle comfortably, the coordinator thins it by removing some pages; the coordinator returns these pages to the record after the patient is discharged. The coordinator arranges pages

Figure 11–13 *Accurate transcription of physicians' orders is important.*

in the required order and sends the complete record to the medical records department for review and storage.

Ordering supplies so workers have what they need to do their jobs effectively is the health unit coordinator's task. Many facilities have developed a system for automatically stocking of sterile items from central service, linen from the linen room, forms from the print shop, and office supplies from the storeroom. If these supplies become depleted or if the unit's needs increase, the coordinator notifies the proper department and arranges delivery.

Organization is a skill that is crucial to the successful performance of the health unit coordinators' role. Activities often occur simultaneously, for example, multiple incoming telephone calls, physician requests, nurses asking for a colleague to be paged, technicians needing requisitions, visitors waiting for assistance, and transport personnel requiring directions. Continually straightening the desk area by putting charts away, filing reports promptly, and checking task completion contributes to increased accuracy and fewer errors. Using a memo pad to list messages and keeping it by the phone is a valuable organizational technique. It helps to remind the coordinator of the information that callers require and to repage someone if he or she does not respond to a page within a reasonable time.

Biography

I always wanted to be a helper. When I was in high school, I volunteered at the local hospital as a Candy Striper. As I delivered mail and flowers to patients, I got to see firsthand how nurses worked with patients, how they helped them. I decided then to become a nurse.

When I was in eighth grade, I began to use drugs. I kept using them even after high school and into college. Eventually, to support my habit, I began to sell drugs. Not long after, I was caught, arrested, and sent to prison—an awful experience! While doing my time, I finally kicked drugs and decided that I was wasting my life. I knew that when I got out, I did not want to come back. I was determined to find a career that would allow me to support myself in a life without drugs. As soon as I was released, I registered at the community college. Since I had flunked out before because of drugs, I had to repeat every course. This time, though, I made it and went on to enroll in a nursing program.

I had to overcome some big obstacles to become an RN. During college, I had to work to support myself. And to qualify for financial aid, I had to be a full-time student. After graduation, I had to petition the State Board of Nursing for permission to take the state board exam. Since nurses administer narcotics, they have access to drugs. So, the state board personnel had to confirm that I had not been arrested for possessing drugs in recent years. When they found that I hadn't, they cleared my record for purposes of licensure, and I took the exam. Now I am a self-supporting registered nurse with a full-time hospital job. It wasn't easy, but I did it! I am clean and proud of becoming the helper I always wanted to be.

Career Search

To discover more about a career and the roles of members in a nursing department, contact the following organizations for online addresses, printed information, and videotapes.

American Nurses Association
600 Maryland Avenue S.W.,
 Suite 100 W.
Washington, DC 20024–2571
Phone: 202–651–7000
Fax: 202–651–7001

American Association of Critical Care
 Nurses
101 Columbia
Aliso Viejo, CA 92656
Phone: 714–362–2000
Toll-free phone: 800–899–AACN
Fax: 714–362–2020

American College of Nurse-Midwives
1522 K Street N.W., Suite 1000
Washington, DC 20005
Phone: 202–728–9860
Fax: 202–289–4395

National Federation of Licensed
 Practical Nurses
1418 Aversboro Road
Garner, NC 27529–4547
Phone: 919–779–0046
Fax: 919–779–5642

American Nurses Assistants'
 Association
Box 165
Ottawa, KS 66067

National League for Nursing
350 Hudson Street
New York, New York 10014
Phone: 212–989–9393
Toll-free phone: 800–669–1656
Fax: 212–989–9256

National Association for Home Care
519 C Street, N.E.
Washington, DC 20002
Phone: 202–547–7424
Fax: 202–547–3540

Association of Rehabilitation Nurses
4700 W. Lake Avenue
Glenview, IL 60025–1485
Phone: 847–966–3433
Toll-free phone: 800–229–7530
Fax: 847–375–4777

National Association of Health Unit
 Coordinators
1821 University Avenue, Suite 104S
St. Paul, MN 55104
Phone: 612–641–8095

National Association of Social
 Workers
750 First Street N.E., Suite 700
Washington, DC 20002–4241
Phone: 202–408–8600
Toll-free phone: 800–638–8799
Fax: 202–336–8312

Range of Annual Incomes

Director of nurses	$70,000–$130,000
Clinical nurse manager, head nurse	$ 45,000–$70,000
RN: staff nurse	$ 32,000–$54,000
RN: clinical nurse specialist	$ 34,000–$55,000
RN: nurse practitioner	$ 37,000–$60,000
RN: midwife	$ 44,000–$68,000
RN: infection control nurse	$ 44,000–$54,000
RN: enterostomal therapy nurse	$ 35,000–$60,000
RN or social worker: utilization review coordinator	$ 31,000–$48,000
RN or social worker: case manager	$ 30,000–$46,000
RN: nurse anesthetist	$ 65,000–$90,000
RN: nurse educator, BSN	$ 34,000–$56,000
RN: nurse educator, MSN	$ 37,000–$52,000
Social worker	$ 30,000–$46,000
Recreational therapist	$ 25,000–$40,000
Licensed practical nurse	$ 20,000–$32,000
Nursing assistant, patient care assistant	$ 14,000–$22,000
Home health aide	$ 14,000–$29,000
Service care associate	$ 13,000–$19,000
Child life specialist	$ 24,000–$33,000
Health unit coordinator (secretary)	$ 16,000–$25,000

What's New

Clinical pathways are guidelines that have been developed for the care of patients with certain diagnoses. They have been developed by health care teams that include physicians and other professional disciplines. They serve as a guide to tests, treatment, therapies, medications, and education. These clinical pathways help case managers track patient progress in the health care system, and determine the need for continued hospital care, placement in another skilled facility, or discharge to home with support systems.

Nurse practitioners will take over more of the tasks that were once done by physicians. These professional nurses have advance practice skills that qualify them to provide much of the routine care of patients in hospitals, nursing homes, clinics, and physician offices. They may develop specialty practices in pediatrics, women's health, family practice, acute care, or geriatrics. They do physical exams, take medical histories, order lab tests and X rays, and see patients for follow-up visits. In some states, they can prescribe medications. They teach patients about chronic diseases and recognize complications before they become serious. Services provided by nurse practitioners qualify for Medicare, Medicaid, and other health insurance reimbursement.

Computer documentation is the latest method of charting. This may be done at the bedside on the nursing units or on a laptop in the home. Checklists and wands facilitate documenting patient care. For each shift and patient, the computer prints out a care plan, treatment list, and medication schedule. The nurse can use this printout as a worksheet. At the end of the shift, a wand is used to touch the screen to indicate that care was given and medications taken. If something was omitted, a multiple-choice screen appears to identify the reason or a note can be written. Access to lab tests and physician reports are available through the hospital's main-frame computer.

Automatic stocking of linen, sterile supplies, disposable equipment, and medications is being done with robotic carts. This robotic equipment is programmed to leave the source department and arrive on the nursing unit without being accompanied by a worker. It delivers stock from the linen room, central service, storeroom, and pharmacy. The robotic cart restocks the shelves or replaces an empty cart, then returns empty to the source department. The robotic action of medication carts changes the drawers before returning to the pharmacy.

Direct menu selection is done by a handheld computer that directly connects with the hospital dietary department. When a service care associate helps a patient select menu choices, they are directly recorded in the dietary computer.

"Robo nurse" is a medication distribution system in which a medication cart automatically arrives on the nursing unit and drives itself into each patient's room to deliver the exact medication for that hour of the day. When the medication is taken out of the specific drawer, it is documented, and the patient is charged. This is especially useful in a senior residence where patients can be depended upon to take their own medication.

Telephone advice from registered nurses is a service offered by medical centers at no charge to the caller and by insurance companies for a monthly fee. Nurses answer questions on general health concerns and specific problems. Advice is given according to established protocols resulting in increased consumer knowledge, problem resolution, or a trip to an emergency room or physician's office. The goal and effect of this service has been to maintain quality health care while lowering costs through reducing visits to physician offices and emergency rooms.

School to Work

In addition to the general academic subjects and workplace skills contained in the "Job Skills" chapter, the following subjects and skills apply specifically to careers in the nursing department.

Academic Subject	Workplace Skills
Arts	—Prepare a pie-shaped chart demonstrating bed utilization.
	—Design bar graphs to show diagnoses by month.

School to Work—continued

Academic Subject	Workplace Skills
Arts (cont'd)	—Prepare line graphs to show that falls increase the length of hospital stays.
Business	
Time Management	—Prioritize patient care to administer medications on time.
	—Assign duties to nursing assistants according to their training.
	—Honor requests for pain medication as soon as possible.
	—Arrange desk work to minimize confusion and expedite orders.
	—Note new orders and direct to the appropriate department promptly.
	—Check to see that new orders were carried out.
Communication	—Explain the application of health care services to patients and families.
	—Clarify the process of moving a patient from acute care to a skilled facility and then home.
	—Contact the case manager to follow new admissions.
	—Renew certification with insurance companies as needed.
Economics	—Explain to patients and families what insurance will cover.
	—Use supplies sparingly; avoid waste.
	—Instruct families in patient care to prepare for patients' discharge.
Career and Guidance	—Work as licensed graduate of the chosen program before advancing on the education ladder.
	—Begin a career in the general field before establishing a specialty.
English and Communications	—Interpret orders and reports.
	—Listen to and accurately record verbal orders.
	—Write clear statements for insurance and disability plans.
	—Document the complete event on incident reports.
	—Understand emergency protocols for cardiac arrests.
	—Know how to make an emergency page.
Science	
Anatomy and Physiology	—Assess normal and abnormal symptoms.
	—Address changes in the patient's physical condition; document.
Biochemistry	—Check the patient's lab results; identify and that are abnormal.
Microbiology	—Swab infected sites for culturing.
	—Administer appropriate antibiotics for the infection.

Academic Subject	Workplace Skills
Nutrition and Food Science	—Teach how diet relates to the patient's disease. —Stress the effects of sodium and sugar on heart disease and diabetes.
Pathophysiology Pharmacology	—Understand the effects of surgery on certain organs. —Administer medications appropriate to the patient's disease. —Watch for side effects of medication. —Notice positive effects of medication.
Radiology	—Instruct patients on preparing for imaging tests. —Read radiology reports. —Administer and teach radiation therapy.
Mathematics	—Measure weight, height, body fat, and skin turgor. —Calculate the amount of body surface. —Mix the diluent with the medication and draw an accurate dose into the syringe. —Administer medication according to schedule. —Calculate a sliding scale of insulin based on blood sugar levels. —Pour an accurate dose of liquid medication into a medicine cup. —Translate body temperature from centigrade to Fahrenheit. —Count pulse and respiration for one-quarter minute and multiply by four. —Measure blood pressure. —Calculate IV drops per minute according to milliliters per hour. —Count and account for narcotics supplies on each shift.

Review Questions

1. What are the goals of a nursing department?
2. What are the minimum numbers of years of education needed after high school to become a registered nurse, a licensed practical nurse, and a social worker?
3. What are six areas of employment for nurses? Six for social workers?
4. List six personal characteristics desirable in nursing personnel and six for social workers.
5. List three academic subjects and two ways each is applied in the nursing department.

OCCUPATIONAL THERAPY DEPARTMENT

Objectives

After completing this chapter, you should be able to:

- ❏ Explain the goals of the occupational therapy department.
- ❏ List the reasons people need occupational therapy.
- ❏ Discuss each career in this department.
- ❏ Describe the skills performed in this department.
- ❏ Recognize how academic subjects apply in this workplace.

Key Terms

Assessment   Activities of daily living   Therapeutic activity planning

---

INTRODUCTION

Occupational therapy helps disabled persons become more confident and self-sufficient in carrying out the **activities of daily living**. It enables them to learn or relearn the performance of basic skills that were interrupted by physical, mental, or emotional illness, traumatic injury, or congenital or developmental disability. In the occupational therapy department, basic life skills are taught, including bathing, dressing, preparing food, shopping, and banking. Job skill require-ments are determined by testing for the necessary levels of manual dexterity required to do a job, then determining if the patient can meet those requirements (Figure 12-1); also, training, retraining, and work-hardening programs are developed after work-related injuries.

GOALS

The goals of the occupational therapy department are to evaluate, diagnose, and treat people with impaired functioning to enable them to achieve optimum living

Figure 12–1 *A test for arm dexterity and strength.*

skills, prevent disabilities, and maintain health.

Career Descriptions

In the occupational therapy department, the assets and deficits of patients of all ages are assessed, patient potential is analyzed, and activities are set up to in-crease patients' ability to function and lessen limitations. Workers teach premature babies to suck. They treat children whose development is slow. They help stroke patients regain cognitive, perceptual, sensory, and physical abilities. They interact with mentally ill persons to give them the confidence and skills needed to return to family and work. They aid patients who have been weakened by the debilitating illnesses of emphysema and multiple sclerosis to organize their activities to conserve energy. They design, construct, and adapt equipment to help patients become more independent (Figure 12-2.)

Occupational therapists determine the extent of problems and available strengths before planning treatment. They confer with other professionals and include patients in setting goals. Occupational therapy assistants help carry out the treatment plan established by the occupational therapists.

Career Hierarchy

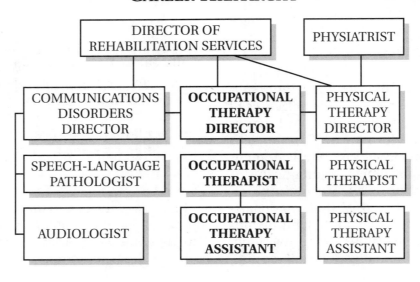

Figure 12–2 Equipment adaptation.

Career characteristics

Employment opportunities include hospitals, clinics, rehabilitation facilities, long-term care facilities, facilities for mentally retarded and handicapped people, schools, camps, private homes, day care centers, mental health facilities, government agencies, and community health centers. Occupational therapists can also work in private practice or with a group of physicians who specialize in a particular field. Areas of specialization include spinal cord injuries, mental retardation, strokes, hand injuries, and mental illness.

Work hours are usually during the day, Monday through Friday, with Saturday hours in some facilities.

Career advancement for occupational therapists includes supervisor, section head, or director in a large department. Occupational therapy assistants can progress to occupational therapist positions with additional education. A master's or doctoral degree is needed to teach in colleges and universities.

Desired personal characteristics include an encouraging, supportive approach to patient care and a nurturing attitude toward people of all ages and backgrounds. Other assets include versatility, adaptability, and sensitivity to patients' needs and moods. Along with a good base of knowledge in science, anatomy, muscles, and nerves, creativity and imagination are needed to develop unique treatment programs. Strength of purpose is needed to surmount the stress and frustration that result from anticipated outcomes of treatment not always being reached. Occupational therapy assistants need good communication, observational, and problem-solving skills; creative thinking; and the ability to follow directions.

Job satisfaction comes from being a part of the health care team with a special body of knowledge. It comes from a feeling of professional accomplishment and the ability to work independently with patients and family members. It also comes from using creativity to develop a rehabilitation plan, serving as a resource to other professionals, teaching preventive measures, and helping patients regain maximum independence. Other sources of gratification are observing patients' progress and taking pride in their continuing efforts to maintain their maximum potential, even though it may be less than full function.

Career roles

Occupational therapists interview and evaluate patients to assess strengths and weaknesses and to determine physical and mental abilities (Figure 12–3). They plan and direct activities specifically designed

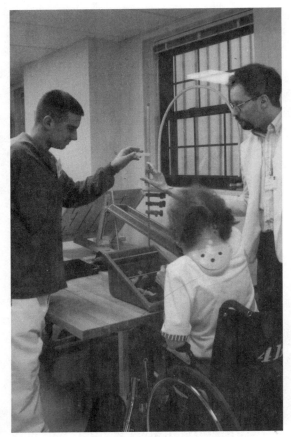

Figure 12–3 *Abilities and limitations are identified.*

for patients with physical, mental, or emotional problems. They devise methods and treatment plans to prevent complications, increase independence, and adjust to residual deficits. They evaluate progress, work with patients to set realistic goals, and share insights into life changes as a part of the daily treatment regimen. Therapists work with patients to develop or improve fine motor coordination, manual dexterity, and small muscle strength. They teach how to prevent complications or deformity from existing medical conditions. They help patients adapt to tempo-

rary or permanent disabilities and function within those limitations.

Occupational therapy assistants work under the direction of the occupational therapist to carry out the treatment plan. They observe patients' tolerance, report improvements, document activities and progress, and work with the occupational therapist to upgrade and adjust patients' treatment plans. Other responsibilities include checking inventory and ordering supplies.

Occupational therapy aides/technicians help the therapists and assistants by carrying out some patient treatments, escorting patients, preparing project parts, and cleaning after arts and crafts projects.

JOB AVAILABILITY

The U.S. Department of Labor estimates the job outlook for occupational therapists is excellent. Job growth is expected to increase faster than average to the year 2005. Demand for services will increase because of expanded rehabilitation programs and growth in skilled nursing facilities and home care. There will be a moderate gain in jobs in school systems because of increased funding for children with disabilities. Though working as a private practitioner is expensive, more therapists will become self-employed because they can bill Medicare directly for services.

SKILLS

Occupational therapy skills are geared to strengthen fine motor skills, improve cognition, prevent complications, and train or retrain in job skills. Treatments

EDUCATION AND CREDENTIALS

CAREER	YEARS OF EDUCATION AFTER HIGH SCHOOL	DEGREE OR DIPLOMA	TESTED BY; LICENSED BY
Occupational therapist (O.T.R.)	4 years plus 6–9 months internship or 5 years plus 6–9 months internship	B.S. in occupational therapy or B.S. in another field plus master's degree in OT	AOTA national exam; State licensure
Occupational therapy assistant (C.O.T.A.)	2 years plus 6 months internship	A.A.S.D. in occupational therapy assisting technology	AOTCB national exam; State registration
Occupational therapy aide or technician	12–14 months plus 6 months internship	Certificate	Vocational or technical schools

Key to abbreviations:

AOTA—American Occupational Therapy Association
AOTCB—American Occupational Therapy Certification Board
A.A.S.D.—Associate of Applied Science Degree
B.S.—Bachelor of Science Degree
C.O.T.A.—Certified Occupational Therapist Assistant
O.T.R.—Registered Occupational Therapist

are based on the assessment of strengths and deficits, medical diagnosis, age, general condition, ability to cooperate, type of surgery, and expected discharge disposition. Treatment plans help patients overcome the restrictions of disability, adjust to residual limitations, and increase independence.

Assessing

Assessment is the skill of interviewing, observing, and testing patients' physical and mental abilities. This process helps therapists determine deficits and needs. Goals and treatment plans are then designed and aftercare needs recommended. Patients' cognitive function, safety factors (such as using a stove), ability to organize thoughts (balancing a checkbook) and carry out steps of a task (preparing a meal), memory, problem-solving skills, and ability to manage medication may need to be evaluated before patients are discharged to a home setting, particularly if they live alone.

Job skill assessment and training are used with patients who have been hurt on the job. This assessment is done to determine if injured patients can return to their previous jobs or if they need to be trained for new jobs. Documentation from occupational therapy is often required before disability or worker's compensation insurance funds can be paid.

Prevention complications

Techniques to prevent complications are planned, based on the medical diagnosis and assessment. Patients are taught methods of doing tasks to minimize damage to joints and tissues. Patients with arthritis can be taught to stand from a sitting position by pushing up with the flat of the hand without using the fingers. This method avoids pressure on the fingers and eliminates joint damage. Therapists design and fit splints and braces to support affected parts.

Encouraging independence

Activities of daily living are skills that relate to self-care and the quality of life. The degree to which these skills can be done alone makes the difference between dependent and independent living. Most adults want to be independent and feed, dress, and bathe themselves. Needing to ask for the help of others to accomplish basic tasks can result in feelings of worthlessness.

Therapists use their creative ability to develop methods and devise or provide special equipment to help patients achieve maximum independence. They teach mobility skills and plan activity schedules so that patients who have low energy can accomplish certain tasks.

Planning activities

Therapeutic activity planning is the skill of selecting games, arts, crafts, and social activities that promote patients' adaptation to handicaps (Figure 12-4). Activities are based on patients' interests and physical and mental capacities. Some activities are used to increase organizational skills and concentration, ability to follow directions, and hand-eye coordination. Some activities may change compulsive behavior and decrease frustration. Also, they can be used to express feelings of accomplishment, particularly in a mental

Figure 12–4   *Finger exercises are therapeutic.*

health setting. Art therapy is especially effective with children.

Exercise is another form of therapeutic activity that can be used to increase fine motor skills of fingers and arms. Activities such as "stair climbing" with fingers and playing catch with a large foam ball can improve dexterity and perception.

Motivating

Motivational techniques are needed to help patients continue to strive for improvement. One technique is setting attainable goals, evaluating progress every day, and changing the goals as conditions progress or regress. Both the therapist and the patient need to guard against discouragement if improvement is slow or limited.

Biography

When I was only twenty-two, I suffered a stroke after taking a prescribed medication. Though this is rare, it happened to me. One side of my body was paralyzed, and I could not speak. This was very frustrating. I knew what I wanted to say, but I could only make sounds. Over time and after much therapy, I regained my speech. But I did not regain the full use of my left arm and leg. I use my cane to walk so I don't fall.

I had many sessions with occupational therapy. I learned to tie my shoes, dress myself, peel potatoes, open cans, and cook dinner with one hand. Since I had a three-month-old baby at the time of my stroke, I needed to learn to change a diaper and dress a wriggly infant. This was really hard to do, but I learned, and fortunately, he finally grew out of diapers.

I was so grateful to the occupational therapy department, that I applied for a job there. I wanted to help others and show them that recovery is possible. I was hired for a few hours a week to assist the therapists with other stroke victims. I am sure that I give those patients hope. I am happy to be of service to people who need encouragement.

Career Search

To discover more about a career and the roles of members in the occupational therapy department, contact the following organization for online addresses, printed information, and videotapes.

American Occupational Therapy
  Association
4720 Montgomery Lane
P.O. Box 31220
Bethesda, MD 20824–1220
Phone: 301–652–2682
Fax: 301–652–7711

Range of Annual Incomes

Occupational therapist	$32,000–$55,000
Occupational therapy assistant	$23,000–$32,000

What's New

Computer programs that increase hand-eye coordination, association, memory, and cognitive recognition will be used with increasing frequency in occupational therapy. These programs will be helpful to patients of all ages with a variety of diagnoses. Therapists will visit patients in their homes to customize these programs, instruct on how to use them, and check on the patient's recovery progress.

Home care will increase because of short hospital stays for patients who have had strokes or orthopedic surgery, particularly joint replacements. Also, more follow-up work with crack babies and premature infants will be done in the home.

School to Work

In addition to the general academic subjects and workplace skills contained in the "Job Skills" chapter, the following subjects and skills apply specifically to careers in the occupational therapy department.

Academic Subject	Workplace Skills
Arts	—Create a progress chart for each patient. —Record range-of-motion goals on a graph.
Business Time Management	—Begin teaching patients immediately because of early discharge. —Determine the number of treatments needed to accomplish goals.
Communication	—Establish detailed goals with patient input. —Write notes that include exact progress to qualify for continued insurance coverage. —Prepare summary reports that detail injuries for disability insurance.
Economics	—Determine the amount of income you need to live each month. —Determine the cost of being an independent contractor. —Include the cost of health and disability insurance in your calculations. —Compare the costs of working for a hospital, an agency, and independently. —Learn how to bill insurance plans for services.
Health Education and Safety Body Mechanics	—Teach patients leverage techniques to use when lifting. —Manage tasks in the home using the least amount of energy. —Handle patients on anticoagulants with care to avoid bruising.
Mathematics Angles	—Document joint flexion and abduction degrees; track progress. —Calculate percentage or degree of improvement in joint movement.
Science Anatomy and Physiology	—Analyze muscle structure. —Know what nerves stimulate each muscle. —Identify the muscles and nerves involved in an injury. —Understand the effects of nerve damage on various parts.

Academic Subject	Workplace Skills
Pathophysiology	—Know the functions of different nerves.
	—Determine the muscle and nerves affected by an injury.
	—Calculate the effect of treatment on certain nerves and muscles.
Psychology	—Work with patients with disfigurements and changes in self-image.

Review Questions

1. What is the goal of the occupational therapy department?
2. How long is the educational program for occupational therapists and occupational therapy assistants after high school?

3. List and explain four skills used in occupational therapy.
4. Name five employment opportunities.
5. List three subjects and two ways each are applied in the workplace.

Chapter 13

PHARMACY DEPARTMENT

Objectives

After completing this chapter, you should be able to:

- ❒ Explain the goals of the pharmacy department.
- ❒ Describe each career in this department.
- ❒ Identify the required education and credentials for each career.
- ❒ Describe the skills performed in this department.
- ❒ Recognize how academic subjects apply in this workplace.

Key Terms

Medication

Drug interaction

Pharmacology

Pharmacokinetics

INTRODUCTION

The hospital pharmacy provides essential services to patients, physicians, and nurses by preparing and providing prescribed drugs in a timely manner so they can be administered by nurses or taken at home by patients. The pharmacy serves as a resource for information on the effects of drugs and **medications** on the human body.

Hundreds of chemical substances affect the body or a disease process (Figure 13–1). If a chemical helps to slow a disease process or improves the body's ability to function, it is manufactured, packaged, and sold as a medication. When more than one medication is prescribed and ingested, a **drug interaction** may result. That is, the chemical makeup changes, producing effects on the body

Figure 13–1 *Hundreds of medications are available.*

that were not intended. Drug interactions may involve food. Some food elements combine with medications and render them ineffective. Some drugs must be taken with food to prevent side effects. **Pharmacology** is constantly changing and expanding because of new discoveries in biochemistry and **pharmacokinetics**. Medicine and drug therapy are becoming more advanced and complex each year, and pharmacists continuously study to keep up with these changes. Computers are helpful for accessing data on drugs and drug interactions and to support clerical tasks.

The pharmacy provides a clean work environment, uniquely free of bacterial and viral contamination, in a hospital setting.

GOALS

The goals of the pharmacy are to prepare and dispense prescribed medications safely and promptly and to advise physicians, nurses, and consumers on the use, action, interaction, and side effects of prescription and nonprescription (over-the-counter) drugs and medications.

CAREER DESCRIPTIONS

Job descriptions in the field of pharmacy vary by the site of employment. Hospital pharmacists interact more frequently with nurses, physicians, and pharmacy staff than with consumers. Although consumer contact is more common in a retail store than in a hospital setting, hospital pharmacists are involved in outpatient education programs and counsel patients who are leaving the hospital and will be taking medications at home.

Career characteristics
Employment opportunities. Most pharmacists are employed in retail drug stores, grocery stores and discount stores, where they fill prescriptions and interact with the public. The majority of these stores belong to a chain, but some are privately owned, often by the pharmacist. Pharmacists also work in hospitals, long-term care facilities, outpatient clinics, universities, and government institutions, and in sales or research for pharmaceutical companies (Figure 13–2). A doctor of pharmacy degree is usually required for administrative, teaching, and research positions.

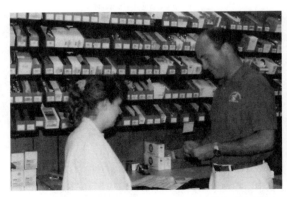

Figure 13–2 *Pharmacists are employed in many sectors.*

CAREER HIERARCHY

```
          ┌─────────────────────────┐
          │   DIRECTOR/PHARMACIST    │
          └─────────────────────────┘
            ┌─────────────────────┐
            │   STAFF PHARMACIST   │
            └─────────────────────┘
   ┌──────────────────┐      ┌──────────────────────────┐
   │    SECRETARY     │      │   PHARMACY TECHNICIAN     │
   └──────────────────┘      └──────────────────────────┘
                              ┌──────────────────────────┐
                              │   PHARMACY ASSISTANT      │
                              └──────────────────────────┘
```

Pharmacy technicians are employed by hospitals, retail stores, long-term care facilities, and clinics. Career advancement depends on additional education or specialized training.

Working hours. Many hospital pharmacies are open twenty-four hours a day, every day of the year. Most of the staff work the day shift; some work evenings, and only a few work the night hours. This reflects the volume of medication orders that are processed on each shift. Pharmacists can work varied hours, scheduling their work to cover the needs of the pharmacy and their personal goals.

Career advancements for pharmacists include becoming a hospital pharmacy director, a research supervisor, or an administrator in a pharmaceutical company. Other opportunities include buying a retail store or serving as program director in a government agency. Career advancement for pharmacy technicians and assistants requires further formal education or on-the-job training.

Desirable characteristics in pharmacists include an aptitude for science, especially math, organic chemistry, and bio-chemistry. Pharmacists must have the capacity to do precision work, have good organizational skills, and strictly follow the U.S. Drug Enforcement Administration's guidelines. A good memory, pleasant manner, and interest in helping people are beneficial. The ability to verbally communicate ideas clearly and inspire confidence are other favorable assets.

Desirable characteristics in pharmacy technicians include an aptitude for detail tasks and routine procedures. They need to work well with people, have a positive attitude and a friendly manner, and take pride in their work.

Job satisfaction comes from providing essential services to patients, physicians, and nurses. Pharmacists gain job satisfaction from being a respected professional member of the health care team with a unique body of knowledge. Physicians, nurses, and the public look to them to identify properties of various medications as therapeutic agents. Pharmacy technicians find satisfaction in assisting pharmacists, interacting with professional people, and facilitating pharmacy services.

Safety is a concern for pharmacists when mixing chemotherapy solutions. Since these solutions are classified as hazardous materials, special protocols must be followed when they are mixed and delivered, as well as when a spill must be cleaned up. Also, certain procedures must be used if the chemotherapy solution accidently contacts the skin or eyes.

Career roles

Pharmacists dispense drugs and medications prescribed mainly by licensed physicians and dentists (Figure 13–3). They continually study the composition, action, interaction, and effect on the body of chemical compounds. They learn how to avoid interactions, but know antidotes if interactions occur. They act as consultants to physicians to ensure optimal drug use for particular conditions; advise patients about drug action, interaction, and side effects; and recommend some drug products and caution against others. They review patients' drug profiles and work with computers to identify safe drug interactions. They participate in patient care conferences and provide

Figure 13–3 *Pharmacists dispense drugs.*

reliable labels and safe drug packaging. They develop methods and systems to process orders, deliver medications to nursing units in a timely manner, manage inventory control, communicate with professionals, and educate patients and health care professionals. In a hospital setting, pharmacists have the added responsibility of overseeing the preparation of sterile products, primarily intravenous solutions. They also mix chemotherapy solutions.

Pharmacy technicians work under the supervision of the licensed pharmacist. In a hospital, they routinely visit nursing units to deliver medications and pick up new prescriptions (if not ordered through the computer). They work with the unit-dose or other drug-dispensing system and replenish medication bins. In a unit-dose system, daily tasks include placing a twenty-four-hour supply of medications into each hospitalized patient's drawer in a "medication cart" designated for a specific nursing unit. The drugs are checked by a pharmacist before being delivered to the nursing unit, where refilled drawers are exchanged for empty ones. Upon return to the pharmacy, technicians credit to patients' accounts drugs left in the drawers.

Technicians enter the patient's drug history and diagnosis into a computerized patient medication record or onto a drug profile card each time a patient is admitted. These records or cards are updated each time a new drug is ordered, changed, or discontinued. Questions about orders regarding dose, route, or frequency are handled by the pharmacist with the physician or nurse taking care of the patient.

Technicians deliver controlled drugs to the nursing units and obtain proper signatures. They assist pharmacists in completing documentation and maintaining records according to the Drug Enforcement Administration's regulations. They monitor the storage of medications according to manufacturer's recommendations. They inventory pharmacy stock and reorder when supplies are low. They review the stock of standard medications on nursing units and resupply as needed.

Technicians mix and add medications to intravenous solutions under the laminar-flow hood to maintain sterility. They label each container carefully. Special solutions and chemotherapy agents are mixed by a pharmacist.

Pharmacy assistants check delivered orders, price items, maintain records, and restock pharmacy shelves (Figure 13–4). They have an aptitude for detail tasks and routine work.

JOB AVAILABILITY

Opportunities for employment in pharmacy continue to be good in spite of unit-dose packaging and an increase in automated drug dispensing. More medications are being used because of the increase in the number of pharmaceuticals available and the size of the elderly population. In some areas of the country, fewer pharmacists are needed because of automation and the availability of pharmacy technicians.

SKILLS

Tasks performed in the pharmacy fall into four categories: management, distributive services, communication, and clinical/cognitive services.

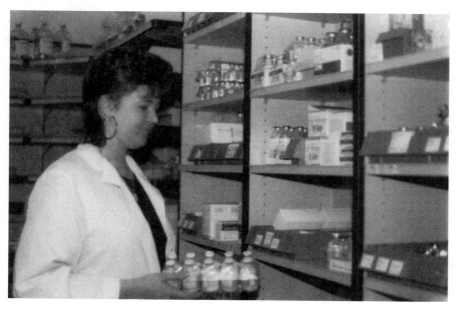

Figure 13–4 *Assistants restock shelves as needed.*

Education and Credentials

CAREER	YEARS OF EDUCATION AFTER HIGH SCHOOL	DEGREE OR DIPLOMA	TESTED BY; LICENSED BY
Registered pharmacist (R.Ph.)	5 years plus 1,500 hours of internship (during three summers)	B.S. in pharmacy	State board of pharmacy exam and pharmacy law exam; State
Doctor of pharmacy (Pharm.D.)	At least 6 years plus 500 hours of internship and residency training	Doctor of pharmacy	State board of pharmacy exam and pharmacy law exam; State
Pharmacy technician	2 years	A.A.S.D. in pharmacy technology	None
Pharmacy assistant	On-the-job training	None	None

Key to abbreviations:

A.A.S.D.—Associate of Applied Science Degree
B.S.—Bachelor of Science Degree
R.Ph.—Registered Pharmacist

Management

Management involves hiring staff, scheduling time, developing personnel policies, delineating roles and responsibilities, and developing safe, cost-effective systems for providing pharmacy services.

Distributive services

Distributive services involve systems of drug inventory, purchasing, dispensing, billing, delivery to nursing units, computer data entry, as well as procedures for mixing intravenous solutions, storing and dispersing controlled drugs, and working with outpatient prescriptions (Figure 13–5).

Figure 13–5 *Distributive services.*

Communication

Communication involves written and oral techniques. Written communications include physician prescriptions, memos on procedures, incident reports on missing drugs or errors, drug and supply orders, and patient and professional educational materials. Oral communications include telephone calls between nursing units, physician offices, outpatients, and the pharmacy; and verification and clarification of prescriptions. It also includes participating in team conferences, consulting services, and interactions between pharmacy staff and nursing unit staff, along with presenting patient and professional education through counseling and seminars.

Clinical/cognitive services

Clinical/cognitive services involve reviewing patient medication profiles and screening for potential allergies, adverse reactions, and drug interactions. Monitoring patient therapy to ensure compliance and providing dosing information to guarantee optimal therapy are additional aspects of clinical services.

Biography

When I was a child, I loved to play with dolls. When they were "sick," I worked hard to "heal" them. I gave them "pills" to bring their temperatures down and help them to feel better.

When I was seven years old, a boy was born into our family. Not long after he came home, he developed meningitis. I watched as my mother gave him medication. It seemed like magic to me, how those medications brought down his fever, cleared up the infection, and allowed him to live. Through that experience, I learned the power of medication and the effects that chemicals can have on the human body.

From then on, I knew I wanted to be part of the world of health care. I wanted to help sick people get well. When I reached high school and took a chemistry course, I discovered the career that would be best for me: being a pharmacist.

In college, I took a biochemistry course. I found it fascinating that so many chemical elements contribute to the human body and that those chemical elements must be exactly in balance for the body to be healthy. I began to understand that illness can occur when there is too much or not enough of certain chemical elements in the body.

The career of pharmacist fits me perfectly. I have a good memory and love to study the effect of chemical elements and medications on the human body. I enjoy teaching patients about their medications and the symptoms of side effects. I know that patients rely on my filling the prescription correctly and giving them instruction. I have classmates that have gone on to research new chemicals that fight killer viruses and medications that control disease-producing genes. But I am content to work at the local hospital and help neighborhood patients.

After I graduated from pharmacy school, I married and had two children. I have adapted my schedule so that I work part time and I am available to my children when they are not in day care or school. My work schedule lets me spend time with my family and maintain my profession as a pharmacist.

Career Search

To discover more about a career and the roles of members in the pharmacy department, contact the following organization for online addresses, printed information, and videotapes.

American Pharmaceutical
   Association
2215 Constitution Avenue N.W.
Washington, DC 20037
Phone: 202–628–4410
Toll-free phone: 800–237–APHA
Fax: 202–783–2351

Range of Annual Incomes

Pharmacist	$40,000–$65,000
Pharmacy technician	$17,000–$25,000
Pharmacy assistant	$12,000–$18,000

What's New

A computer-generated system of record keeping allows physicians' orders to be entered in the computer on the nursing unit, filled by the pharmacy, and recorded in a patient profile and medication record during each shift. This system tracks medications dispensed, flags stock that needs to be reordered, records patient drug charges, and monitors drug interactions. Specific reports can be printed on request.

Automated prescription filing is a system of packaging a patient's daily medications mechanically. A computer scanner reads the bar code on the unit-dose medication packages, and a machine gathers together all the drugs to be taken by each patient each day. This is an efficient and cost-effective system of dispensing medications. Though the initial investment for the automated system is high, it replaces several pharmacy technicians, eventually paying for itself. This system works in institutional settings as well as in pharmacies that package medications for skilled nursing, extended care, and residential facilities.

The development of drugs that influence genes is a new field of exploration. Research is underway to isolate, test, and manipulate the genes that cause obesity and Alzheimer's disease. One of the goals of this research is to develop drugs that influence those genes and prevent those conditions.

School to Work

In addition to the general academic subjects and workplace skills contained in the "Job Skills" chapter, the following subjects and skills apply specifically to careers in the pharmacy department.

Academic Subject	Workplace Skills
Business	
Time Management	—Deliver medications to patients in a timely manner.
Computer Skills	—Enter each patient's medications accurately.
	—Investigate drug interactions.
	—Print a patient's daily drug profile for nursing documentation.
Economics	—Use generic medications when the effects are the same as those of trade drugs.
	—Understand insurance drug plans.
Communications	—If a physician's handwriting is not legible, call the physician for clarification.
	—Take verbal orders accurately from a physician over the phone.
Health Education and Safety	—Instruct patients on the actions of medications.
	—Teach patients about side effects to watch for.
	—Use careful techniques to prevent harm from chemotherapy.
Mathematics	—Check that the dose is appropriate for the size of the patient.
	—Dilute IV antibiotics according to the recommended dosage.
	—Understand the metric and apothecary systems.
Science	
Biochemistry	—Discuss replacing low chemical elements in the blood with the physician.
Microbiology	—Prepare the most effective antibiotic against the cultured bacteria.
Nutrition and Food Science	—Recommend foods containing elements depleted by medications.
Pharmacology	—Understand the effects and interactions of medications.

Review Questions

1. What is the goal of the pharmacy department?
2. How long is the educational program for a pharmacist after high school?
3. Where are pharmacists employed?
4. List the four category of skills needed in a pharmacy.
5. List three academic subjects and two ways each are used in the pharmacy department.

PHYSICAL THERAPY DEPARTMENT

Chapter 14

INTRODUCTION

The physical therapy department specializes in helping patients regain strength in large muscle groups to improve **mobility** and function. It helps patients get back **flexibility**, **coordination**, and functional independence lost to disabilities that impede normal activity. These **disabilities** may be new or old, acute or chronic, congenital or acquired, painful or not painful.

They may have started slowly or suddenly and may be mild and temporary, severe and permanent.

Under the direction of patients' physicians, treatment and assistance are provided to people who are unable to move, have limited range of motion, have musculoskeletal pain or dysfunction, or have had surgery on bones or muscles. Patients may need physical therapy for

Figure 14–1 *Physical therapy is needed for a variety of conditions.*

muscle, nerve, or joint diseases, such as multiple sclerosis, stroke, and arthritis (Figure 14–1). Others have disabilities caused by spinal cord injuries, brain lesions, and musculoskeletal or neuromuscular problems. Babies needing physical therapy may have been born with physical defects, or children may experience developmental delays. Other patients have become disabled by illnesses, sports injuries, work-related incidents, or other accidents.

Members of the physical therapy department are part of the rehabilitation team. Also on this team are representatives of the occupational therapy, speech therapy, nursing, dietary, and social service departments.

GOAL

The goal of the physical therapy department is to help patients achieve their highest level of independence by increasing mobility and function through strengthening large muscles, reducing pain, and improving balance and endurance.

CAREER DESCRIPTIONS

Physical therapists, physical therapy assistants, and physical therapy technicians work directly with patients to

CAREER HIERARCHY

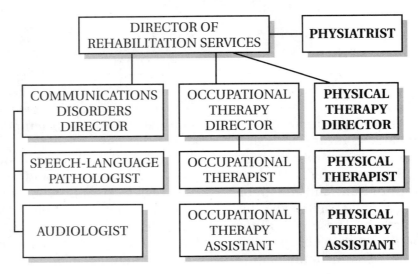

strengthen muscle tone, increase joint function, decrease pain, retrain muscles, stimulate nerves, improve balance, and regain strength. They work toward preventing complications of disuse, overcoming disabilities, and restoring physical health. This is done through an individualized plan of care developed by the patient's therapist and carried out by the therapists, assistants, and technicians.

Career characteristics

Employment opportunities include acute and chronic care hospitals, skilled nursing facilities, long-term care facilities, rehabilitation units, burn units, outpatient centers, school systems, home care, athletic facilities, and professional sport teams. Other sites are centers for mentally retarded and physically handicapped patients, and residences for the aged.

Work hours in a hospital and skilled nursing setting may be from five to seven days a week during daytime hours. Outpatient clinics, physician offices, and home care are usually open during the day, Monday through Friday, with some Saturday and evening hours.

Career advancements for physical therapists include supervisor and director positions. With an advanced degree, teaching is an option. Assistants can become therapists, and aides can become assistants with additional education.

Desired personal characteristics include the ability to work well with people of all ages and temperaments. Courage and emotional strength are helpful in confronting the sad and traumatic events

Figure 14–2 *It takes courage and emotional strength to work with patients.*

that can happen to good people (Figure 14–2). Insight and sensitivity are assets needed to help patients deal with feelings of anger, frustration, helplessness, and hopelessness that arise from their disability. Tolerance, patience, and a relaxed manner are valuable attributes under the pressure of heavy workloads. Strength and stamina are needed because physical therapy workers must stand most of the day, lift heavy equipment, and move and raise weighty extremities.

Job satisfaction arises in helping people achieve the highest level of independence possible. Gratification comes from seeing patients' efforts, physical improvement, and goal achievement. Improving the quality of patients' lives is rewarding. Being a member of the rehabilitation team with a unique body of knowledge and working with other professionals to plan and achieve goals are also satisfying.

Safety measures to protect patients from harm are a high priority. Procedures for preventing falls, burns, pressure injuries, joint dislocations, and muscle strains are followed carefully.

Career roles

Physiatrists are physicians who specialize in physical medicine and rehabilitation. They have studied methods of caring for patients with spinal cord injuries, brain lesions, musculoskeletal and neuromuscular problems, and sports injuries. They understand the relationship of exercise and its effect on bone, muscles, and circulation. They are knowledgeable in the principles of sports medicine and the psychosocial aspects of patients with disabilities. They meet with other rehabilitation team members to plan treatment, teach and counsel patients and families, and serve as a resource to staff. They may be employed by facilities to direct rehabilitation activities or serve as consultants.

Physical therapists interview new patients; review their records; assess their physical strengths, disabilities, and capabilities; and identify problems and needs. They set treatment goals with patients, develop a plan of care to meet those goals, administer treatments, and document therapy and progress. They monitor the effectiveness of care, change the treatment plan as needed, and teach patients methods of self-help, safety and preventive measures, and rehabilitation strategies. Therapists encourage patients and point out realistic accomplishments.

Physical therapy assistants carry out patient treatment plans developed by the physical therapist and give direct patient care under professional supervision. They perform all major treatment procedures, including gait training, exercise, and heat, massage, electrical stimulation, and ultrasound therapies, as well as give home instruction. They document treatments and report progress to the therapist.

Physical therapy aides/technicians help therapists and assistants carry out selected treatments, transport and converse with patients, prepare equipment for use, clean equipment after use, order and obtain supplies, and answer the department telephone (Figure 14–3).

Athletic trainers use strength and conditioning principles to develop programs that go beyond rehabilitation into the maintenance and improvement of physical condition. They work with school and professional sports teams. They work as personal trainers and in rehabilitation departments. They administer and analyze cardiac tests and prescribe appropriate exercise for patients in compliance

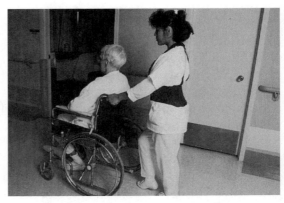

Figure 14–3 *Physical therapy aides transport patients.*

with physicians' orders. They help develop physical conditioning programs for communities and corporations.

Exercise physiologists study how the body reacts to exercise and determine a protocol to maximize effectiveness. Their focus is on research for athletes rather than on actually working with athletes. For example, they might work with the U.S. Olympic rowing team to determine the most effective training strategy. They check muscle reaction and conduct molecular studies after exercise. They work more with principles than with people.

JOB AVAILABILITY

Physical therapy is one of the fastest growing health care occupations. Therapists are in short supply because only a few graduate each year. Entrance into a physical therapy program is highly competitive. Some programs require up to six hundred volunteer hours in a physical therapy department before an application is considered.

Other reasons for the shortage of therapists are that many choose to work part-time and as independent contractors. The number of facilities providing physical therapy programs also has grown in cities and rural areas. Some corporations have employed physical therapists to develop worksite evaluations, exercise programs, and safe work habit instruction for employees to decrease on-the-job injuries.

SKILLS

Certain skills are required to help patients regain strength, flexibility, mobility, coordination, and independent function. The types of treatment selected for each patient depend on age, physical and emotional conditions, kind of surgery, strength, medical diagnosis, ability to help, degree of cooperation, presence of pain, and capacity to understand.

Therapy

Kinds of therapy include exercise, massage, manual therapy, hydrotherapy, electrical, ultrasound, heat and cold, traction, and exercise machines. Among the exercise equipment that may be used are stairs, weights and pulleys, dumbbells, and stationary bicycles. If a muscle is very weak, the injured limb may be moved under water. Therapists teach techniques of ambulation with walkers, crutches, canes, and sometimes with braces and artificial limbs.

Exercise is essential for the maintenance of joint motion and muscle strength (Figure 14–4). Active exercise is necessary

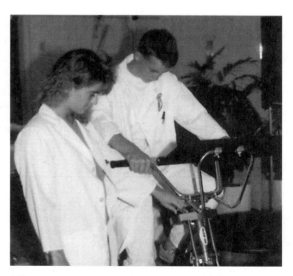

Figure 14–4 *Exercise is essential for joint motion and muscle strength.*

Education and Credentials

CAREER	YEARS OF EDUCATION AFTER HIGH SCHOOL	DEGREE OR DIPLOMA	TESTED BY; LICENSED BY
Physiatrist (M.D.)	4 years of college, 4 years of medical school, 1 year of general internship, and 4 years of residency in physical medicine and rehabilitation	M.D.	Certified by ABPMR; State
Physical therapist (PT or RPT)	4 years of school plus volunteer hours*	B.S.	National exam; State
Sports medicine**	5 years of school plus internship and volunteer hours*	Master's	—
Physical therapy assistant (PTA)	2 years	A.A.S.D. in physical therapist assisting technology	National exam; State
Physical therapy aide or technician	On-the-job-training or 12 to 14 months plus 6 months internship	Certificate	Vocational or technical school
Athletic trainers	2 to 5 years plus 1,500 clinical hours under supervision of a certified trainer	B.Ed. degree	State certified; U.S. Department of Education (certified to teach gym in schools); A.S.M.A. certified
Exercise physiologist	4 years (no clinical hours)	B.Ed. (not certified to teach in schools) or Master's degree in exercise physiology. Ph.D. programs also available	American College of Sports medicine as Exercise Specialist

*Applicant must have 200 to 300 volunteer hours in a hospital physical therapy department before being accepted into a physical therapy program. The number of hours is determined by the school.

**Sports medicine is a specialty of physical therapy. To gain this expertise, a candidate may spend a 6 to 8 week rotation in the sports medicine section of a physical therapy department during the basic physical therapy program. Another option is to spend the internship of a master's degree program in exercise physiology in the sports medicine section of a physical therapy department.

Key to abbreviations:

A.A.S.D.—Associate of Applied Science Degree
ABPMR—American Board of Physical Medicine and Rehabilitation
A.S.M.A.—American Sports Medicine Association
B.Ed.—Bachelor of Education Degree
B.S.—Bachelor of Science Degree
M.S.—Master of Science
PTA—Physical Therapist Assistant
PT—Physical Therapist

to increase strength. Passive exercise keeps muscles pliant and joints mobile. The goal of exercise is to increase the strength, flexibility, and coordination of the muscles. Paralysis is caused by nerve damage, not muscle damage. Passive exercise will not return active motion to the part. Instead, it will maintain joint motion so that if motion does return, the patient will not have to overcome contractures. Facilitation techniques help stimulate muscle function.

Stair climbing, weights and pulleys, dumbbells, and stationary bikes are used to increase muscle strength and endurance (Figure 14–5).

A small electrical current is used to produce contractions. The goal of this treatment is to reeducate the patient in using weak muscles. Electrical currents are also very effective in reducing pain.

Gait training is used to teach patients to walk using whatever strength or restrictions they have. After hip or leg surgery, many patients are only allowed to put a little weight on the injured leg. The therapist teaches them to use a walker to protect the injured leg (Figure 14–6). After a stroke, many patients are unable to move one leg. The therapist teaches them to walk using what is known as a "quad

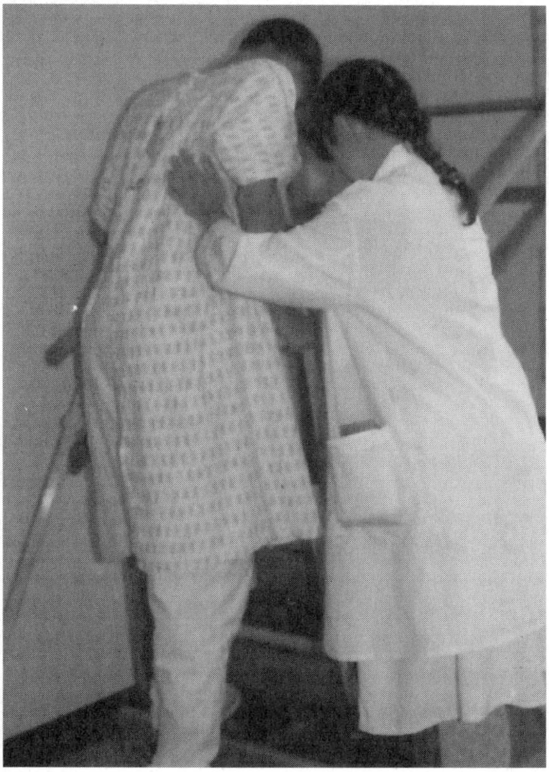

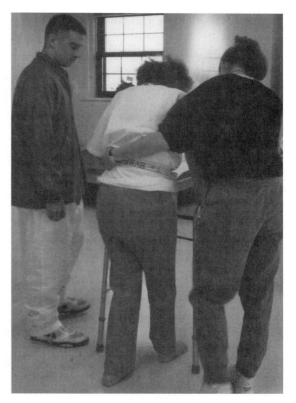

Figure 14–5 *Climbing stairs is part of the exercise program.*

Figure 14–6 *Learning to use a walker is also part of Physical Therapy.*

cane," or a four pronged cane, so they can protect the weak leg. The therapist uses parallel bars, walkers, crutches, and canes to teach patients to walk as independently as possible (Figure 14–7).

Massage is used to relax tight muscles and promote circulation.

Applications of heat increase circulation and relieve muscle tension. Cold applications decrease pain and prevent muscle swelling.

Mechanical traction mobilizes the spine and helps reduce pressure on pinched nerves.

Hydrotherapy can be used to decrease pain and increase ability to move muscles. It is also frequently used to cleanse open wounds.

Mobilization and stretching techniques are used to increase range of motion in joints after surgery or injury.

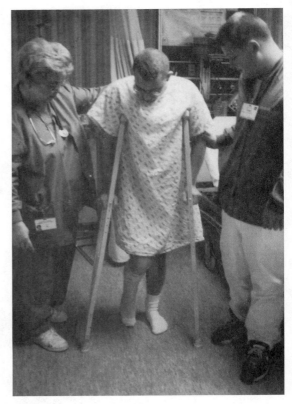

Figure 14–7 *Learning to walk with crutches.*

Biography

When I was five years old, my big brother went hunting for deer with some buddies. As they were heading back to the hunting cabin, one of his friends tripped over a tree root, and his rifle accidentally discharged. The bullet struck my brother in the leg, shattering his thigh bone.

While my brother was recovering, my Mom and I spent a lot of time at the hospital. I watched my brother struggle to regain his mobility. His leg had to be operated on many times. Because the bullet was not sterile, bacteria got into the wound, and his muscle and thigh bone became infected. The surgeon had to cure the infection before she could get a bone from the bone bank to patch my brother's shattered femur. Physical therapy was begun early because my brother could bear weight on his unaffected leg. He needed to get out of

Career Search

To discover more about a career and the roles of members in the physical therapy department, contact the following organizations for online addresses, printed information, and videotapes.

American Physical Therapy
    Association
1111 N. Fairfax Street
Alexandria, VA 22314
Phone: 703–684–2782

American College of Sports Medicine
P.O. Box 1440
Indianapolis, IN 46206–1440
Phone: 317–637–9200
Fax: 317–634–7817

Aerobics and Fitness Association of
    America
15250 Ventura Boulevard, Suite 200
Sherman Oaks, CA 91403
Phone: 818–905–0040
Toll-free phone: 800–446–AFAA
Fax: 818–990–5468

World Sports Medicine Association
    of Registered Therapists
206 Marine Avenue
P.O. Box 5642
Newport Beach, CA 92662
Phone: 818–574–1999
Fax: 818–447–5667

Range of Annual Incomes

Physiatrist	$120,000–$190,000
Physical therapist	$ 35,000–$60,000
Physical therapy assistant	$ 22,000–$35,000
Exercise physiologist	$ 27,000–$40,000
Athletic trainer	$ 20,000–$40,000

Biography (continued)

bed and stand on his good leg to avoid losing this strength. It was a long time, though, before he could bear any weight on his wounded leg.

I was really impressed with how the physical therapists and their assistants helped my brother. I watched them work with other young people, too, helping them regain movement in their limbs. Even patients with spinal cord and brain damage from car and bicycle accidents made amazing progress with the help of these professionals. I decided then that I wanted to help kids walk again or at least gain the most mobility possible after their injuries. So after high school, I went to a junior college and earned an associate degree as a physical therapy assistant. Now I can help people like others helped my brother.

What's New

Exercise programs to maintain health and fitness as well as for cardiac and pulmonary rehabilitation have been developed because people have come to recognize the value of exercise. These programs may be associated with health care institutions as well as private organizations such as the YMCA and YWCA. Some health insurance plans pay the fees for these programs. Some corporations provide these programs as a benefit for their employees.

School to Work

In addition to the general academic subjects and workplace skills contained in the "Job Skills" chapter, the following subjects and skills apply specifically to careers in the physical therapy department.

Academic Subject	Workplace Skills
Business	
Time Management	—Schedule patients so they don't get tired waiting for their turn.
	—Arrange to work with inpatients between outpatient visits.
	—Allow time for instruction during the exercise program.
English	—Write clear, explicit notes for disability insurance.
	—Document improvements precisely for insurance reimbursement.
Computer Skills	—Enter treatment data for billing purposes.
English and Communications	
Speech Class	—Give careful directions to patients on weight-bearing activities.
	—Teach families exercises to do at home with patients.
	—Instruct patients and their families in the use of crutches and other appliances.
Health Education and Safety	
Body Mechanics	—Use the proper technique when doing range-of-motion exercises.
	—Use leverage when helping a hemiplegic victim to stand.
	—Instruct patients in how to help themselves without injuring the therapist.
	—Exercise caution when applying a leg brace to a paralyzed limb.

Academic Subject	Workplace Skills
Mathematics	—Take the pulse of a patient after exercise and compare to the patient's normal rate. —Set a goal on the treadmill according to the patient's previous ability. —Document the degree of improvement in limb movement. —Monitor the degree of heat in a paraffin bath. —Set the degree of heat in a whirlpool.
Science	
Anatomy and Physiology	—Identify muscle and nerve functions and deficits. —Understand the differences between various age groups.
Pathophysiology	—Recognize the tolerance of a patient to exercise after surgery. —Teach a patient to wrap a sprained ankle with an Ace bandage. —Encourage a patient to stop exercising when cardiac symptoms occur. —Instruct patients on the proper use of equipment to prevent harm.
Pharmacology	—Understand the effects of muscle relaxants on back pain. —Instruct patients on value of taking pain medications before exercising.

Review Questions

1. What is the difference between physical therapy and occupational therapy?
2. How long is the educational program after high school for a physiatrist, a physical therapist, and a physical therapy assistant?
3. List and explain three skills used in the physical therapy department.
4. What five personal characteristics are needed to become a physical therapist or physical therapy assistant?
5. Identify four academic subjects and two ways that each is used in the physical therapy department.

RADIOLOGY DEPARTMENT

Chapter 15

Objectives

After completing this chapter, you should be able to:

❏ Explain the goals of the radiology department

❏ Define the major imaging techniques.

❏ Describe each career in this department.

❏ Identify the required education and credentials for each career.

❏ Recognize how academic subjects apply in this workplace.

Key Terms

X ray

Ultrasound

Magnetic resonance imaging

Computerized axial tomography

Nuclear scans

INTRODUCTION

Radiology is an essential department in every health care facility where patients come for treatment. Diagnostic and treatment procedures both are performed in this department. However, only a few facilities have the special equipment needed to treat malignancies with radiation therapy.

Procedures done in the radiology department produce images that visualize bones, organs, and vessels of the body. They do this by using **X rays**, sound waves, **magnetic resonance imaging (MRI)**, and radioactive nuclear material (Figure 15–1). Most of these methods are enhanced by computer technology. Diseases can be diagnosed earlier and with

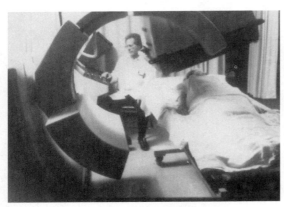

Figure 15–1 *C-arm portable fluoroscope is used in surgery when a pacemaker is being inserted. It is named because of its shape and can take images at either end of the "C".*

more certainty with this high-tech equipment. Treatment of diseases has changed because of new procedures that allow simultaneous viewing of internal structures with the administering of treatment strategies. Other treatment changes have

occurred because of new discoveries and refinements in the use of radiation therapy as a tool to stop malignant cell growth.

GOALS

The goal of the radiology department is to produce images of interior body structures for diagnostic purposes and to guide the treatment of injury or disease. Departments that provide radiation therapy have the additional goal of administering treatments safely to control the growth of malignant cells.

CAREER DESCRIPTIONS

The roles and responsibilities of radiology professionals are determined by the education and experience of the staff, type of facility, policies of the department, and available equipment (Figure 15–2). There are several specialties in ra-

Figure 15–2 *Many responsibilities fall on the radiologist.*

CAREER HIERARCHY

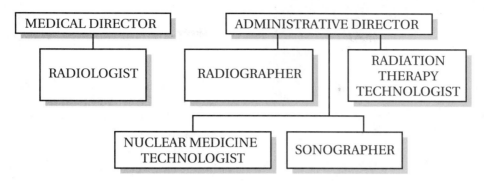

```
┌─────────────────────┐        ┌─────────────────────────┐
│  MEDICAL DIRECTOR   │        │ ADMINISTRATIVE DIRECTOR │
└─────────────────────┘        └─────────────────────────┘
          │                         │            │
┌─────────────────┐     ┌──────────────┐   ┌───────────────┐
│   RADIOLOGIST   │     │ RADIOGRAPHER │   │   RADIATION   │
└─────────────────┘     └──────────────┘   │    THERAPY    │
                                           │ TECHNOLOGIST  │
                                           └───────────────┘
              ┌──────────────────┐   ┌──────────────┐
              │ NUCLEAR MEDICINE │   │ SONOGRAPHER  │
              │  TECHNOLOGIST    │   └──────────────┘
              └──────────────────┘
```

diology. Radiographer is the basic educational program. Additional formal education can lead to a career as a radiation therapy technologist, nuclear medicine technologist, or sonographer. Other specialties that require additional on-the-job training are **computerized axial tonography (CAT)**, positron emission tonography (PET), MRI, angiography, cardiac catheterization procedures, and mammography.

Career characteristics

Employment opportunities are many. Positions are available in health screening clinics with patients who are healthy, in acute care settings with patients who are critically ill, and in treatment centers where radiation treatments are administered to patients who have been diagnosed with malignancies. In acute care settings, X rays are taken in all departments of the hospital, including the emergency room, nursing units, cardiac catheterization lab, and surgery (Figure 15–3). Other positions are in physician offices, clinics, industry, the military, the Veterans Administration, education, freestanding emergency centers, and mobile vans.

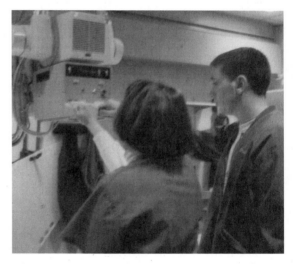

Figure 15–3 *Moving a ceiling-mounted X-ray machine in the ER.*

Work hours vary by the work site. Radiology departments are open twenty-four hours a day in acute care facilities. Positions are available there on day, evening, and night shifts. Workers are in such demand that a choice of full-time, part-time, flextime, or independent agency placement is possible for qualified radiographers. Office, clinic, and mobile unit positions are available during the day shift on weekdays.

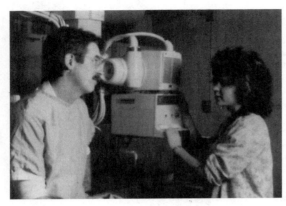

Figure 15–4 *Good rapport with the patient is important.*

Job satisfaction comes from obtaining quality images and establishing good patient rapport in a short time (Figure 15–4). In most settings, radiographers render a complete service at one meeting with a patient. They take one X ray or perform one test and do not meet the patient again. Radiation therapy technologists, however, have the opportunity to develop relationships with patients and their family members because treatments are given over time. Rewards come from the friendships that evolve as technologists and patients work together to contain the malignancy. Professionals and patients are partners in the fight for survival and share in the hope that life will be spared and health will return. Job satisfaction also comes from the mutual respect of peers.

Career advancement can be in moving into a supervisory or staff development position in a large department, changing specialties, learning new techniques, or changing facilities. Radiology is a rapidly expanding career because of the explosion of knowledge in the visualization of internal body structures, advancing techniques, and the development of new equipment. Career opportunities will continue to grow for those who keep up with new procedures.

Desirable characteristics of workers in the radiology department include a warm, compassionate manner, pleasant personality, ability to work with others, accurate work habits, patience, and an interest in science and computer-assisted medical technology. The ability to follow instructions, painstakingly complete procedures, work in emergency situations, and maintain safety standards is essential. Physical strength to lift equipment and patients, manual dexterity to manipulate instruments, and audio, visual, and verbal skills to observe and communicate with patients are necessary assets.

Career roles

The radiologist is a physician with a specialty in interpreting X rays and other diagnostic tests (Figure 15–5). This specialty is achieved by completing years of

Figure 15–5 *The radiologist's specialty is interpreting X rays.*

study and practice after medical school in the field of radiology and passing specific exams. A radiologist may specialize by working exclusively in an area of diagnosis, treatment, or nuclear medicine. Responsibility and liability are great because patients' medical diagnoses and treatment are based on this professional's interpretation of tests. The radiologist studies the results of each test, comes to diagnostic conclusions, and sends a report to the ordering physician. The radiologist also serves as a resource to the department helping to develop policies and procedures that will improve patient care. Responsibilities also include continuing education, learning new techniques, and updating diagnostic equipment. The radiologist is either employed by a facility or works in private practice.

Radiographers or radiologic technologists use X rays to produce body images on film or a video monitor as an aid to physicians in diagnosis (Figure 15–6). These technologists have completed a basic educational program before specializing in this expanding field. Responsibilities include patient identification and instruction, positioning the part to be studied, protecting parts that are not to be X-rayed, manipulating equipment, positioning the film, adjusting the exposure, taking the X ray, processing the film, and inspecting the image for quality. The radiographer also calibrates, runs daily maintenance checks, cleans, and disinfects the equipment. Additional responsibilities include filing films, maintaining reports, and copying and sending radiographs according to policy.

Figure 15–6   *A video monitor aids in diagnosis.*

Nuclear medicine technologists work with radioactive compounds that are absorbed by particular body tissues to diagnose and treat certain diseases. In a lung scan, a radioactive solution is injected into the blood and absorbed by the lungs. Then the uptake by the lung of the radioactive material is recorded on a special film by a scanner and used to diagnose lung disease.

The Nuclear Regulatory Commission has developed strict guidelines on the use of radioactive materials to protect workers, patients, and the environment. Though only tiny amounts of radioactive materials are used for each test, technicians are careful with technique and wear protective gear. Techniques for storing, handling, transporting, using, and disposing of these materials are strictly mandated to minimize risks associated with radiation. Because of risk to the fetus, special care is taken if a female patient is pregnant.

The sonographer works with sound waves (ultrasound) and a computer to create images of soft tissues, vessels, or organs on film or videotape and a monitor (Figure 15–7). Ultrasound is a noninvasive technique used to identify and diagnose various conditions. It is a safe procedure that uses no X rays or radioactive materials. A physician reviews the images and reports to the patient's doctor. Sonographers specialize in cardiac, vascular, or abdominal areas. The abdominal specialty includes obstetrics, gynecology, and general conditions in the abdominal cavity. In obstetrics, a baby's abnormalities can usually be detected before birth. Depending on the position

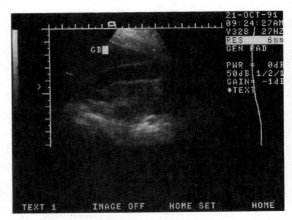

Figure 15–7   A sonogram.

and age of the developing fetus, the gender also can be determined.

The radiation therapy technologist works with patients who were diagnosed with cancer or other malignancies. Administration of radiation involves careful patient preparation, the operation of complex machines, exact patient positioning, the marking of specific zones for treatment, and creation of individualized masks and blocks to ensure precision in targeting the area to be radiated. Responsibilities include patient assessment, education, comfort, reassurance, and emotional support. Duties include documenting physical symptoms, procedure tolerance, and treatment administration. The technologist also therapeutically interacts with the patient's family members.

JOB AVAILABILITY

There will be no shortage of radiologic technologists to the year 2005. As a result, schools may limit their enrollment.

EDUCATION AND CREDENTIALS

CAREER	YEARS OF EDUCATION AFTER HIGH SCHOOL	DEGREE OR DIPLOMA	TESTED BY; LICENSED BY
Radiologist M.D. or O.D.	4 years of college, 4 years of medical school, 4 years of radiology internship, and 1 year fellowship	M.D. or O.D.	National boards exam by American College of Radiology; State based on ACR exam; some states require an additional test
Radiographer (radiologic technologist) RT	2 years (8 quarters) plus basic life support-CPR (recommended)	A.A.S.D. in radiography	National ARRT exam; national registry exam; State; some states require tests every year to renew state license
Nuclear medicine technologist RT and CNMT	2 years plus 1 year nuclear medicine course	A.A.S.D. in radiography or allied health certificate	Same as radiographer plus national exam by NMTCB; some states have an additional test in nuclear medicine
Sonographer RT and RDMS	2 years plus 1 year	A.A.S.D. in radiography or allied health certificate	Same as radiographer
Computed tomography technologist (CT) RT	2 years college plus 6 month on-the-job training or course at manufacturer	A.A.S.D. in radiography	Same as radiographer
Magnetic resonance imager (MRI) technologist RT	2 years of college plus 6 months on-the-job training or course at manufacturer	A.A.S.D. in radiography	Same as radiographer
Positron emission tomography technologist (PET) RT	2 years college plus 6 months on-the-job training or course at manufacturer	A.A.S.D. in radiography	Same as radiographer
Radiation therapy technologist RT	2 years plus 1 year course in radiation therapy	A.A.S.D. in radiography or allied health certificate	Same as radiographer

Key to abbreviations:

A.A.S.D.—Associate of Applied Science Degree
ARRT—American Registry of Radiological Technologists
CNMT—Certified Nuclear Medicine Technologist
CPR—Cardiopulmonary Resuscitation
CT, CAT—Computer Assisted Tomography
M.D.—Medical Doctor
MRI—Magnetic Resonance Imaging

NMTCB—Nuclear Medicine Technology Certification Board
O.D.—Osteopathic Doctor
PET—Positron Emission Tomography
RDMS—Registered Diagnostic Medical Sonographer
RT—Radiation Therapist

Competition will be stiff for acceptance into a program and employment in the field. Though new techniques are being developed, the equipment is so expensive that only major medical centers will have it. The need for nuclear medicine technologists will increase, but because it is a small occupation, jobs will be few in number.

SKILLS

Skills learned by radiographers relate to imaging techniques and treatment techniques. After completing the basic educational program and becoming licensed, radiographers often specialize in certain techniques that may require additional education.

Imaging techniques

Imaging techniques are procedures that allow visualization of the interior of the body. This is done through four techniques: X ray, **ultrasound**, magnetic resonance imaging, and nuclear scans.

X ray involves the use of radiation that penetrates the skin, muscle, organs, and bones (Figure 15–8). As X rays pass through the body, a picture like a photograph is taken of the inside of the body on a special kind of film. The film is developed, evaluated by a physician, and stored as a permanent record. It shows the condition of the anatomical part at the time of the X ray. The picture is called a radiograph.

This technique is used to diagnose a broken bone or the presence of stones in the gallbladder or kidney. Sometimes a liquid contrast medium is needed to visualize soft tissue organs. The contrast

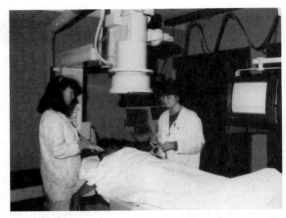

Figure 15–8 *The X ray penetrates the body and leaves the body's imprint on the film plate under the patient.*

medium can be seen on the X ray as it defines the structure. The contrast medium of a barium solution is swallowed to visualize the stomach; an iodinized solution is injected to visualize kidneys or blood vessels.

X-radiation is the ray that allows the inside of the body to be seen on X-ray film. Because this ray is potentially harmful to the body, care is taken to use only enough to visualize the affected part. Other areas of the patient's body are protected from rays by a shield made of lead. X-radiation cannot penetrate lead. The technician also needs to be protected from rays. This is done by wearing a lead apron, leaving the room, or standing behind a lead shield when the X ray is taken. The lead apron used in the radiology department is the same type that is placed over a patient in a dentist's office when teeth are X-rayed.

Fluoroscopy is a technique that produces X ray-like images in motion on a television monitor (Figure 15–9). When the area that best shows the internal problem is seen, an X ray is taken.

The computerized axial tomography scanner (CAT scan), also called computed tomography (CT scan), combines advanced X-ray scanning with a high-speed computer to visualize cross-sectional views of the body. Each cross section can be compared to a slice (axial) of the body (Figure 15–10). Cross sections are pictured from the top of the body downward. The X-ray beam rapidly enters the body while the computer transfers the information about tissue density into numerical or pictorial displays. This type of X ray is at least one hundred times more sensitive than conventional X rays due to computer enhancement. It is used

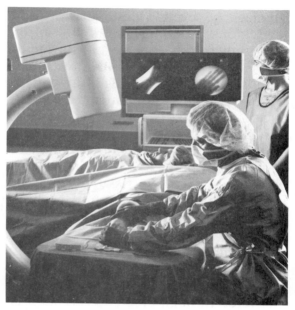

Figure 15–9 *The fluoroscope is X-ray images in motion.*

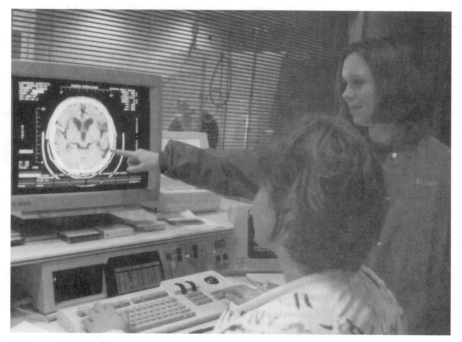

Figure 15–10 *Reviewing images during a CAT scan.*

to diagnose several types of diseases and conditions, including tumors and cancer. It directly pictures organs and surrounding tissues. Sometimes a contrast medium is administered to "light up" certain structures so they are not confused with other body parts. An oral contrast medium allows identification of the bowel; an intravenous contrast enhances kidneys. Use of the CAT scan often eliminates the need for risky exploratory surgery. The average exam time is about fifteen minutes.

Standard angiography is a diagnostic procedure for studying the condition of the arteries and veins. A catheter is maneuvered through blood vessels while a contrast medium is intermittently injected into the bloodstream. The contrast medium illuminates blood vessels to produce images of the vessels on X-ray film and a video monitor. The picture continually changes as the heart pumps. Throughout the injection of the contrast medium, films are taken and developed. After viewing these films, the physician decides if the vessels are satisfactorily visualized or if more contrast medium and films are needed before the standard angiography is completed.

Digital subtraction angiography (DSA) uses the same basic technique as standard angiography, except the pictures of veins and arteries are stored in the computer. The pictures can then be recalled to identify where blood vessel problems are located, eliminating the need to wait for films to be developed. One of the advantages of the DSA test is the production of sustained pictures, using less contrast

medium than with standard angiography. Newer equipment allows structures to be visualized from many different angles without changing the patient's position. In addition, the computer can store up to twenty-eight thousand images that remain available for review either one at a time or in a motion picture format.

Ultrasound and magnetic resonance imaging are other diagnostic techniques that visualize the inside of the body without the use of radiation. These techniques involve the use of computers. Computer-enhanced equipment rapidly produces clear, sharp images of all body parts with no radiation exposure to the patient. These tests are called noninvasive because they are done without performing surgery. Organs such as the brain and heart can be systematically examined and studied by the computer as it visualizes, organizes, and evaluates millions of messages received during each test. Imaging

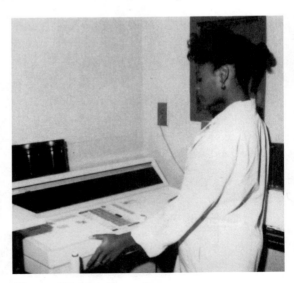

Figure 15–11 *X ray in progress.*

techniques will continue to evolve and change as equipment becomes more sophisticated.

Ultrasound uses high-frequency sound waves with a computer to visualize the inside of the body. This procedure is done on the adrenal glands, heart, aorta, gallbladder, kidneys, liver, uterus, pancreas, pelvis, spleen, and blood vessels. When it is done on a pregnant uterus, the fetus is visualized. The technologist is called a sonographer.

Cardiac catheterization is a diagnostic procedure that is done by passing a catheter through a major vessel of the body into the heart. This test can determine heart function and circulation to the heart muscle (Figure 15–12). Also, a contrast medium can be inserted through the catheter into the coronary vessels and angiography and angioplasty can be done in the same procedure.

During the cardiac catheterization procedure, an ultrasound probe can be threaded through the artery of the leg into the coronary artery. Then an ultrasound is done to measure the size of opening of the coronary artery and show any atherosclerosis plaques in the wall of that vessel.

Angiography may reveal that a coronary artery in the heart is either partially or completely obstructing circulation. This means the patient is experiencing a heart attack. A repair procedure called angioplasty may be done. Angioplasty is a procedure that enlarges the lumen (inside) of the blood vessel and restores circulation to that area of the heart muscle. The procedure is done while the coronary arteries are visualized. The patient is awake throughout the procedure.

Figure 15–12 *The control room during a cardiac catheterization.*

To do the angioplasty, a tiny catheter is passed into a vessel in the groin and threaded through the major vessels and into the coronary artery until the blockage is reached. A balloon catheter is inserted and inflated against the blockage. The inflated balloon pushes the arterial wall outward and reopens the clogged vessel so blood can again flow through. If the artery is totally blocked, a hole can be made through the blockage so the balloon can be positioned and inflated. Other treatments that can be done during this procedure include removing pieces of the blockage and placing supporting meshwork to prevent the vessel reclosing. Angioplasty is done to reestablish circulation in the heart muscle to decrease angina (pain), minimize damage from an existing heart attack, and provide improved circulation to the heart muscle.

Figure 15–13 *MRI in progress.* (Courtesy of Cleveland MetroHealth Medical Center Medical Photography Department.)

The magnetic resonance imager (MRI) uses magnetic fields with a computer to show inner body structures (Figure 15–13). No radiation is involved. The patient is placed in a high-magnetic field. In the body, atoms in each cell spin and give off energy at certain radio frequencies. This energy forms images on film. In this way, the proton structure of every cell is evaluated by the computer. Because of the clarity and high quality of its imaging capabilities, MRI is especially useful in the evaluation and diagnosis of aneurysms, congenital cardiac abnormalities, brain and spine diseases, and orthopedic conditions. It is also useful in assessing and evaluating the liver, pancreas, uterus, and kidneys. MRI is the future of imaging because the patient is exposed to no harmful rays.

Magnetic resonance angiography (MRA) provides information about blood flow and the anatomy inside blood vessels, such as the carotid artery, without the injection of a contrast medium. MRA is used to determine vascular pathology and flow abnormalities.

Positron emission tomography (PET) is a nuclear imaging technique used to detect receptor abnormalities of the brain and nerves. It also validates drug effects and drug metabolism. Specially tagged chemicals that cross the blood-brain barrier are administered so that the brain can be visualized and studied to determine nerve function and the effects of certain drugs on those nerves. PET is used to study neuropsychiatric disorders, cancer, and coronary artery diseases. It can also be used to determine the effectiveness of chemotherapy by following the metabolic response of the tumor. In the future, it may be used to identify brain, lung, and breast cancers. PET is used in conjunction with mammography when breast cancer treatment is being evaluated.

Single photon emission computed tomography (SPECT) is another nuclear imaging technique that can be used in brain studies after strokes, in Alzheimer's patients, and after drug use. SPECT detects abnormalities in brain metabolism and blood flow with the use of radioactive glucose and brain scanning. Following strokes, the effect of speech and other therapies can be evaluated. In Alzheimer's patients, the brain's reaction to specific thinking tasks can be evaluated. SPECT can detect long-term and probably irreversible changes in brain function from the use of cocaine, crack, and marijuana.

Mammogram is a diagnostic X ray of the breasts. Images are produced on sensitive film for early detection of any cancer, about two years before a lump is felt. With early detection, over 90 percent of breast cancers can be successfully treated. Needle localization mammography involves the insertion of a sterile needle into the site of the cell changes immediately before the surgical biopsy. The needle is left in place until the biopsy is completed to identify the exact spot to be excised because the lump is not palpable.

Nuclear scans use radioactive materials to help diagnose and treat diseases and disorders. **Nuclear scans** are performed to study the structure and test the function of certain organs and to determine the extent of some conditions. Radioactive isotopes are administered by in-halation, swallowing, or injection, depending on the part to be studied. This radiopharmaceutical gives off gamma rays. Though these rays are invisible, a gamma camera records them as bursts of light. These bursts are translated by the computer into images. Scans are done on the brain, thyroid gland, lungs, liver, gallbladder, bone, and cardiac muscle and vessels. A commonly used material is radioactive thallium. It is given to facilitate blood flow studies during and after a stress test. The heart and coronary vessels are visualized while the patient exercises on the treadmill and again a few hours later. This test is done to determine blood flow to the myocardium and to detect a recent heart attack.

The densitometer is an X-ray machine that measures bone density. It detects the loss of bone solidity, thus identifying osteoporosis. This is important so treatment can be started to prevent fractures.

Treatment techniques

Radiation treatment consists of the use of a radioactive agent to control the growth and prevent the spread of malignant cells. Several agents are available for this increasingly successful treatment. Routes of administration vary according to the agent and the area to be treated. Some radioactive agents, such as cobalt, are encased in a machine external to the body, and the rays are fired into the affected spot. Other agents are taken into the body by mouth, vein, or direct injection into the body part. Treatment may be a one-time procedure or repeated several times during a set time period.

Radioactive implants can be used to shrink or destroy some types of tumors.

In this case, the patient is hospitalized so a capsule containing a radioactive agent can be placed inside the body, adjacent to the tissue to be destroyed. After a few days, the capsule is removed, and the patient is discharged.

Biography

When I was a junior in high school, my grandmother developed breast cancer. Though she had surgery to remove the tumor, she needed to undergo radiation therapy to ensure that the tumor would not reoccur. She had cobalt treatments five days a week for six weeks. I remember that it drained her energy and made her skin sore. It worked, though, because the cancer never recurred.

Since my grandmother lived with our family, I and my brother and sisters went through that difficult time with her. Sometimes I would drive her to the hospital for the treatment. Once the technologist showed me the plate that was made to protect my grandmother from stray rays so the cobalt would affect only the targeted tissue.

The experience of my grandmother's illness and treatment so impressed me that I decided to become a radiation therapy technologist. I wanted to help others the way the technologist had helped my grandmother. She not only administered the therapy, she also taught my grandmother taking care of her skin, pacing her activity and getting rest, eating a good diet, and managing the pain. During the course of therapy, the technologist and my grandmother became friends. After the therapy was completed, the technologist called my grandmother every few months to see how she was doing. The therapist took a lot of pride in her work and obviously felt that she made a difference in each patient's life. I wanted to have that same feeling. I wanted to make a difference in the life of others.

When I graduated from high school, I entered junior college and earned an associate degree in radiography. Then I went on for one more year in radiation therapy. I am doing just what I want to do now. I recognize that patients who have cancer are under considerable stress. Besides administering their treatments, I help them by being kind and thoughtful and teaching them what they need to know. I know that I am effective in my job. I am good at what I do, and I love it.

Career Search

To discover more about a career and the roles of members in the radiology department, contact the following organizations for online addresses, printed information, and videotapes.

American College of Radiology
1891 Preston White Drive
Reston, VA 22091
Phone: 703–648–8989
Toll-free phone: 800–ACR–LINE

Society of Nuclear Medicine
1850 Samuel Morse Drive
Reston, VA 22090
Phone: 703–708–9000
Fax: 703–708–9015

American Society of
Echocardiography
1100 Raleigh Building
P.O. Box 2598
Raleigh, NC 27602

American Society of Radiologic
Technologists
15000 Central Avenue S.E.
Albuquerque, NM 87123
Phone: 505–298–4500
Fax: 505–298–5063

American Institute of Ultrasound in
Medicine
14750 Sweetzer Lane, Suite 100
Laurel, MD 20707–5906
Phone: 301–498–4100
Toll-free phone: 800–638–5352

Society of Diagnostic Medical
Sonographers
12770 Coit Road, Suite 508
Phone: 214–239–7367
Fax: 214–239–7378

Range of Annual Incomes

Radiologist	$150,000–$240,000
Cardiac catheter lab RN	$ 33,000–$50,000
CAT scan technologist	$ 27,000–$40,000
Darkroom technician	$ 14,000–$20,000
Department director or supervisor	$ 32,000–$55,000
Film librarian	$ 16,000–$23,000
MRI technologist	$ 29,000–$43,000
Nuclear medicine technologist	$ 30,000–$44,000
Radiation therapy technologist	$ 29,000–$43,000
Radiologic technologist	$ 28,000–$42,000
Receptionist	$ 16,000–$23,000
Sonographer or ultrasound technician	$ 29,000–$41,000
Special procedures technician	$ 26,000–$37,000
Transcriptionist	$ 17,000–$21,000
X-ray assistant or transporter	$ 14,000–$21,000

What's New

Digital machines, computers, and laser printers are being used increasingly in the radiology department. The latest equipment makes images clearer and faster.

High-density imaging is done with ultrasound to detect masses. It differentiates between a solid mass and a fluid-filled cyst. It can detect cancer of breast tissue. Because of its sensitivity to types of tissue, it can replace a biopsy procedure.

Densitometer registration is the latest specialty available to radiographers. These radiation therapists specialize in measuring bone density using the densitometer.

School to Work

In addition to the general academic subjects and workplace skills contained in the "Job Skills" chapter, the following subjects and skills apply specifically to careers in the radiology department.

Academic Subject	Workplace Skills
Computer Skills	—Manipulate the computers of MRI, CAT, and other tests.
	—Update skills as new computer programs are developed.
	—Attend workshops on new equipment and procedures.
Mathematics	—Calculate the patient's size related to the darkness of the image or picture.
	—Compute the distance between the X-ray tube and the film in inches.
	—Calculate the amount of radiation needed to penetrate a tumor.
	—Estimate variance in radiation when visualizing an enlarged heart.
Physics	—Understand how imaging machines (MRI, CAT, X-ray) work.
	—Explain how electrons bounce off the body.
	—Define the paths of various electronic circuitry.
	—Clarify the effects of radiation on the body.
Science	
Anatomy and Physiology	—Position body parts in normal alignment.
	—Identify abnormal positions of limbs and internal organs.
	—Recognize fractures on X rays.
	—Position a patient most favorably for imaging.
	—Identify unclear images that need to be repeated.
Pathophysiology	—Vary imaging techniques with diseased parts.
	—Identify the area that needs visualizing according to the physician's diagnosis.
Pharmacology	—Realize the effects and side effects of dyes used for imaging.
	—Understand the need for pain medication before some X rays are taken.
	—Move patients receiving blood thinners with caution.
Radiology	—Explain the effects of radiation therapy to patients.
	—Instruct patients in caring for the skin during radiation therapy.
	—Make a protective shield for tissue around the radiation site.

Academic Subject	Workplace Skills
Social Sciences	
Mental and Social	—Empathize with patients experiencing a change in body image.
	—Encourage patients who are receiving cobalt treatments.
Psychology	—Keep a positive attitude regarding a cancer prognosis.
	—Maintain a cheerful atmosphere in the radiation department.
	—Support patients' efforts with exercise and diet.

Review Questions

1. What are the goals of the radiology department?
2. How many years after high school are needed to attain each career in the radiology department?
3. What are two sources of job satisfaction in this department?

4. What is the difference between a CAT scan and an MRI?
5. List four academic subjects and two ways each is used in the radiology department.

RESPIRATORY THERAPY DEPARTMENT

Objectives

After completing this chapter, you should be able to:

❑ Explain the goals of the respiratory therapy department.

❑ Describe each career in this department.

❑ Identify the required education and credentials for each career.

❑ Describe the skills performed in this department.

❑ Explain how academic subjects apply in the workplace.

Key Terms

Oxygen therapy

Aerosol treatment

Incentive spirometer

Artificial respiration

Pulmonary function test

INTRODUCTION

Tests and treatments of patients with heart and lung problems are performed by the respiratory therapy department. These therapists are concerned with the exchange of gases in the life-sustaining process of breathing and with the circulation of oxygenated blood throughout the body.

The respiratory therapy department provides lifesaving and therapeutic procedures to acutely and chronically ill patients of all ages (Figure 16–1). Diagnostic tests and treatments are performed in the department for outpatients and on nursing units throughout the facility for hospitalized patients. Tests and

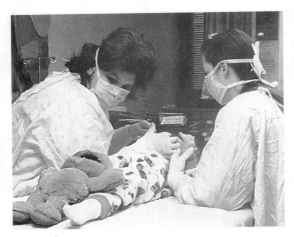

Figure 16–1 Respiratory therapists work with patients of all ages.

procedures are ordered by physicians, and results are reported to them.

Breathing is the act of inhaling oxygen and exhaling carbon dioxide. This function is essential to life, but an increasing number of people have problems with this process (Figure 16–2). Respiratory problems can be caused by smoking, air pollution, allergies, chronic illness, or poor nutrition and health practices. Respiratory illnesses such as asthma, chronic bronchitis, emphysema, and lung cancer can seriously affect breathing.

When breathing is adversely affected, oxygen may need to be administered (Figures 16–3 and 16–4). Patients may need to inhale certain medications and moisture to ease their breathing. Sometimes, breathing is so seriously impaired that patients cannot move air in and out without mechanical assistance. At that time, an endotracheal or tracheostomy tube may be inserted to provide an artificial airway. Then, manual or mechanical ventilation can be used as a temporary substitute for the natural breathing process until the patient's condition improves and natural breathing resumes.

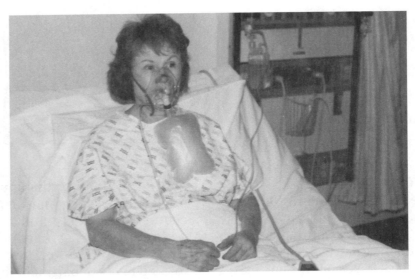

Figure 16–2 Oxygen administered through a high-concentration oxygen mask.

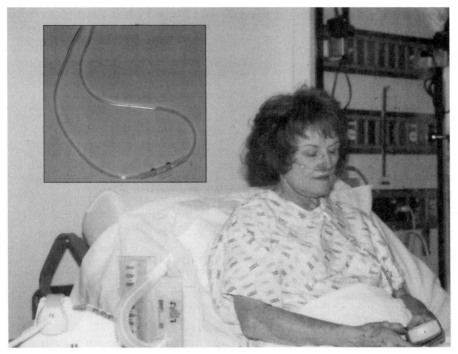

Figure 16–3   *Patient wearing oxygen cannula.*   ***Insert*** *A nasal cannula.*

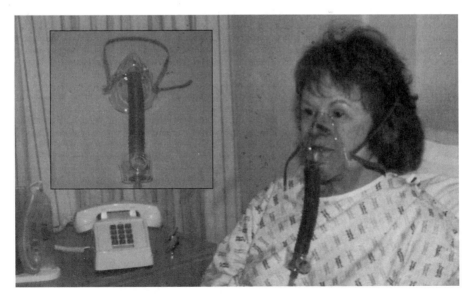

Figure 16–4   *Oxygen administered through a Venturi mask.*
Insert   *A Venturi mask.*

GOALS

The goals of the respiratory therapy department are to provide pulmonary assessment, perform diagnostic tests, administer treatments, and provide artificial respirations when needed. Also included is the development of health education and rehabilitation programs.

CAREER DESCRIPTIONS

Respiratory therapy involves the assessment, diagnosis, treatment, management, and rehabilitation of people with breathing problems. Some procedures are done routinely to ease breathing, and some are done as emergency measures to save lives. Respiratory therapy also includes health education programs for maintaining healthy breathing and preventing diseases.

Career characteristics

Employment opportunities include hospitals, skilled nursing facilities, rehabilitation facilities, physician offices, clinics, home care, and medical equipment companies. Respiratory therapists can specialize by age group or facility. Some specialties are neonatal, rehabilitation, and acute care.

Work hours vary according to the facility and type of job. Respiratory therapists are needed in acute care facilities twenty-four hours a day, every day of the year. Full- and part-time positions are available, and flextime is often an option. Work in offices, clinics, and home care and sales is usually during the day, with some Saturday and evening hours.

Career advancement comes from promotion within the department to a supervisory position. With additional education, section head or department director positions may be an option. Career promotion can come from developing a clinical specialty or by changing

CAREER HIERARCHY

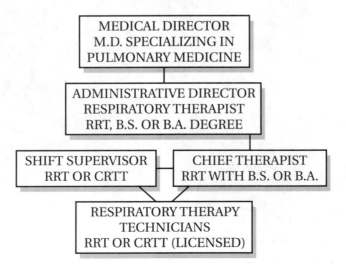

MEDICAL DIRECTOR
M.D. SPECIALIZING IN
PULMONARY MEDICINE

ADMINISTRATIVE DIRECTOR
RESPIRATORY THERAPIST
RRT, B.S. OR B.A. DEGREE

SHIFT SUPERVISOR
RRT OR CRTT

CHIEF THERAPIST
RRT WITH B.S. OR B.A.

RESPIRATORY THERAPY
TECHNICIANS
RRT OR CRTT (LICENSED)

to a position in education, research, or pharmaceutical sales. Respiratory therapy is a good basis for other careers within health care, such as perfusionist or physician assistant.

Desired personal characteristics include a strong desire to help people who are struggling to breathe. Patience, sympathy, empathy, and ability to work in a stressful environment are useful attributes. Physical endurance and tolerance for working with respiratory secretions are other helpful characteristics. Therapists constantly move from patient to patient administering treatments. They often participate in resuscitations.

Job satisfaction comes from helping people who are in physical crisis and knowing that they might die if the therapist's assistance were not available. A sense of pride is generated by performing lifesaving measures and being valued members of the health care team. Therapists know that patients and other professionals depend on them for lifesaving and life-sustaining procedures. In addition, therapists work with some patients over a long time because of repeated hospitalizations for chronic lung disease. Feelings of job satisfaction come from helping these patients accept their conditions and showing them how to live with their disease. Therapists recognize that these patients depend on their therapeutic care, good advice, and calming influence.

Safety is a concern in the respiratory department. Respiratory therapists are considered to be in a high-risk career because they consistently work with body substances, specifically sputum and blood.

Career roles

Pulmonologists are physicians who specialize in breathing problems. These physicians are either employed by an institution as the medical director of the respiratory therapy department or are in private practice and serve as a resource to the department. They interpret the pulmonary function tests and prescribe medications and treatments to improve respiratory status. They work with department members to develop policies and procedures for effective patient care.

Respiratory therapists work under the supervision of a pulmonologist. They work with people of all ages, from premature infants to the aged. They work with some patients who are healthy and others who are critically ill. They assess patients' respiratory status, carry out diagnostic tests and therapeutic procedures, participate in pulmonary rehabilitation, and perform cardiopulmonary resuscitation. They visit patients before surgery to instruct them in deep breathing and inform them of postoperative respiratory treatments. Respiratory therapists adjust the ventilator equipment necessary to support life. In some facilities, they intubate patients in respiratory distress. Other responsibilities include education to improve the quality of life and postpone complications and deterioration. Carrying out quality assurance and control procedures, maintaining equipment, and documenting and reporting are other duties. Tasks may include doing electrocardiographs during the evening, night, and weekend shifts. Respiratory therapists are in charge of the department activities and direct the work of respiratory technicians.

Respiratory technicians work under the direction of respiratory therapists and report to them. Technicians perform most of the procedures that therapists do, depending on training, job performance, and amount of experience. Technicians are responsible for cleaning equipment, billing patients, purchasing equipment, and stocking the department.

Job Availability

Job availability should remain good through 2005 for respiratory therapists.

Therapists experienced with adult and infant patients who have pulmonary and cardiac problems are especially in demand. An increasing number of jobs are available in home care, extended care facilities, skilled nursing facilities, rehabilitation centers and with companies that sell respiratory equipment.

Skills

Skills performed by respiratory therapists and technicians relate to diagnostic tests and treatments of the pulmonary system.

Education and Credentials

CAREER	YEARS OF EDUCATION AFTER HIGH SCHOOL	DEGREE OR DIPLOMA	TESTED BY; LICENSED BY
Pulmonologist (M.D. or D.O.)	4 years of college, 4 years of medical school, 3 years internal medicine internship and residency, and 2 years of pulmonary medicine residency	M.D. or D.O.	ABIM certified in internal medicine; exam in pulmonary disease; State licensure
Registered respiratory therapist (RRT)	2 years (7 quarters)	A.A.S.D. in respiratory therapy	Entry-level exam by NBRC and registry exam (written and simulation); State; advanced cardiac life support (recommended); basic CPR (required)
Certified respiratory therapy technician (CRTT)	1 year (12 months)	Diploma from vocational, technical school, community college, hospital program, or job experience	Entry-level exam by NBRC; State; basic life support (required)

Key to abbreviations:

A.A.S.D.—Associate of Applied Science Degree
ABIM—American Board of Internal Medicine
CRTT—Certified Respiratory Therapy Technician
D.O.—Doctor of Osteopathy

M.D.—Medical Doctor
NBRC—National Board for Respiratory Care
RRT—Registered Respiratory Therapist

In some facilities, respiratory therapists are trained to do electrocardiographs.

Respiratory therapists work with sophisticated equipment with newborn, pediatric, and adult patients in intensive care units, on nursing units, and in patient homes. They administer medications and treatments, provide resuscitation, and instruct in preventive and rehabilitation measures.

Therapies

Oxygen therapy is the administration of a specific percentage of oxygen through a gauge from a tank or wall-mounted unit. A humidifier is attached to the gauge to moisturize the gas. Disposable tubing delivers oxygen to the patient through a nasal cannula, mask, endotracheal tube, tracheostomy tube, tent, or ventilator.

An aerosol treatment is a procedure that delivers medication directly into the patient's respiratory tree through the inhalation of tiny droplets. The liquid medication is converted into a mist and topically delivered through the act of inhaling (Figure 16–5). Aerosol treatments improve breathing by relaxing and dilating the bronchi so that air can pass with greater ease.

Incentive spirometer is a device used to encourage deep breathing. Respiratory therapists instruct patients in the use of this instrument before surgery, then follow up with regular therapy sessions postoperatively to prevent pneumonia (Figure 16–6).

Metered-dose inhalers are handheld medicated atomizers used to dilate

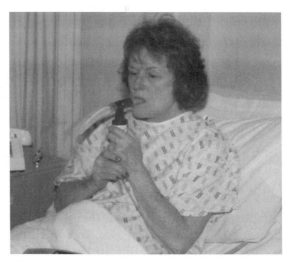

Figure 16–5 *Patient receiving an aerosol treatment.*

breathing passages and ease respirations. These inhalers are prescribed for patients with obstructive lung disease. Respiratory therapists teach patients how to use inhalers correctly.

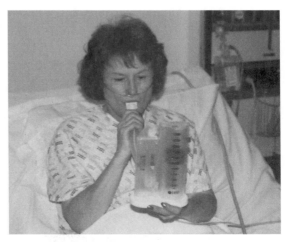

Figure 16–6 *Patient using an incentive spirometer. A humidified oxygen setup is mounted on the wall behind the bed.*

Intermittent positive pressure breathing is a procedure that forces a measured amount of air into the lungs during inhalation. This procedure is ordered for a short period of time (ten minutes) to increase the amount of air exchanged. A bronchodilator medication may be given topically in aerosol form with this procedure. The machine used to accomplish this may be a CPAP or a BIPAP ventilatory support system (Figure 16–7).

Cardiopulmonary resuscitation is the process of reviving a person by administering breaths manually and doing cardiac compressions. It is the treatment prescribed for cardiac and respiratory arrest. Respiratory therapists administer both artificial respiration and cardiac compressions.

Artificial respiration is manually breathing for a patient by forcing air into the lungs when breath is not spontaneous. Artificial respiration can be done mouth to mouth or with a bag-and-mask apparatus. Whatever the method, oxygen needs to be given (and circulated) within four to five minutes to avoid brain damage. If resuscitation efforts need to continue for an extended period of time, a ventilator may be used to continue mechanical respirations (Figures 16–8 and 16–9).

Figure 16–8 *Assembling a ventilator.*

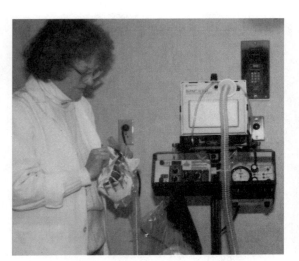

Figure 16–7 *Preparing a BIPAP ST-D ventilatory support system.*

Figure 16–9 *Ventilator with a waveform monitor.*

Intubation is the insertion of an endotracheal tube through the mouth into the trachea using a laryngoscope. This tube provides an airway for a patient in respiratory distress. It may be attached to a ventilator to provide mechanical support for respirations.

Cardiac compressions consist of depressing the lower third of the sternum one and one-half inches in an adult patient sixty times a minute with the heel of the hand. This action forces the blood out of the heart, simulating the natural heartbeat. The heart refills between each compression.

Bronchopulmonary treatment is the process of helping the patient clear the airway passages to improve breathing. The procedure involves chest percussion (clapping) and postural drainage. Chest percussion is the firm but gentle clapping on the chest to loosen secretions that clog airways. Once loosened, they can be coughed out of the lungs and bronchi. Postural drainage is the positioning of a patient so that gravity can help remove those secretions that have been loosened by an aerosol treatment and percussion.

Tests

Arterial blood gas is a test done on blood from an artery to determine the oxygen and carbon dioxide levels. This test determines the effectiveness of natural breathing and mechanical ventilations. Based on the test results, the physician will decide the amount of oxygen and medication to be administered.

Biography

When I was a child, I had asthma. I was especially vulnerable to attacks in the fall, when molds abounded. During that season, I was late to school a lot because I had to have a respiratory treatment before I could leave home. I took a lot of kidding because of my asthma, and sometimes it hurt me. I felt different from the other children and deficient in some way. Also, I had to be careful around those who had a cold or flu so I would not get sick, too.

My asthma diminished as I grew up, but my memory of feeling inferior did not. I vowed that I would help others with their breathing problems, especially asthmatic children. I felt that I had something special to offer because I had experienced what they go through.

I'm working now as a counselor at a camp for asthmatic children. Kids come here to learn to live with their disease. They learn to assess their condition and take appropriate medication according to their breathing status. This helps them gain more control of their disease, with guidance from their parents. Of course, very young children must have their parents assess their condition and administer medication accordingly. It is good to work with people who want to take charge of their life, to understand the illness, and to minimize the influence of the disease in their everyday life. I wish that someone had been available to help me when I was growing up like I am helping these children.

Vital capacity is a test measuring the amount of air that passes in and out of the lungs when a patient breathes. The test consists of exhaling completely, inhaling deeply, then exhaling all breath into a machine that measures the amount of air exhaled. The total volume of exhaled air is the vital capacity.

A pulmonary function test is a series of tests that measure and record the breathing ability of a patient. The first test is done without medication. If the test shows an abnormality, a second test is done after inhaling medication to dilate the bronchi. The physician compares test results to determine if the bronchodilator medication improved the patient's breathing. A pulmonary function test helps the physician identify the nature of respiratory problems so that appropriate treatment can be prescribed.

Career Search

To discover more about a career and the roles of members in a respiratory therapy department, contact the following organization for online addresses, printed information, and videotapes.

American Association for Respiratory Care
11030 Ables Lane
Dallas, TX 75229–4593
Phone: 214–243–2272
Fax: 214–484–2720

Range of Annual Incomes

Pulmonologist	$100,000–$190,000
Respiratory therapist	$ 27,000–$45,000
Respiratory technician	$ 23,000-$32,000

What's New

BIPAP treatment is used to decrease the incidence of intubation and use of ventilators. It forces air in and out of the respiratory system using a tightly fitting face mask.

Clinical pathways are specific courses of treatment used with patients who have certain diagnoses such as pneumonia, congestive heart failure, and chronic obstructive pulmonary disease. They have been agreed upon by physicians and other professionals. The pathways include treatments, medications, and education. Specific guidelines are set out for each day of treatment for all who are involved in caring for the patient. They serve as evaluation tools for case managers when examining the quality of care and length of hospital stay.

Therapist-driven protocols are specific actions preapproved by the medical director and respiratory therapists. These responses can be taken by respiratory therapists when confronted by certain symptoms and conditions. Examples of these protocols are changing therapy from aerosol treatment to a metered dose inhaler or discontinuing oxygen when a patient meets certain criteria. These accepted actions allow therapists to make professional judgments regarding care based on science, rationale, and experience without contacting the physician for direction.

School to Work

In addition to the general academic subjects and workplace skills contained in the "Job Skills" chapter, the following subjects and skills apply specifically to careers in the respiratory therapy department.

Academic Subject	Workplace Skills
Arts	—Draw arterial blood gases. —Monitor the graph on a ventilator screen.
Business	
Time Management	—Schedule pulmonary function tests with outpatients. —Plan with inpatients for aerosol treatments. —Return to inpatients as scheduled.
Communication	—Report the need to purchase equipment to the appropriate person.
Computer Skills	—Enter information for patient billing.
Health Education and Safety	
Universal Precautions	—Wash hands between administering treatments to each patient. —Wear gloves when treating patients.
CPR	—Report to each cardiac arrest and emergency page. —Intubate patients when necessary. —Set up ventilators and attach to endotracheal tubes when needed. —Prepare oxygen setups as needed.
Mechanical Maintenance	—Diagnose malfunctioning of ventilators and other machines. —Run tests on arterial blood gas computers according to protocol.
Mathematics	—Compute oxygen liter setting according to oxygen saturation. —Determine need for bicarbonate according to blood gases. —Figure dosage of inhaled medication according to the size of the patient.

School to Work—continued

Academic Subject	Workplace Skills
Mathematics (cont'd)	—Translate milligrams into micrograms to calculate dosages. —Adjust ventilator settings according to the mathematical formula. —Calculate how long a tank of oxygen will last according to the remaining pounds of pressure and the flow rate.
Science Anatomy and Physiology	—Understand respiratory structures to intubate. —Know the effects of chest trauma on the ability to breath.
Biochemistry	—Realize the effects of elements on the respiratory system. —Relate the effects of acid-base balance on respirations.
Microbiology	—Relate the effects of sepsis on the respiratory system. —Understand the responsibility of keeping bacteria away from patients who have a compromised respiratory system.
Pathophysiology	—Calculate ventilator settings according to blood gases. —Know how lung disease affects the overall body. —Explain to patients how they can live with diseased lungs. —Instruct patients on the effects of medications on their lungs. —Determine the need for humidity according to the oxygen liter flow.
Pharmacology	—Understand the effects of inhaled drugs on the respiratory tree. —Explain the best way to use a metered-dose inhaler. —Instruct patients on the side effects of respiratory medications.
Radiology	—Explain the effects of radiation treatments on lungs. —Identify the condition of a patient's respiratory system from a chest X ray.
Social Sciences Psychology	—Understand that the inability to breathe causes panic. —Help the patient to relax as treatment is administered.

Review Questions

1. What are the goals of the respiratory therapy department?

2. What is the role of a respiratory therapist?

3. What are the sources of job satisfaction in this department?

4. List and explain six skills associated with respiratory therapy.

5. List four academic subjects and two ways each is applied in the respiratory department.

SUPPORT DEPARTMENTS:
ADMITTING, BUSINESS, MATERIEL MANAGEMENT, AND HOUSEKEEPING

Chapter
17

Objectives

After completing this chapter, you should be able to:

❐ Explain the goals of the support departments.

❐ Describe each career in these departments.

❐ Identify the required education for each career.

❐ Describe the skills performed in these departments.

❐ Describe how academic subjects apply in the workplace.

Key Terms

Direct admission   Emergency admission   Conversion admission
Sterilization

INTRODUCTION

Support departments are essential to the existence of a health care facility. In a hospital setting, admitting, business, and central service are a few of those support departments. Others include data processing, housekeeping, and maintenance.

The admitting department is the "front door" of the hospital. Workers greet patients, conduct confidential interviews, and direct patients to their proper destinations. They make registration as easy and efficient as possible.

Two business departments are patient accounting, and credit and collection. These divisions take care of billing and collecting money to pay for staff salaries and supplies and to ensure the financial solvency of the facility.

Materiel management departments order, prepare, stock, and deliver supplies needed by workers at the facility. Divisions include central service, linen room, print shop, purchasing, and storeroom (Figure 17–1).

Figure 17–1 *Central service is one of the many support departments.*

Members of the housekeeping department maintain a clean and comfortable environment. Their tasks help to keep the facility safe for patients and pleasant for family members and staff. This department reports to the assistant administrator in charge of the facility.

GOALS

Support departments facilitate quality patient care. The goal of the admitting department is the smooth, expeditious processing of patients' entry into the hospital for diagnostic tests, care, same-day surgery, and outpatient treatments. The goals of the business department include issuing precise bills and arranging for payment. The goals of materiel management include developing effective methods for ordering, stocking, processing, dispensing, inventorying, replacing, and charging items used by facility workers. The goals of the housekeeping department include maintaining a clean, safe environment.

CAREER DESCRIPTIONS

Support departments help health care workers do their jobs. Workers interact with staff in other hospital departments; only admitting and collection clerks interact with patients.

Career characteristics

Employment opportunities are found in hospitals, large skilled nursing facilities, and clinics. In most facilities, workers are trained on the job.

Work hours vary according to the department and the facility. Admitting departments are usually open five days a week during day hours, with some evening and weekend hours. Business offices are usually open during the day shift. Materiel management departments are usually open seven days a week during day and evening shifts. Some large facilities provide twenty-four-hour central service coverage. Housekeeping personnel work during the day and evening shifts.

Career advancement includes a coordinator position within the department or a lateral move within the facility. To move up the career ladder, education beyond high school or additional job training is usually necessary.

Desired personal characteristics include good verbal skills, a courteous manner, good organizational skills, and ability to work under pressure. Communication needs to be calm, clear, pleasant, and

CAREER HIERARCHY

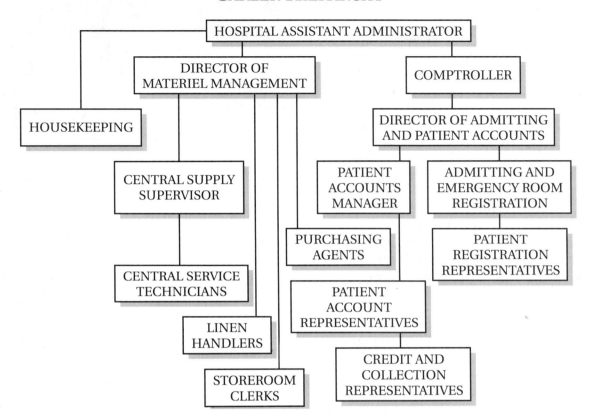

positive—even in stressful situations. Ability to accept responsibility and work independently are other desirable traits. Strong math skills and aptitude for detail tasks are helpful in business departments. Creative planning is important in credit and collections.

Job satisfaction in the support departments comes from doing a job well and pride in service. It comes from knowing that good performance makes it possible for those who give direct patient care to do their jobs better, from perfecting job skills, and from achieving a standard of excellence. It comes from making a difference in the lives of patients and fellow workers. Workers in the admitting and credit and collection departments gain satisfaction from making the admission process and payment process as smooth as possible.

Career roles

Admitting department workers are patient registration representatives. They do a variety of tasks to ensure prompt, thorough service as receptionists, preregistration scheduling clerks, precertification agents, and bed allocation clerks. They interact with patients, physicians, staff nurses, and insurance clerks to process patient admissions. Admissions, which must be ordered by a physician, are classified as direct, emergency, or conversion.

A **direct admission** occurs when a patient comes to the hospital from home, long-term care facility, or a physician's office. In this case, the physician calls the admitting department to request a bed. An **emergency admission** occurs when a patient was seen by the emergency room physician and is too sick to go home. A **conversion admission** occurs when a patient was scheduled for same-day surgery but had a more extensive operation or is too unstable to go home.

Interaction with physicians is an important facet of the work of patient registration representatives. Physicians want patients admitted and served promptly and will direct their patients to those hospitals that give courteous and expedient service. They also need to be kept informed of their patients' room assignments and changes.

Receptionists greet patients when they come to the facility, interview patients for personal data, enter health insurance information into the computer, and direct patients to appropriate locations (Figure 17–2). They confirm that patients' physicians are active and in good standing on the medical staff and have admit-

Figure 17–2 *A receptionist station.*

ting privileges. Receptionists work in the admitting department and the emergency room where, in addition to other duties, they help identify unknown patients and locate relatives. They prepare patient identification bracelets and imprinter plates for identifying chart forms.

Preregistration scheduling clerks register outpatients and arrange for their diagnostic tests. They confer with patients on the telephone about the date, time, and instructions for the test. Though some departments schedule tests directly with patients, most outpatient tests are arranged through this central scheduling service. Preregistration clerks also schedule diagnostic tests before planned admissions and elective surgeries.

Precertification agents call insurance companies to verify coverage for patients' charges. Insurance companies may refuse to pay for hospitalization, surgery, diagnostic tests, and physicians' services unless they approved the procedures before patients were treated. Some insurance policies require patients to call for precertification.

Bed allocation clerks assign newly admitted patients to nursing units and rooms. Many factors must be considered when doing this complex task, including acuity level, age, gender, and presence of infection. Most hospital rooms are doubles, that is, they house two patients. Patients may be very sick, dying, confused, and calling out. Bed allocation clerks may not know the mental and physical status of new patients or potential roommates on the nursing units. Another consideration is diagnosis. If the facility has specialty units, patients should be assigned accordingly. For example, those with cancer should be assigned to the oncology unit.

Bed allocation clerks handle all bed assignments for inpatient transfers as well. When patients become stable, they are moved out of intensive care to the step-down unit. Often, other patients may need to be moved off the step-down unit to make that possible. When most hospital beds are full, it is hard to assign and relocate patients. Sometimes the nurses and nursing supervisor become involved, particularly if a critical change has occurred in a hospitalized patient, necessitating immediate transfer to the intensive care unit.

Business departments are essential to the existence of a facility. Without efficient functioning of the patient accounts, credit and collection, and purchasing departments, the facility could go into bankruptcy and close.

Patient account representatives are responsible for billing. Charges are entered into the computer by workers in each department, and the final bill is compiled by the computer (Figure 17–3).

Figure 17–3 *Patient account representatives are responsible for billing.*

Approximately seven days after the patient is discharged or treated, a patient account representative sends a computer-generated bill to the insurance company or the patient. Patient account representatives post payments in patients' computer files and send a computer-generated follow-up letter if payments are not received on time. They check the percentage of payment against the insurance company's policy or contract with the hospital to be sure that each payment is correct. If bills become delinquent, the accounts are assigned to the credit and collection department.

Patient accounts representatives correspond with attorneys, balance all payments to patient accounts, and develop form letters and flowcharts. Each day, patient charges are downloaded from the mainframe computer so representatives can send a bill to the proper insurer or person. Tasks also include checking microfiche to see that daily reports and billing are accurately recorded. In a paperless department, records are kept on microfiche, not on paper.

Credit and collection representatives also work to keep the facility financially solvent. They follow up on bills that are rejected by insurance companies and document the amounts to be paid by patients. If insurance carriers pay only a portion of the medical bills, patients may be responsible for the remaining part.

Representatives work with patients in person or over the phone to explain charges and devise a payment plan. Workers need to be particularly aware of the stresses associated with illness and recovery. They need to be careful in how they approach the issue of indebtedness and sensitive when developing a payment schedule.

Materiel management workers perform tasks in purchasing, central service, the linen room, and the storeroom.

Purchasing agents order hospital equipment and supplies requested by members of other departments of the hospital. Agents work with staff to operate an efficient system for inventorying, ordering, receiving, storing, and paying for necessary items.

Purchasing agents assign a number to each order submitted to suppliers, ascertain a delivery date, monitor the delivery, and affirm satisfaction with the product. They may be responsible for presenting information on and coordinating evaluations of new products before establishing these items as standard equipment in the facility.

Purchasing agents coordinate presentations of new equipment by hospital supply sales representatives. These agents may contact suppliers when searching for a product.

Central service clerks provide reusable supplies and machines for patient care. Workers are responsible for decontaminating, cleaning, sterilizing (Figure 17–4), and assembling small equipment, such as treatment trays for biopsies, and large equipment, such as suction machines and IV pumps. They clean and replenish emergency carts used in cardiac arrests and disinfect and refurbish resuscitation manikins used to teach CPR. They package equipment according to protocol and operate the steam autoclave, gas sterilizer, and aerator. The process of **sterilization** kills all microorganisms. They keep records on preventive maintenance procedures done on major equipment.

Figure 17–4 *Central service workers place equipment into a sterilizer.*

Figure 17–5 *Linen handlers furnish patient linens.*

Linen handlers furnish linens for patient care, treatments, and surgery (Figure 17–5). Workers deliver clean or sterile linens to patient care units, surgery, and other departments, and collect soiled linen in a manner compatible with infection control standards. Workers in this department fold and package linens to be sterilized and used to cover patients in the operating room (if disposable drapes are not used). Workers either launder soiled linen or deliver it to a designated location to be picked up for processing by a commercial laundry. Workers wear protective coverings, such as gloves, when handling soiled linen. In some facilities, the linen room or laundry is part of the housekeeping department.

Storeroom workers maintain a stock of paper materiels and commercially packaged supplies for the facility. They distribute sterile disposable treatment kits, dressings, intravenous fluids and tubing, bath and other personal hygiene items, secretarial supplies, medical record forms, and other items ordered by requisition. In many facilities, storeroom workers automatically stock specific items in designated departments. They also fill individual orders, follow protocol for supply charges, and deliver materials as requested. Special instruments for surgery may be ordered directly by the surgery department.

Housekeeping workers perform tasks in the offices, lobbies, nursing units, and all departments of the patient care facility. Housekeeping is an important department. Maintaining areas that are free from dirt is essential to prevent the spread of bacteria. Also, patients and family members need to see that the institution values cleanliness. Housekeepers wash the surfaces of countertops and furniture with antibacterial solutions. Floors are scrubbed with disinfecting solutions. When the floors are cleaned, signs identifying the "wet floor" status are put in place as a safety factor to prevent falls. In some facilities, the housekeeping department has been decentralized and the housekeeper's role has been expanded to that of a service care associate. This employee is a part of the nursing unit staff.

JOB AVAILABILITY

Because computers are being used to track and transmit information, jobs for admitting clerks, patient accounting clerks, and credit and collection agents will be fewer to the year 2005. Since more disposable equipment is used in patient care, fewer jobs will be available in central service as well. Automated stocking will keep job demand at the current level for storeroom workers. Housekeepers

Education and Credentials

CAREER	YEARS OF EDUCATION AFTER HIGH SCHOOL	DEGREE OR DIPLOMA	TESTED BY; LICENSED BY
Patient registration representative	On-the-job training; medical terminology and computer knowledge are helpful	—	—
Patient account representative	On-the-job training; medical terminology, math skills, and a typing course are helpful	—	—
Credit and collection representative	On-the-job training; a business course is helpful	—	—
Central service technician	2 years or on-the-job training	A.A.S.D. in sterile processing and distribution technology	—
Linen handlers	On-the-job training	—	—
Purchasing agent	4 years	B.S. in business	
Housekeeper	On-the-job training	—	—

Key to abbreviations:

A.A.S.D.—Associate of Applied Science Degree
B.S.—Bachelor of Science Degree

will increase because of the growth in the number of patient care facilities and assisted living residences for the elderly.

SKILLS

Tasks done in support departments vary according to the facility. Some workers are trained to do more than one job within a department in case of illness, absence, or a heavy workload.

Admitting

In the admitting department, the skill of communication is used with patients, physicians, nurses, and insurance company clerks. Interviewing incoming patients, providing clear directions, and keeping physicians informed of the room assignments are necessary tasks. Documenting insurance approval is also required.

Tactful investigative skills are used to confirm that patients' physicians are active and in good standing on the medical staff and have admitting privileges. These skills also are needed to help identify unknown patients and locate relatives.

Organizational skills are used to register outpatients and arrange for their diagnostic tests.

Negotiation skills are helpful with bed allocation. If one site is not available or acceptable, another plan must be worked out.

Purchasing

In the purchasing department, accuracy is essential. Tasks include accurate ordering and documentation of requisitions, along with determining receiving dates. Making price comparisons, reviewing quality, and coordinating product evaluation are some of the organizational skills needed in this department.

Patient accounting

In patient accounting, accuracy in math and detail tasks is necessary. Computer entry and data retrieval are skills used as departments become paperless, that is, workers use computers so no hard copy is printed, and no paper files are used. Organizational skills and accuracy in gleaning and collating information from face sheets of medical records are other talents used.

Credit and collection

In the credit and collection department, telephone courtesy and the ability to give clear explanations are necessary communication skills. Imagination and creativity are helpful when developing payment plans.

Central service

In central service, following detailed routine tasks and established practices is a skill needed to ensure cleanliness, safety, and completeness of issued equipment (Figure 17–6).

Storeroom

In the storeroom, logical organization, careful rotation of items, and attention to expiration dates ensure the stocking of equipment that is safe and usable. A spirit of service and accuracy in ordering and receiving supplies is a valued asset.

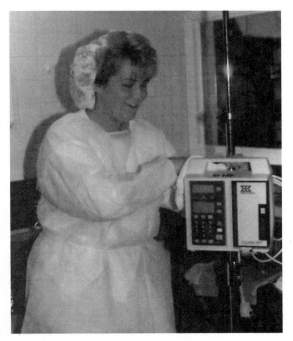

Figure 17–6 *Central service worker disinfects a computerized IV pump between patient uses.*

Housekeeping

In housekeeping, conscientiously following the department cleaning techniques for floors, furniture, and countertops is essential for infection control and a pleasant atmosphere. Scrubbing, polishing, and waxing floors, along with stripping off old wax and removing scrape marks, are some tasks that may involve heavy equipment. Cleaning sinks, countertops, bathroom fixtures, and utility rooms is another chore. Dusting and preparing patient units are also included in the role. A positive attitude toward tasks is important to maintain a good rapport. Chores may include cleaning up accidents that involve spills of food or body fluids. Safety measures are important to prevent harm to one's self and others. Self-motivation is an important characteristic because only one housekeeper is assigned to an area. Ordering supplies is another job that department members perform.

Biography

I moved to this country from Hungary when I was sixteen years old. I came alone to live with my aunt and uncle. Since their house was near the community hospital, I applied to work at the facility part time while I was going to high school. Though I spoke some English, I was not comfortable with the language.

I was lucky to be hired to work in the housekeeping department. There, I learned about what many kinds of workers did in their health care careers. I decided that I wanted to be a doctor. All I did during my high school years was study and work because I wanted to realize my dream.

Over time, my English improved. So did my income. I was such a good housekeeper that my supervisor recommended me to some physicians to clean their offices on weekends. I worked for these doctors all through college and did a good job. When I applied to medical school, these doctors wrote good recommendations for me and gave me some money to supplement my scholarships and student loans. Even when I was young, I understood the value of a conscientious, honest worker and a job well done. Now I am a physician looking for a conscientious worker to clean my office. I would help that person just like the doctors I worked for helped me.

Career Search

To discover more about a career and the roles of members in a support department, contact the following organizations for online addresses, printed information, and videotapes.

American Society for Health Care
   Materials Management
c/o American Hospital Association
1 N. Franklin, 30th floor
Chicago, IL 60606
Phone: 312–422–3840
Fax: 312–422–3573

American Society for Healthcare
   Engineering
c/o American Hospital Association
1 N. Franklin, Suite 2700
Chicago, IL 60606
Phone: 312–422–3800
Fax: 312–422–4571

International Association of
   Healthcare Central Service
   Materiel Management
213 W. Institute Place, Suite 307
Chicago, IL 60610
Phone: 312–440–0078
Toll-free phone: 800–962–8274
Fax: 312–440–9474

Range of Annual Incomes

Admitting Department:

Patient registration representative	$18,000–$25,000
Patient account representative	$18,000–$27,000

Business Department:

Credit and collection representative	$18,000–$27,000

Materiel Management Department:

Central service technician	$12,000–$24,000
Linen handlers	$12,000–$24,000
Purchasing agent	$17,000–$24,000
Storeroom technician	$14,000–$24,000

Housekeeping:

Housekeeper	$13,000–$19,000

What's New

Service care assistants have replaced housekeepers on the nursing units. They are a part of the nursing unit staff. They keep the environment clean and pleasant and give indirect patient care. (More information about this position is contained in Chapter 11 on the nursing department.)

School to Work

In addition to the general academic subjects and workplace skills contained in the "Job Skills" chapter, the following subjects and skills apply specifically to careers in the support departments.

Academic Subject	Workplace Skills
Arts	
Business Departments:	—Develop flowcharts.
Business	
Communication	
Admitting:	—Take a gentle approach with apprehensive patients.
	—Use a kindly manner with anxious relatives.
	—Carefully obtain information regarding health insurance.
Credit and Collection:	—Speak tactfully when collecting money owed.
	—Keep calm in the face of evasive or angry clients.
	—Meet with patients to set up a payment schedule.
Materiel Management:	—Service the nursing units with a positive attitude.
Housekeeping:	—Do not give medical advice to patients.
	—Speak pleasantly to the patients and personnel on the units.

School to Work—continued

Academic Subject	Workplace Skills
Housekeeping (cont'd):	—Leave the patient's room when the physician enters. —Maintain confidentiality about a patient's illness. —Avoid making judgments about unit activities.
Computer Skills *Admitting:*	—Respect patient confidentiality regarding diagnosis and illness. —Enter insurance and patient identification information. —Obtain permission to admit from the patient's insurance company via modem.
Credit and Collection:	—Respect the confidentiality of patients' financial state. —Post payments accurately so accounts are up to date. —Print bills of patients who are in arrears. —Correspond with attorneys.
Mathematics *Business:* Accounting Addition, Subtraction	—Bill clients and insurance companies. —Post insurance and client payments. —Determine balances owed. —Prepare deposit slips and receipts. —Pay suppliers or authorize payment by another department.
Housekeeping: Division	—Calculate supplies needed. —Dilute liquid cleansers according to directions.
Science *Housekeeping:* Microbiology	—Use techniques that avoid cross contamination of patient rooms. —Perform special cleaning of isolation rooms. —Use universal precautions when cleaning up emesis.
Central Service:	—Sterilize instruments according to procedure. —Disinfect equipment too large to be autocleaned between patient uses.

Review Questions

1. What are the goals of the admitting, business, materiel management, and housekeeping departments?

2. What are four sources of job satisfaction for workers in the support departments?

3. What are five personal characteristics desired in persons who work in support departments?

4. List the jobs in the support departments for which post-high school courses are available.

5. List three academic subjects and two ways each is applied in the support departments.

Chapter 18

SURGERY DEPARTMENT

Objectives

After completing this chapter, you should be able to:

- ❐ Explain the goals of the surgery department.
- ❐ Describe each career in this department.
- ❐ Identify the required education and credentials for each career.
- ❐ Describe the skills performed in this department.
- ❐ Explain how academic subjects apply in the workplace.

Key Terms

Emergency procedure

Elective procedure

INTRODUCTION

The surgery department is often pictured as a place of mystery and miracles. It is. Wonderful things happen there because of the education, training, teamwork, and dedication of the surgical team.

Even members of the surgical team are sometimes impressed by activities in the operating room. They see how vital organs are cut, sewn, restructured, and replaced so that the body can function and patients continue to live.

During minor surgical procedures, such as the removal of a skin mole or a cataract, patients may remain awake. During major surgical procedures, such as stomach removal, hip replacement, or heart surgery, patients are anesthetized into an unconscious, unfeeling state.

Surgical procedures may be done in emergency and nonemergency situations. Repairing major blood vessels after a gunshot wound or automobile accident is classified as an **emergency procedure** because the patient's life depends on immediate action. Removing cysts or cataracts is classified as a nonemergency or **elective procedure** because it relieves a patient's discomfort and improves the quality of life, but these conditions are not life-threatening.

GOALS

The goals of the surgery department include the successful performance of necessary operative procedures, administration of medication and anesthetics, and the monitoring and supporting patients' vital functions to sustain life.

Goals in the same-day surgery unit, preoperative holding area, and recovery room include preparing patients for designated procedures and monitoring their conditions afterward until they are stable and their mental status is clear.

The goal of the perfusion section of the department is to support the vital functions of blood circulation and gas exchange when the heart is not pumping and the patient is not breathing.

CAREER DESCRIPTIONS

Many careers are associated with the care of patients before, during, and after surgery. The surgery department includes the same-day surgery unit, preoperative holding area, operating rooms, and recovery room. Specialties within surgery include neurosurgery, thoracic/open heart surgery, abdominal surgery, vascular surgery, gynecology, urology, orthopedic surgery, plastic surgery, and eye, ear, nose, throat, and maxillofacial surgery. Except for the physicians, most workers in a hospital setting are employed by the institution.

Nurses in the same-day surgery unit and preoperative holding area discuss procedures with patients, administer preoperative medications, and begin intravenous fluids. Anesthesiologists and surgeons may meet with their patients there. The staff in the operating room greet patients and prepare for the surgery. The circulator does a preoperative assessment that includes checking patients' understanding of the operative procedure, reviewing lab results and

PATIENT CARE FLOWCHART

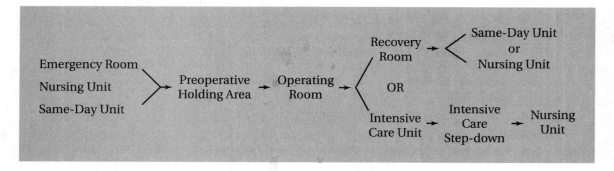

CAREER HIERARCHY

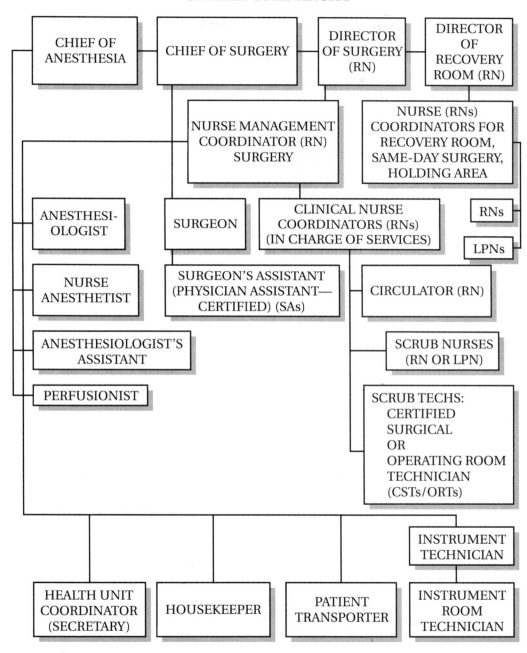

physical and mental status, and making sure that permissions are signed. Once the surgeons, surgeon's assistants, nurses, and technicians have scrubbed and dressed in sterile gowns and gloves, they cannot touch anything that is not sterile. They depend on the circulator to obtain items and position patients.

In the recovery room, staff nurses monitor patients' conditions and help them awaken from anesthesia. In some hospitals, recovery room nurses meet hospitalized patients and establish a relationship the day before surgery is scheduled.

Career characteristics

Employment opportunities include hospitals, freestanding surgical clinics, and surgeon and oral surgeon offices. Other options are health maintenance organizations, research centers, the Veterans Administration, the military, and private industry.

Work hours. In a hospital setting, surgery is usually scheduled Monday through Saturday on day and evening shifts, with on-call duties during the night and on Sunday. If an emergency arises, on-call staff come to the hospital. Freestanding surgical clinics are open Monday through Friday during the day. Generally, clinics perform less complicated types of surgery than hospitals do because they have limited resources for coping with emergencies.

Job satisfaction comes from having special knowledge and skills that contribute to improving the patients' quality of life and, in some cases, saving lives. It comes from making good decisions in stressful situations, functioning in emergencies, associating with technically talented professionals, and enjoying the respect of colleagues and the admiration of other health care staff. Though surgery is sometimes stressful, it is always a prestigious place to work.

Career advancement may depend on returning to school for further education or obtaining more on-the-job training. Nursing assistants may become surgical technicians; practical nurses and surgical technicians may become registered nurses or surgeon's assistants; registered nurses may become specialty coordinators or directors of surgery. A surgeon may work in private practice, a health maintenance organization, government or industry, or as an advisor to institutions, chief of surgery, or chief of a specialty. Some of these may be lateral moves rather than career advancements.

Desired personal characteristics include an aptitude for detail tasks, ability to work under stressful conditions, and react constructively in emergency situations. Good vision, manual dexterity, good hand-eye coordination, self-confidence, a sense of humor, and team spirit are other helpful traits. The stamina to stand in one place for many hours is necessary.

Career roles

Anesthesiologists are physicians who administer agents that induce muscle relaxation, drowsiness, and loss of consciousness. Anesthetic agents are administered by intravenous, inhalation, or spinal routes to ensure freedom from pain during surgery or delivery of a baby. Anesthesiologists meet with patients before surgery, review their medical records, then choose anesthetic agents. When the patient reaches unconsciousness, an airway is established by inserting an endotracheal tube to facilitate gas exchange and to administer anesthesia. Throughout surgery, anesthesiologists monitor patients' vital signs, state of hydration, level of consciousness, skin color, and pupil reaction. They look for symptoms of shock, respiratory distress, arrhythmias, and other adverse conditions (Figure 18–1).

Job responsibilities include administration of anesthesia, oxygen, intravenous fluids and blood transfusions, along with constant observation of the patient's physiological condition as the body reacts to the stress of surgery. Heart function, vital signs, and blood oxygen levels are monitored, recorded, and reported to the surgeons. While surgeons concentrate on the technical aspects of the operation, anesthesiologists are responsible for the patient's overall condition. The first responsibility of the surgical team is the patient's survival.

Nurse anesthetists and anesthesiologist assistants work under the direction of anesthesiologists and perform the same tasks. They administer anesthesia by spinal, intravenous, and inhalation methods, and give intravenous fluid, blood transfusions, and oxygen. They monitor and record patients' conditions, record anesthesia and medications, and report to the anesthesiologist and to the surgeon. Questions are addressed to the supervising (physician) anesthesiologist.

Surgeons are physicians who have completed extra studies in general surgery or a specialty, such as orthopedic or plastic surgery. The number of years to become

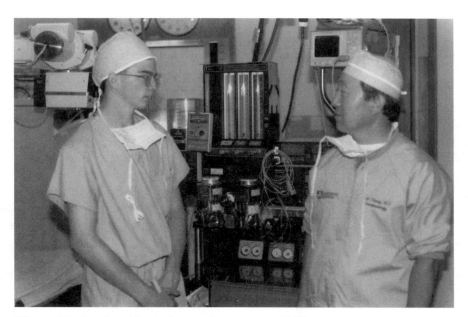

Figure 18–1   *Anesthesia is a serious responsibility.*

board certified depends on the specialty. Neurosurgery is the longest program of study, requiring seven years after medical school.

Surgeons usually specialize in a particular area. Family physicians refer patients to them when operations are needed (Figure 18–2). Surgeons meet with their new patients, examine them, review diagnostic tests, and explain how procedures will be done.

Surgeons study every nerve, muscle, and blood vessel of each organ and section of the human body. The procedure of surgery includes making an incision and tying off or cauterizing blood vessels to stop bleeding and ensure a clear visual field. Then the problem part is located, cut, or stapled and sewn until it is repaired, removed, replaced, or revascularized. When this is done, the incision is sewn or stapled closed.

The surgeon is the head of the surgical team. Surgeons depend on others for help, but they make the decisions about procedures and techniques, designate tasks, and determine the equipment to be used.

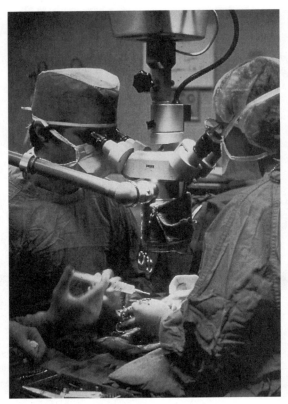

Figure 18–3 *Surgeon's assistants work alongside the physician.* Credit: Cleveland MetroHealth Medical Center–Medical Photography Department.

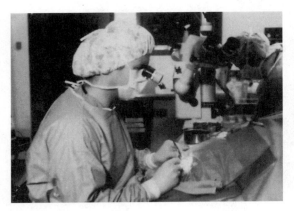

Figure 18–2 *Surgeons usually specialize.*

Surgeon's assistants are physician assistants who specialize in surgery. They work in the operating room as a first or second assistant to the surgeon, doing tasks that would otherwise be done by a resident physician (Figure 18–3). This role includes tying off blood vessels and retracting the incisional opening to enlarge the visual field inside the patient. They sew, handle special instruments, irrigate, and hold organs and parts for the surgeon (Figure 18–4). Some may sew together layers of tissue to close the inci-

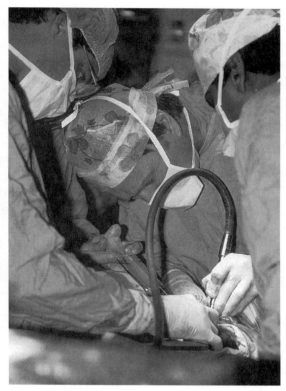

Figure 18–4 *The surgical team works closely together.* Credit: Cleveland MetroHealth Medical Center–Medical Photography Department.

sion and finish with skin sutures, staples, or clips. After surgery, surgeon's assistants visit patients to remove sutures or staples.

Surgeon's assistants are also trained to work with patients before and after surgery. They may be responsible for meeting with patients before surgery, obtaining medical histories, assessing physical conditions, requesting laboratory and diagnostic tests for pre- and postoperative assessments, performing therapeutic procedures, explaining the operative and postoperative course, and answering questions.

Surgeon's assistants have some of the same technical skills as the surgeons. The difference is in the depth of education, technical skill, and responsibility to patients. Surgeons have had more in-depth education of anatomy and physiology, more practice in surgical techniques, and actually perform the operation. Surgeons are responsible to patients for the surgical diagnosis, professional decisions, and the technical quality of the operation.

Certified surgical technicians, operating room technicians, and scrub nurses prepare the room, assist with positioning patients, and prepare and drape the operative site. They pass instruments, drains, sponges, and dressings to surgeons and surgeon's assistants. They need to learn the name and function of each instrument, anticipate when each instrument will be needed, and pass that instrument when appropriate without being asked. They set up instrument tables, prepare sutures, count sponges before use, pass and retrieve sponges, and maintain the sterile field during the procedure (Figure 18–5).

It takes time to learn the many instruments for each surgical service. Different instruments are needed to remove a cataract than to perform open heart surgery or replace a hip joint. But when staff members are on call, they work on any case that presents an emergency.

Surgeons expect that operating room technicians or scrub nurses will place (not slap) correct instruments into their extended palms. Ideally, the surgeon's eyes never leave the operative site, never look at the instruments. Placing incorrect instruments into the surgeon's palm

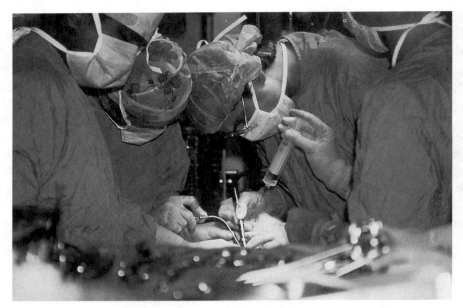

Figure 18–5 *Instruments are handed up by surgical or operating room technicians and scrub nurses.* Credit: Cleveland MetroHealth Medical Center–Medical Photography Department.

interrupts thought processes and breaks concentration.

Circulators are registered nurses who meet the needs of the scrub team that is dressed in sterile attire. Members of the scrub team cannot obtain extra supplies and sutures from storage cupboards, position X rays on the lighted viewer, or use the telephone without contaminating their whole outfit. Circulators prepare the rooms, help transfer and position patients, open sterile supplies, obtain additional supplies and special instruments, and call for additional support when needed. Other responsibilities include administering intravenous medications, ordering blood components, sending specimens to the lab, calling the pathology department for biopsy results, obtaining X rays, and counting used sponges,

needles, instruments, and sharps to be sure all are accounted for before the incision is closed. They complete some forms that document the procedure and assist anesthesiologists who cannot leave unconscious patients.

Perfusionists operate the heart-lung machine that is used during open heart surgery when the heart is not beating. In this procedure, the patient's blood is passed through this machine in special tubing. This machine temporarily replaces the heart and lungs, pumping blood, adding oxygen, and removing carbon dioxide.

Perfusionists, or extracorporeal circulation technologists, monitor blood gases and electrolytes during heart surgery. They interact with patients, surgeons, anesthesiologists, and nurses. Responsibilities include preoperative patient assessment, the setup and management of the heart lung-machine during the repair or replacement of the heart, and monitoring oxygen, carbon dioxide levels, and other substances in the blood. Other duties entail monitoring vital signs; administering blood, anesthetic agents, and other drugs; and inducing hypothermia (lowered body temperature) by reducing the temperature of the blood. At the end of surgery, the technologist is responsible for weaning the patient from the machine when the heart resumes pumping. The technologist specializes in adult or pediatric perfusion.

Job satisfaction comes from competent performance. Perfusionists know that patients' lives depend on their technical ability to keep oxygenated blood flowing throughout the body and brain while the heart is not functioning. Respect from fellow professionals, particularly surgeons and anesthesiologists, is also gratifying. Financial compensation is another source of satisfaction. The perfusionist is well paid—most heart surgery cannot be performed without this professional.

Surgery transporters bring patients from same-day surgery, hospital rooms, and the emergency department to the preoperative holding area. To ensure proper identification of each patient, the name and hospital number on the transport card are compared with the name and number on the chart and on the patient's identification wrist bracelet. This procedure eliminates the chance of transporting the wrong patient to surgery.

Instrument room technicians clean, wrap, and sterilize instruments and stock operating rooms. They inspect instruments for wear and replace worn parts or the whole instrument. After cleaning, instruments are packaged and readied for sterilization. Technicians have been trained in the proper use of the steam autoclave and gas sterilizer. These procedures are crucial for killing organisms, creating a sterile field in the operating room, and preventing infection that would result if unsterile instruments were used.

Health unit coordinators (**secretaries**) are an integral part of the surgical department. Telephone management is a central task in this role. Coordinators call to inform nurses when to administer preoperative medication. They call for patients to be transported to the holding area, then to the operating room. They call the visitors' waiting room to tell the visiting room coordinator to inform family members when patients have gone to the recovery room and when surgeons will meet them.

Some facilities have a scheduling secretary/coordinator for the operating room. This complex scheduling procedure requires knowing what surgeons operate on what days, how long each procedure lasts, and what rooms are needed for what specialty cases. If an emergency arises, cases may have to be shifted to a different time or day, depending on other procedures, patients' conditions, and surgeon and staff availability.

RNs and LPNs in same-day surgery assess patients, instruct them in the impending procedure, answer their questions, inform them and family members about scheduling details, affix patient identification bracelets, and transport patients to the holding area.

RNs in the preoperative holding area start intravenous fluids, check patient understanding, give preoperative medications, facilitate the patient's meeting with the anesthesiologist, and transport the patient to the operating room.

RNs and LPNs in the recovery room monitor patients' vital signs, monitor cardiovascular and respiratory status, check dressings, connect drains and tubes, and apply ice bags and traction as needed. They carry out physician's orders and remain with patients until stability is ensured.

JOB AVAILABILITY

Job availability is excellent for positions in surgery. Though hospitals are still the primary employers of surgery personnel, jobs are becoming increasingly available at the ambulatory surgery centers. The number of jobs will grow for nurse anesthetists and anesthesiologist's assistants, surgical technologists, surgeon's assistants, registered nurses, and licensed practical nurses. Positions for perfusionists are increasing at this time. In the future, some types of heart surgery may be done using a scope procedure rather than opening the chest and stopping the heart. That will mean fewer positions available for perfusionists. Only twenty schools for perfusionists exist in the United States, so the number of graduates each year is limited.

SKILLS

Staff in the department of surgery develop special skills according to their education, position, and work site. Tasks required in same-day surgery are not the same as those required in the operating room.

Airway management

Airway management is an important responsibility of those who administer anesthetic agents. To manage an airway safely in an unconscious patient, endotracheal tube may be inserted to facilitate gas exchange and administer anesthetic agents.

Intubation is the procedure of inserting a laryngoscope and an endotracheal tube into a patient's windpipe through the mouth or nose to maintain the airway. This tube is connected to the anesthesia machine and ventilator. It remains in place until the operation has been completed and the patient can breathe without mechanical assistance. The procedure is done by anesthesiologists, their assistants, or nurse anesthetists.

Insertions

Insertion of intravenous and arterial lines is another skill performed by anesthesia team members (Figure 18–6). Central venous pressure monitoring and insertion of special catheters are other procedures done. Health history, type of surgical procedure, and anticipated length of unconsciousness are all factors considered before determining what lines are necessary.

Scrubbing

Surgical scrub is the procedure of washing hands and forearms to the elbow for ten minutes with antibacterial soap, a scrub brush, and a nail file or orange sticks. This procedure is done by every staff member who will dress in sterile attire for the operation. Anyone performing

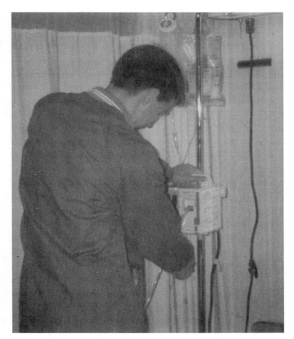

Figure 18–6 *IV pumps control fluid administration.*

surgery or passing sterile instruments will scrub. Though the skin is never sterile, scrubbing decreases the number of bacteria present on the hands and forearms.

Sterile technique

Sterile technique is a skill learned by all professional staff members who work in surgery. Sterile implies the absence of bacteria. Introduction of bacteria into a patient's incision can cause a serious infection, debilitation, and sometimes death. Only instruments that have been sterilized by steam or gas or purchased in a prepackaged sterile container are used in the operating room (Figure 18–7). Staff wear masks to avoid breathing into the incision or on the sterile field, which includes the instrument tables and drapes that cover the patient.

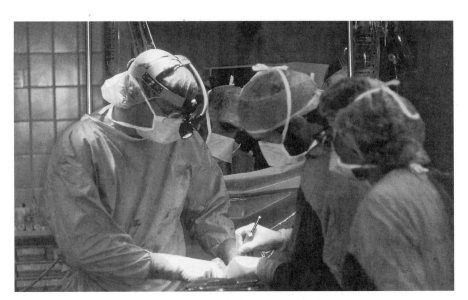

Figure 18–7 *Only sterile instruments are used in surgery.* Credit: Cleveland MetroHealth Medical Center–Medical Photography Department.

Education and Credentials

CAREER	YEARS OF EDUCATION AFTER HIGH SCHOOL	DEGREE OR DIPLOMA	TESTED BY; LICENSED BY
Anesthesiologist (M.D. or D.O.)	4 years of college, 4 years of medical school, 1 year of internship, 3 years of residency in anesthesia	M.D. or D.O.	Board exams by ASA; State
Nurse anesthetist (CRNA)	4 years college plus, 1 year of critical care plus 2–3 years of anesthesia program	B.S.N. degree plus M.S.N. in anesthesia	Exam for certification by AANA Council of Certification; State
Anesthesiologist's assistant (AA)	4 years of college plus 2–3 years of anesthesia program	B.S. in health science plus M.S. in anesthesia	Exam for certification by AAAE and AAAA
Surgeon (M.D. or D.O.)	4 years of college, 4 years of medical school, 1 year of internship, and residency (number of years varies with specialty: 2 for general surgeon, 7 for neurosurgeon)	M.D. or D.O.	Certified by ACS plus board exams given by the specialist medical organization; State
Surgeon's assistant (SA)	3–5 years before program; applicant must have 1 year of health care experience and A.A.S.D. in health field or a baccalaureate degree in a related field, plus 2 years of SA program or (with previous experience in a health career) 2 years of college, 2 years A.A.S.D. in SA program	A.A.S.D. in SA	Certification exam by NCCPA
Certified surgical technician (CST) or operating room technician (ORT)	9–12 months in hospital or school program or on-the-job training	Certificate	Certification through AST to become a CST (optional)
Scrub nurse (RN or LPN)	1, 2, 3, or 4 years: nursing program	2 year: A.A.S.D. in nursing, 3 year: diploma from hospital school, 4 year: B.S.N. from college or university	State board exam; State
Circulator (RN* or ORT with an RN present)	2, 3, or 4 years: nursing program	(See above for nursing programs)	Same as for RN or ORT

Education and Credentials (continued)

CAREER	YEARS OF EDUCATION AFTER HIGH SCHOOL*	DEGREE OR DIPLOMA	TESTED BY; LICENSED BY
Perfusionist or extracorporeal circulation technologist (CCP)	4 years; 5 years: 4 years, 1 year; 4 years: 2 years, 2 years	Bachelor of science in circulatory technology or bachelor of science plus perfusion program or college courses plus perfusion program	National license American Board of Cardiovascular Perfusionists (ABCP)
Surgical transporter	On-the-job training or HOE program	—	—
Instrument room technician	On-the-job training	—	—
Health unit coordinator (secretary)	(See Chapter 11, "Nursing Department")	—	—
Recovery room nurse (RN, CPAN)	2, 3, 4 years: nursing program plus workshops, continuing education courses, or on-the-job training	2 years: A.A.S.D. in nursing; 3 years: diploma from hospital school; 4 years: B.S.N. from college or university	Certification from ASPAN

*JCAHO and AORN require that an RN be the circulator in the operating room.

Key to abbreviations:

AA—Anesthesiologist's Assistant
AAAA—American Academy of Anesthesiologists' Assistants
AANA—American Association of Nurse Anesthetists
A.A.S.D.—Associate of Applied Science Degree
AAAE—Association for Anesthesiologists' Assistants Education
ABCP—American Board of Cardiovascular Perfusionists
ACS—American College of Surgeons
ASPAN—American Society of Post Anesthesia Nurses
AST—Association of Surgical Technicians
ASA—American Society of Anesthesiologists
AORN—Association of Operating Room Nurses
B.S.N.—Bachelor of Science in Nursing
CCP—Certified Cardiovascular Perfusionist

CRNA—Certified Registered Nurse Anesthetist
CST—Certified Surgical Technician
D.O.—Doctor of Osteopathy
HOE—Health Occupation Education Program
JCAHO—Joint Commission on Accreditation of Healthcare Organizations
M.S.—Master of Science
NA—Nurse Anesthetist
NCCPA—National Commission on Certification of Physician's Assistants
ORT—Operating Room Technician
RN—Registered Nurse
SA—Surgeon's Assistant

Principles of sterile technique need to be strictly followed in the operating room. If something becomes contaminated, it is not used. If a fly landed on a sterile table that contained 150 instruments, the entire table would be considered contaminated and removed from use. Another set of instruments would be obtained and readied for use as quickly as possible.

Passing instruments

Passing instruments is the technique of handing the right instrument to the right surgeon at the right time (Figure 18–8). It also includes wiping used instruments with a sterile sponge and returning them to the sterile field. Instruments are passed back and forth from incision site to table during an operation.

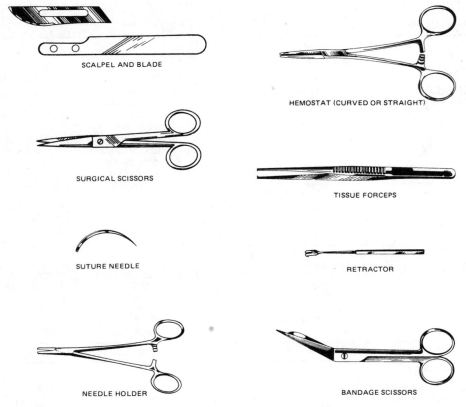

SCALPEL AND BLADE

HEMOSTAT (CURVED OR STRAIGHT)

SURGICAL SCISSORS

TISSUE FORCEPS

SUTURE NEEDLE

RETRACTOR

NEEDLE HOLDER

BANDAGE SCISSORS

Figure 18–8   *Commonly used surgical instruments.*

The skill of passing instruments depends on learning the names and functions of more than one hundred instruments. Because each specialty has its own instruments, the name and function of each are different, though there are similarities. About twelve instruments are commonly used in each specialty. There is time during the training program and orientation period to learn the name and function of each instrument.

The goal of the person passing the instruments is to know the technique of the surgical procedure well enough so that the next instrument to be used is anticipated, selected, and pressed into the extended hand of the surgeon without it being requested. The surgeon expects the correct instrument to be passed without looking away from the operative site or, at the instrument and without asking for it.

Surgical technique

Surgical technique is the procedure of cutting into, dissecting, repairing, removing, and closing—the step-by-step process of performing the operation. It is the surgeon's method of getting the job done with the least amount of trauma to the patient in the least amount of time. Surgical technique is important to the patient. After the surgery, it may matter to the patient where the surgeon placed the incision; how the organs were cut, stapled, and stitched; how the laser was used; how blood vessels were tied or cauterized; how much tissue was removed; how gently were the surrounding organs and tissues handled; and how much time the operation took.

Positioning

Positioning the patient is an important skill carried out by several of the operating room team members. The surgeon directs positioning for the best view of the operative field. The anesthesiologist is concerned about lung expansion and the maintenance of an open airway. The circulator protects the patient from stress on pressure points and overextension of joints and muscles. The patient needs to be positioned on the surgical table with the least amount of trauma to the body. Pressure points need to be padded and cushioned, and safety cuffs and straps need to be carefully placed to avoid tissue damage and restriction of circulation. Special techniques need to be used to move an unconscious patient to avoid skin, muscle, and joint damage.

Monitoring

Monitoring is an important skill performed by everyone in the operating room (Figure 18–9). Each team member is responsible for certain aspects of the monitoring process, but the patient's overall physical status is the primary consideration of the entire surgical team. Anesthesia team members monitor pulmonary and cardiac status through electrocardiograph, arterial blood gas measurements, and vital signs. Surgeons monitor the procedure and progress of

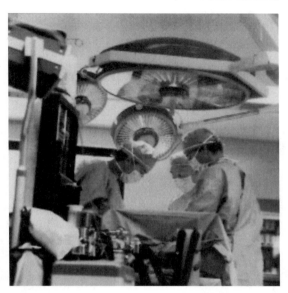

Figure 18–9   *Anesthesia and monitoring equipment is placed near the patient's head.*

the operation to ensure the best technique is used and the operative goal is accomplished. Scrub nurses or operating room technicians monitor the surgical procedure to pass the correct instruments to the surgeons. Circulators monitor the needs of the team and perform unsterile tasks for sterile-suited team members. Recovery room nurses monitor the patient's vital processes, check to see that all systems and all equipment are working properly, and observe the patient's return to consciousness and a physically stable state. Though team members carry out their specific tasks, they are interdependent and work together to make the operative experience successful for the patient.

Extracorporeal circulation

Extracorporeal circulation is the pumping of blood out of the body, through the heart-lung machine, and back into the body, bypassing the human heart and lungs. The word *extracorporeal* means "outside the body." While the heart is not functioning, blood is pumped by the machine. This machine can monitor the oxygen, carbon dioxide, and electrolyte levels and can deliver anesthetic agents.

Biography

When I finished high school, I had no idea of what I wanted to do. The thought of going on to school did not appeal to me. I wanted to earn money, though. So I got a job in the dietary department of a community hospital. I soon realized that if I wanted to move up financially, I would need more education.

When a unit secretary job was posted, I applied for and won the position. I was very happy. Since I worked during the day, I was able to take evening classes at the junior college. I did not have a career goal, but I knew that core courses like English would be a requirement in any program. For three years I worked as a unit secretary on a critical care nursing unit. When other secretaries were unavailable, I floated to all the critical care units. I loved the excitement of acute care, especially the surgical intensive care unit. I decided that I wanted to be a part of surgery. When an opening there occurred, I applied for and got a full-time job as a scrub tech. I loved every minute in the operating room. I had found my niche! I checked the community college catalogue to determine the prerequisites for the surgeon's assistant program and worked toward completing them.

After two years as a scrub tech, I was accepted into the surgeon's assistant program. I was thrilled! I was able to do part of my clinical practice at the hospital where I worked. I graduated last May and continue to work at the same hospital but with more responsibility. It was a very hard program, but I am glad that I completed it.

Career Search

To discover more about a career and the roles of members in a surgery department, contact the following organizations for online addresses, printed information, and videotapes.

American College of Surgeons
55 E. Erie Street
Chicago, IL 60611
Phone: 312–664–4050
Fax: 312–440–7014

American Association of Nurse
    Anesthetists
222 S. Prospect Avenue
Park Ridge, IL 60068–4001
Phone: 847–692–7050
Fax: 847–692–6968

Association of Operating Room
    Nurses
2170 S. Parker Road, Suite 300
Denver, CO 80231
Phone: 303–755–6300 or
    303–750–3212
Toll-free phone: 800–755–2676
Fax: 303–750–3212

Association of Surgical Technologists
7108-C S. Alton Way
Englewood, CO 80112
Phone: 303–694–9130
Fax: 303–694–9169

American Society of Extracorporeal
Technology
1148 Sunset Hills Road, Suite 210E
Reston, VA 22090
Phone: 703–435–8556
Fax: 703–435–0056

American Academy of
Anesthesiologists' Assistants
P.O. Box 33876
Decatur, GA 30033–0876

Association of Operating Room
Technicians
1100 W. Littleton Blvd., Suite 201
Littleton, CO 80120

American Society of Surgeon
Assistants
1730 N. Lynn Street, Suite 502
Arlington, VA 22209
Phone: 703–525–1191
Fax: 703–276–8196

Range of Annual Incomes

Anesthesiologist	$ 150,00–$250,000
Nurse anesthetist	$ 60,000–$ 90,000
Anesthesiologist's assistant	$ 60,000–$ 90,000
Surgeon (depends on specialty)	$160,000–$350,000
Surgeon assistant	$ 25,000–$ 50,000
Operating room or scrub technician	$ 20,000–$ 30,000
Scrub nurse (LPN)	$ 24,000–$ 34,000
Circulator (RN)	$ 29,000–$ 45,000
Perfusionist	$ 60,000–$130,000
Surgical transporter	$ 11,000–$ 15,000
Health unit coordinator (secretary)	$ 17,000–$ 25,000
Recovery room nurse	$ 29,000–$ 45,000

What's New

Outpatient surgery centers are becoming popular. These freestanding surgical offices save money because their overhead is less than that of a surgery department in a hospital. In the event of an emergency, however, they offer less access to critical care personnel and facilities. These centers also do not provide accommodations for an overnight stay.

In in-and-out surgery, the patient reports for the operation in the morning and goes home in the evening. This type of surgery is less involved than the kind that requires a patient to remain at the hospital overnight. With the new types of anesthesia, patients recover more quickly so more can return home at night if their condition is stable.

Many technical advances are being developed for use in surgery. Some of the improvements include sophisticated equipment using fiber optics and laser technology.

Fetal surgery is being done in some medical centers. In this surgery, a baby is operated on before birth, while still in the uterus of the mother. The baby is reached through an incision in the mother's abdomen and uterus. After the procedure, the baby is returned to the mother's uterus. The placenta is not disturbed. This type of operation may be done if permanent damage to an organ or death would occur without it.

School To Work

In addition to the general academic subjects and workplace skills contained in the "Job Skills" chapter, the following subjects and skills apply specifically to careers in the surgery department.

Academic Subject	Workplace Skills
Business	
Time Management	—Schedule surgeries allowing for enough but not too much time.
	—Work with the admitting department to schedule outpatient surgeries.
	—Assign personnel to each operating room.
	—Assign staff fairly to on-call time.
Communication	—Call the lab for frozen-section biopsy results.
	—Dictate surgery summaries.
	—Send a copy of the surgery summaries to the referring physician.
Computer Skills	—Enter the time of surgeries.
	—Enter staff time for payroll processing.
Economics	—Order supplies on a timely basis.
	—Assign transporters, rather than higher-paid workers, to transport patients.
English and Communications	—Read carefully to check patient identification.
	—Note patient allergies and report them to the anesthesiologist.
Medical Terminology	—Perform the correct surgery on the correct patient.
	—Prepare the appropriate instruments for the specific surgery.
Speech	—Introduce yourself to the patient in the operating room.
	—Confirm the type of surgery to be done.
	—Ask if the patient has any questions regarding the procedure.

Academic Subject	Workplace Skills

Health Education and Safety

Universal Precautions
—Use careful techniques with blood and body fluids.
—Handle specimens carefully.

Personal Hygiene
—Request a circulator to mop your brow if you are perspiring.
—Cover beards during sterile procedures.

Body Mechanics
—Arrange for a team to move the patient from the operating table.
—Lift rather than drag an unconscious patient to avoid harm.

Mathematics

Accounting
—Post the time the patient enters and leaves the operating room.
—Document all medications given to the patient.
—List chargeable items on the patient's record.

Addition, Subtraction
—Calculate medication according to the patient's age and weight.

and Division
—Administer anesthesia according to the patient's body surface, weight, and age.
—Set the IV pump to deliver drops per minute according to the cubic centimeters per hour ordered.
—Dilute IV medications according to the order.

Science

Anatomy and Physiology
—Locate a moderately large vein and start intravenous fluids.
—Insert an endotracheal tube (if necessary) after the patient is anesthetized.
—Cut through the skin and stop bleeding according to procedure.
—Identify the body structure that needs to be repaired.
—Remove the diseased part of the organ.
—Sew together the ends of an open organ.
—Place artificial parts appropriately.
—Stitch blood vessels, muscle, and skin.

Biochemistry
—Administer chemical elements according to bodily needs.
—Track acid-base balance as necessary.

Microbiology
—Use sterile instruments and technique during surgery.
—Cover skin around incision area with sterile drapes.
—Wear mask, and sterile gloves and clothing at operative site.

Pathophysiology
—Identify the diseased organ to be removed.
—Check the patient's X ray to confirm the part to be removed.

School to Work—continued

Academic Subject	Workplace Skills
Pathophysiology (cont'd)	—Check with the lab for the pathology report on the biopsy. —Remove only what is necessary. —Sew with proper stitching material for the part.
Pharmacology	—Administer medication before anesthesia. —Prepare medications for the induction of the anesthesia. —Give medications to allow the ventilator to take over the breathing function. —Administer anesthesia through the endotrachael tube. —Monitor anesthesia to prevent an overdose. —Awaken the patient after surgery with oxygen and medications if needed.
Radiology	—Study X rays in the operating room to check the location of the diseased part. —Take an X ray in the operating room to see if the artificial part is properly placed.
Social Sciences	
Ethics	—Maintain patients' confidentiality. —Respect patients' physical privacy. —Perform the procedure listed on the signed permit.
Teamwork	—Maintain a positive attitude toward all. —Help other team members without being asked. —Be willing to take on-call hours. —Volunteer to cover lunch breaks.
Law	—Document events in surgery accurately. —Count sponges and record carefully.

Review Questions

1. How long are the education programs for anesthesiologists, surgeons, nurse anesthetists, surgeon's assistants, and perfusionists?
2. What are four sources of job satisfaction for those who work in surgery?
3. What six characteristics are desirable in people who work in surgery?
4. What six skills are performed in the operating room?
5. List three academic subjects and two ways that each is applied in the work site

Chapter 19

VETERINARY MEDICINE

Objectives

After completing this chapter, you should be able to:

❏ Explain the goals of veterinary medicine.

❏ Describe the careers in this field.

❏ Identify the required education and credentials for each career.

❏ Describe how academic subjects apply in the workplace.

Key Terms

Avian	Aquatic	Equine
Canine	Caprine	Feline
Ovine	Porcine	

INTRODUCTION

Veterinary medicine involves the care of animals. Care giving includes assessing the animal, identifying its needs, planning to care for those needs, administering that care, then evaluating and adjusting that plan. Since animals cannot verbally relate symptoms to the owner or care giver, the veterinarian must rely on careful observations and objective symptoms (Figure 19–1). Care givers specialize in large or small animals.

Veterinarians and their technicians interact with both the animals and their owners. Safety is a major concern because sick and wounded animals that are fearful or in pain can harm people (Figure 19–2).

EDUCATIONAL PROGRAMS

Education for a career as a veterinarian includes a four-year program that follows the completion of prerequisite college courses and volunteer experience with animals. There are twenty-seven schools of veterinary medicine in the United States. They accept approximately one out of every three applicants with a college or

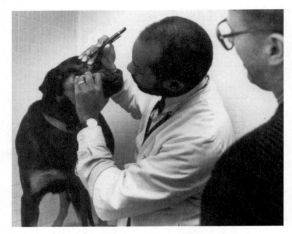

Figure 19–1 *Observation skills are important when examining an animal.* Credit: The Ohio State College of Veterinary Medicine.

Figure 19–2 *A sick animal may need to be transported to a veterinary hospital.* Credit: The Ohio State College of Veterinary Medicine.

preveterinary program grade point average of around 3.5. Each school accepts about 100 students a year. The degree is recognized worldwide. Students attend full-time during the day, Monday through Friday. Third- and fourth-year students obtain clinical experience in a veterinary hospital or laboratory. Veterinarians who choose to specialize must complete a three-year residency program (Figure 19–3).

GOALS

The goals of veterinary medicine are to practice preventive medicine to keep animals in good health, to diagnose and treat sick animals, and to counsel owners, community leaders and the public to maintain the public health.

CAREER DESCRIPTIONS

The care and treatment of animals parallels the care of humans. When studying to

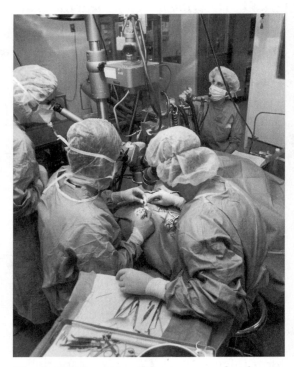

Figure 19–3 *Animal surgery may be chosen as a specialty.* Credit: The Ohio State College of Veterinary Medicine.

EDUCATIONAL LADDER

> **DVM WITH PH.D.:**
> DVM PROGRAM
> PLUS
> MASTERS PROGRAM
> PLUS
> 5 YEARS IN PH.D. PROGRAM

> **DVM WITH MASTER'S DEGREE:**
> DVM PROGRAM
> PLUS
> 3 YEARS MASTER'S PROGRAM

> **DVM:**
> 2-3 YEARS PREVETERINARY COLLEGE
> PLUS
> 4 YEARS DVM PROGRAM

> **ANIMAL HEALTH TECHNICIAN**
> 2 YEARS IN ASSOCIATE DEGREE PROGRAM

> **VETERINARIAN ASSISTANT**
> ON-THE-JOB TRAINING

become a veterinarian or assistant, courses of anatomy, physiology and pharmacology are much the same as humans, especially mammals. Medical therapy and surgical interventions are the same as well. One of the major differences is the size of the patients. Another difference is the inability to speak and understand the spoken word.

Veterinarians are in charge of the team of caregivers. They plan and direct other team members in the treatment of animals in their care. All team members interact with animal owners.

Career characteristics

Employment opportunities for veterinarians depend on the specialty. A general veterinarian can work in private practice alone, join a group, or work on salary for a corporation. Opportunities exist in the same specialties as medical doctors have, such as internal medicine, cardiology, dentistry, dermatology, pathology, and radiology. Other specialties include small animal care (Figure 19–4), large animal care, livestock, fish and wildlife, and research. Positions are available in zoos, corporate farms, racetracks, government, public health, agriculture departments, and state fish and wildlife agencies. Opportunities to work with animals exist in cities, suburbs, and rural areas. Teaching opportunities exist at colleges of veterinary medicine.

Employment opportunities for technicians and assistants include private practice, corporate employers such as Pet Smart or Vet Centers of America, zoos, and university or corporate research centers.

Work hours depend on the job site and type of work. In private practice, the veterinarian works a sixty-hour week Monday through Saturday. When two or

CAREER HIERARCHY

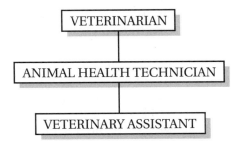

> VETERINARIAN

> ANIMAL HEALTH TECHNICIAN

> VETERINARY ASSISTANT

Figure 19–4 *Pet owners love their animals.*
Credit: The Ohio State College of Veterinary
Medicine.

Career advancements vary. A veterinarian may begin as an employee in a large practice with many veterinarians, then buy into the practice to have equity in the business. A veterinarian may also join a practice owned by a corporation. In research, the veterinarian may move up to be the chief of research for an institution. A veterinarian may decide to specialize and change focus. Animal health technicians may work up to a supervisory position in a large institution. Veterinary assistants may make a lateral move to another work site. A grooming business is an option for independent income.

Desirable personal characteristics include a love of animals and liking people (Figure 19–5). People who work with ani-

more veterinarians share a private practice, they may have a five-and-a half-day work week with an on-call schedule of every other Sunday. Zoo hours depend on the size of the facility and the number of veterinarians on staff. In a large zoo, work hours are usually regular. In research, the hours may be regular though long when a particular project involves monitoring animal responses to a given treatment or medication. In rural areas, the veterinarian may live next to the facility where sick animals are housed and be on call twenty-four hours a day.

Animal health technicians and veterinary assistants may work a variety of shifts if the setting requires twenty-four-hour coverage. In an animal hospital or research center, seven-day coverage may be necessary.

Figure 19–5 *A love of animals helps to establish a rapport.* Credit: The Ohio State College of Veterinary Medicine.

mals need patience and a calm manner because they interact with owners who are anxious, worried, and possibly irritable. They need a sense of community service. The ability to work long hours, solve problems quickly, and adapt to new situations also is important. They must use their intuition and be sensitive to changes in the animals. They need to be dependable, accurate, and thorough.

Job satisfaction comes from seeing the animals regain health and from serving the owners. It comes from protecting and comforting animals and from teaching appropriate safety measures and care-giving techniques to others (Figure 19–6). Those who work in public health know that they are preserving the health of the people who live in the community, the country, or the world, depending on their job.

Safety is an issue when dealing with animals. Veterinarians are at high risk for exposure to rabies. Though bites present the most danger, exposure to the diseased animals' saliva or objects containing the saliva can also result in infection. Veterinarians need to be experienced in methods of physically and chemically restraining animals. Both large and small animals, whether they are sick, hurt, or well, can harm the practitioner if not handled carefully. Besides rabies, tetanus and tuberculosis also are concerns. Bruises from kicks and bites are another hazard.

Some techniques that ensure the safety of workers are being careful when handling sharps to avoid getting cut, wearing a lead apron and gloves in the presence of radiation, and wearing goggles and gloves when working with certain chemicals.

Figure 19–6 *Teaching dairy farm workers about the care of cows.* Credit: The Ohio State College of Veterinary Medicine.

EDUCATION AND CREDENTIALS

CAREER	YEARS OF EDUCATION AFTER HIGH SCHOOL	DEGREE OR DIPLOMA	TESTED BY; LICENSED BY
Veterinarian (DVM)	2–3 years of college for prerequisite courses and volunteer experience plus 4 years of veterinary college	DVM	National licensing exam; each state sets acceptable score; State
Animal health technician (ATR)	2 years	A.A.S.D. in animal health	State; (required in some states)
Veterinary assistant	On-the-job training	Certificate from HOE program	

Key to abbreviations:

A.A.S.D.: Associate of Applied Science Degree
ATR: Animal Technician Registered
B.S.: Bachelor of Science Degree
DVM: Doctor of Veterinarian Medicine
HOE: Health Occupations Education (in high school or vocational school)

Career roles

Veterinarians perform physical exams, assess objective symptoms, perform diagnostic tests, administer medical treatments, and perform surgery (Figure 19–7). They interact with animal owners, zookeepers, livestock breeders, research associates, community leaders, and technicians and assistants. About seventy percent of veterinarians work in private clinical practice. About thirty percent work in research, administration, teaching, public health, zoos, exotic animals, and specialties. Areas of specialization include internal medicine, pharmacology, nutrition, dermatology, allergy, cardiology, theriogenology (animal reproduction), industrial research, laboratory diagnostics, parasitology, wildlife (in state and federal agencies), ophthalmology, pathology, radiology, surgery, dentistry, and animal behavior. Practitioners may specialize in **avian** (bird), **aquatic** (marine life),

equine (horse), **canine** (dog), **caprine** (goat), **feline** (cat), **ovine** (sheep), and **porcine** (pig) pathology (Figure 19–8).

Animal health technicians assist the veterinarian and work with animals. They

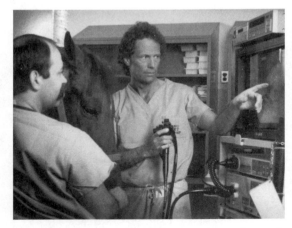

Figure 19–7 *Diagnostic tests are performed on animals.* Credit: The Ohio State College of Veterinary Medicine.

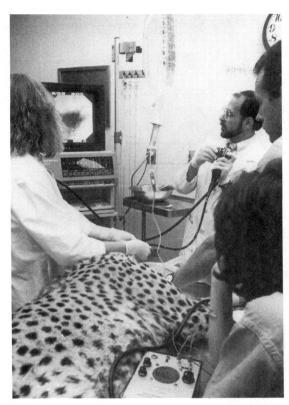

Figure 19–8 *Performing a scope procedure on a large cat.* Credit: The Ohio State College of Veterinary Medicine.

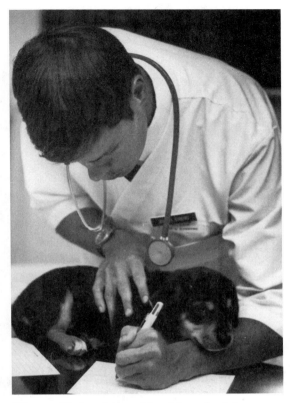

Figure 19–9 *Animal health technicians are responsible for documentation.* Credit: The Ohio State College of Veterinary Medicine.

take the temperature, pulse, and respirations. They record the health history. They monitor the conditions of sick and wounded animals. They interact with animal owners. They assist the veterinarian in performing physical exams and surgery. They document care and treatments (Figure 19–9).

Veterinary assistants perform maintenance tasks for the animals and their environment. They may be assigned to feed and groom the animals, clean the cages, prepare the examining room, prepare animals for procedures, and assist with examinations and surgery (Figure 19–10). They may document care and treatments and maintain office records.

JOB AVAILABILITY

The job market is good for veterinarians. About three jobs are available for each graduating student. The job market is good for animal health technicians and fair for assistants. The job market is particularly influenced by the economy. In times of recession when money is tight, people

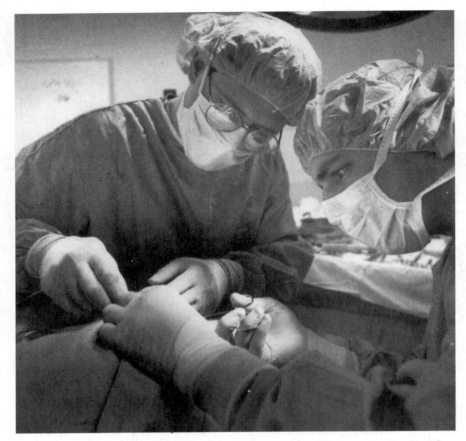

Figure 19–10 *Animal health technicians assist with surgery.* Credit: The Ohio State College of Veterinary Medicine.

do not take their pets to the veterinarian. This significantly affects the income of people who work with animals.

SKILLS

Veterinarians and assistants have the opportunity to develop skills in working with animals during their educational programs. Volunteering in an animal shelter or at a veterinarian's office before entering a caregiving program is another way of developing skills and is highly recommended.

Observation

Keen powers of observation and attention to detail are necessary. People who work with animals must notice changes in their condition by visual and tactile perceptions. They need to develop a specific technique of observation and inspection (Figure 19–11).

Solving problems

Solving problems and carrying out a plan of care based on the process of deduction are two essential skills needed by people who work with animals.

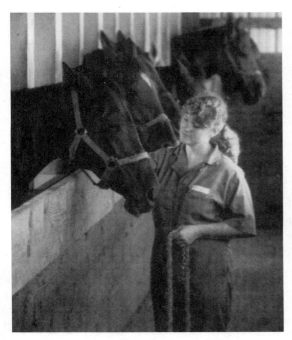

Figure 19–11 *Establishing a rapport precedes the physical exam.* Credit: The Ohio State College of Veterinary Medicine.

Figure 19–12 *An owner may be anxious about the sick animal.* Credit: The Ohio State College of Veterinary Medicine.

Sensitivity

Emotional sensitivity to the needs of owners is especially important. Spoken communication and gentle care of the animals will help to relieve their anxiety.

Careful handling

Careful handling of animals is essential to gain the confidence of the owners and to calm the animal (Figure 19–12).

Restraining

Physical and chemical restraint of all sizes and types of animals must be learned and practiced so the care giver is safe during treatment. Specific methods are followed for domestic, farm, exotic, and zoo animals.

Preventive medicine

Preventive medicine such as vaccinations, parasite control programs, and nutritional support are important for the animal as well as the owner or handler.

Immobilization

Immobilization for a surgical procedure, selection of anesthesia, and use of equipment to administer and monitor anesthesia are skills to be developed. These skills are also needed for some diagnostic testing (Figures 19–13 and 19–14).

Testing

Diagnostic testing for different types of animals is important to understand and practice (Figure 19–15). Methods vary

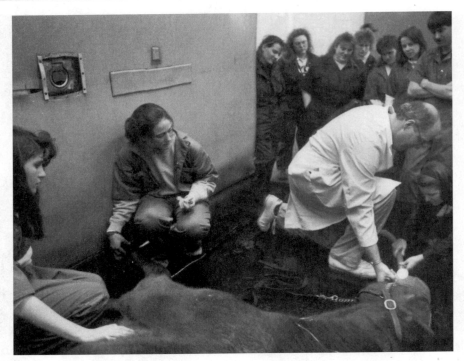

Figure 19–13 *Dr. John Hubbell intubates an equine surgical case.* Credit: The Ohio State College of Veterinary Medicine.

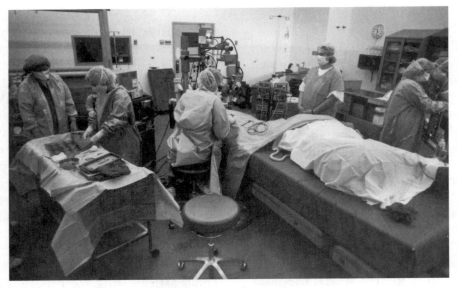

Figure 19–14 *Equine surgery.* Credit: The Ohio State College of Veterinary Medicine.

Figure 19–15 *Radiology is a veterinarian specialty.* Credit: The Ohio State College of Veterinary Medicine.

Figure 19–16 *Owners are happy when a pet is returned to health.* Credit: The Ohio State College of Veterinary Medicine.

from birds to fish to mammals. Understanding lab tests, pathology results, and parasitology testing is an important facet of working with animals.

Treating

Treating diseases and injuries is a large part of the veterinarian's role. Manipulating the animals and prescribing the correct medication or performing the correct surgical procedure are essential components of professional practice. Owners want their pet's condition to improve (Figure 19–16). Zookeepers expect the animal to be able to return to its habitat. Exotic animals may repre-

sent a large financial investment to the community.

Communication

Professional communication including documentation and speaking to owners, handlers, and care givers is essential. Instruction about the care of the animals is an important part of a veterinarian's role. Computer programs are used to track the care, including vaccinations, of domestic and zoo animals.

Regulations

Regulatory matters that influence the practice of animal medicine must be understood.

Biography

I grew up on my grandfather's dairy farm. My father helped on the farm but was really a veterinarian. He helped the neighboring farmers diagnose and treat their animals. Besides dogs and cats, he treated cows, sheep, hogs, and horses. They were hard to handle because they were large and not domesticated like pet dogs and cats. It was fun to help him birth lambs and calves, and rewarding to see how thankful the farmers were when their animals regained their health.

I wanted to join my father in the world of veterinary medicine and work the farm.

Earning a living by being a vet in the country is hard. Patients live far apart, so it is necessary to drive great distances to see them. Most farmers help birth their animals when the mother cannot manage alone. So it is only when a medical problem arises that I am needed. I have a little storefront office in town where I treat pets and small animals. I travel to the surrounding farms when I am called for assistance. I love animals and enjoy their owners. I have made some good friends of the owners and am happy that I chose this profession.

Career Search

To discover more about a career and the roles of members in veterinary medicine, contact the following organizations for online addresses, printed information, and videotapes.

American Veterinary Medical
  Association
1931 N. Meacham Road, Suite 100
Schaumberg, IL 60173–4360
Phone: 708–925–8070
Toll-free phone: 800–248–2862
Fax: 708–925–1329

American Animal Hospital
  Association
P.O. Box 150899
Denver, CO 80215
Phone: 303–986–2800
Toll-free phone: 800–252–2242
Fax: 303–986–1700

Range of Annual Incomes

Veterinarian	$30,000–$95,000
Animal health technician	$14,000–$20,000
Veterinary assistants	$10,000–$16,000

What's New

High-tech veterinary hospitals are being established by corporations. Such facilities have a twenty-four-hour intensive care unit. Veterinarians perform canine hip replacements (costing $3,500 each), CAT scans, MRIs, root canals, and orthodontia. Americans spend $10 billion a year in veterinary medicine, including DNA paternity tests on purebred dogs for accurate breeding papers and DNA gender tests on pet birds such as cockatoos, whose sex is impossible to determine by sight.

Mobile veterinary clinics bring health care to the animal. The clinic is in a twenty-six-foot-long vehicle equipped for examinations, diagnostic testing including X rays and ultrasounds, dental cleaning, anesthesia administration, surgery, and dispensing medications and prescription diets. These clinics are especially useful for owners who have more than one animal that needs to be seen and perhaps immunized.

Diagnostic ultrasound is used on animals. A portable ultrasound device can be brought to large animals in rural areas. It visualizes soft tissues and organs in the chest and abdomen. The animals may need to be sedated for the procedure.

School to Work

In addition to the general academic subjects and workplace skills contained in the "Job Skills" chapter, the following subjects and skills apply specifically to careers in veterinary medicine.

Academic Subject	Workplace Skills
Arts	—Graph the occurrence of diseases related to meats eaten by humans.
	—Make a chart relating animal reproduction to age, weight, and gestation period.
	—Graph the effectiveness of certain feeds based on the size of animals.
Health Education and Safety Precautions	—Use careful handling techniques with rabid animals.
	—Wear a lead apron and gloves when x-raying an animal.
	—Wear goggles and gloves when handling certain chemicals.

School to Work—continued

Academic Subject	Workplace Skills
	—Use care to avoid kicks and bites.
Body Mechanics	—Use the proper technique to lift an unconscious animal.
	—Use a hoist to lift a large animal.
Mathematics	
Addition, Subtraction, and Division	—Calculate medication dose by size and weight of the animal.
	—Obtain the correct lifting equipment for the weight of the animal.
	—Dispense the correct number of tablets and cubic centimeters of medication according to order.
Science	
Anatomy, Physiology, and Pathophysiology	—Identify body structures during the physical exam.
	—Observe objective symptoms of a dysfunctional organ.
	—Understand how each organ and system works.
	—Remove a diseased organ and reconstruct the system as necessary during surgery.
Biochemistry	—Obtain the appropriate specimen to determine illness.
	—Understand lab test results.
	—Administer nutritional supplements as needed.
	—Prescribe medications according to need.
Microbiology	—Identify the organisms causing an infection.
	—Prescribe antibiotics if needed.
	—Instruct the owner or the public on how to avoid illness from sick animals and their flesh or milk.
Nutrition and Food Science	—Give dietary supplements to satisfy the animal's need.
	—Recommend a diet for the age and size of the animal.
	—Be sure that chemicals prescribed for the animal will not harm a human if the animal's meat is to be eaten.
Pharmacology	—Understand the effects of medications on the animal.
	—Prescribe necessary medication.
	—Inform the owner if no medication is available to treat the animal's condition.
Social Sciences	
Ethics	—Perform complete care for the animal knowing that the animal cannot complain.
	—Charge only for the care that was given to the animal.
Human Relations	—Communicate patiently and gently with animal owners.
	—Treat owners with respect and care.

Review Questions

1. What are the goals of veterinary medicine?
2. What are the numbers of years of education after high school needed to become a veterinarian and animal health technician?
3. What are six areas of employment for veterinarians?
4. List six personal characteristics desirable for working with animals.
5. List three academic subjects and two ways each is applied in veterinary medicine.

VISION CAREERS

Objectives

After completing this chapter, you should be able to:

- ❏ Explain the goals of workers in various vision careers.
- ❏ Describe the careers in this field.
- ❏ Identify the required education and credentials for each career.
- ❏ Describe the skills performed in vision careers.
- ❏ Explain how academic subjects apply in the workplace.

Key Terms

Myopia

Hyperoptic

Refraction

INTRODUCTION

Vision is an important asset that is often taken for granted. People may come to realize they have a vision deficit when they cannot read street signs, a computer screen is noticeably blurred, or lights are intolerably haloed. Most vision deficits can be corrected with lenses (Figure 20–1). Some problems, such as glaucoma, can be improved with medication; some can be corrected with lasers, such as nearsightedness; and some require surgery, such as cataracts.

Over half of the people in the United States wear glasses or contact lenses (Figure 20–2). Thus, sooner or later, the majority of the population will need regular eye examinations and health education if not vision correction and surgery. During a person's midlife (his or her forties), eyes change shape, altering the vision. **Myopia** is the vision defect known

Figure 20–1 Prescription lenses can correct most vision problems.

Figure 20–2 Comfortably fitting eyeglasses are more likely to be worn.

as nearsightedness. In myopia, objects can be seen distinctly only when they are very close to the eyes. **Hyperoptic** is the vision defect known as farsightedness. Hyperoptic is a refraction error.

Refraction is the deflection or change in direction of a light ray. To present a clear image, light rays from each eye are meant to meet and focus directly on the retina. In nearsightedness, the rays meet before reaching the retina. In farsightedness, the rays pass through the retina and meet beyond the retina. Measures to correct errors in refraction include surgical and mechanical means.

Informing the public about the Eye Bank is an important responsibility of all professionals in health care (Figure 20–3). The Eye Bank harvests the eyes of a newly expired person so the corneas can be used in other individuals' eyes. This organ procurement program requires permission from the deceased's closest relative

Figure 20–3 *Teaching is an important part of vision centers.*

or holder of the power of attorney. This permission is required even if the deceased requested organ donation on his or her driver's license.

GOALS

The goals of workers in vision careers are to test vision, diagnose and correct abnormal vision, identify and treat diseases of the eye, and teach methods to maintain healthy eyes and good vision. Other goals include ensuring the proper fit of eyewear and using lasers and surgery to correct vision defects.

CAREER DESCRIPTIONS

Careers associated with vision vary according to the individual's education level, associated responsibilities, and work site. In most sites, the atmosphere is relaxed and happy. People receiving services are healthy and pleased to obtain prescription glasses or contacts that will improve their vision (Figure 20–4). In the ophthalmologist's office, some patients are in the process or at risk of losing their vision. These people may be any age but are usually middle aged and older. Their anxiety level is high, and they need special nurturing and counseling to prepare for blindness.

In an office setting, health maintenance organization, or clinic, there may be more than one ophthalmologist and several other certified workers. These may include an optician or ophthalmic laboratory technician. Both are able to

CAREER HIERARCHY

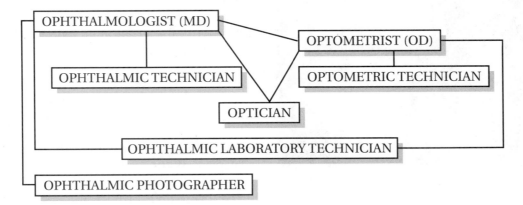

Figure 20–4 *Learning to insert a contact lens.*

put certain kinds of prescriptive lenses into eyeglass frames on site. In addition, opticians may do preliminary eye exams (Figure 20–5), fit frames, and instruct on using contact lenses.

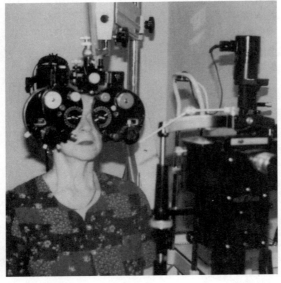

Figure 20–5 *A phoropter determines the exact correction needed in a lens.*

Career characteristics

Employment opportunities for ophthalmologists include independent practice, group practice, and employment by a managed care corporation. Others include becoming a consultant to government, school systems, or corporations. Some positions exist in research with pharmaceutical makers and major medical centers. Teaching in a medical school and mentoring medical students, interns, and residents are other opportunities.

Optometrists may be in independent practice, work for a national chain at a retail outlet (Figure 20–6), and consult to pharmaceutical or manufacturing companies. They may work in a community outreach program and bring their expertise to long-term care facilities, people who are homebound, and school systems.

Ophthalmic technicians work in ophthalmologists' offices and may assist the physician during surgery in the operating room. Optometric technicians work in optometrists' offices. Opticians work in a retail outlet or office setting where glasses are fitted and made. Opportunities for opticians also exist in commercial optical laboratories. Other jobs include working as a sales representative for optical products or pharmaceutical companies. Optical laboratory technicians may work for a national chain of retailers, a local laboratory, or a research facility.

Work hours depend on the career and responsibilities. Ophthalmologists usually work during the day Monday through Friday, with some Saturday and evening office hours. Typically, they perform surgery at the hospital in the mornings on one or two days a week, then have office hours. Ophthalmologists within a

Figure 20–6 *Optometrists or opticians can own a retail outlet that is a franchise of a national chain.*

community share on-call responsibilities for emergencies at the local hospital. Ophthalmic technicians work the same hours as the physician.

Optometrists, optometric technicians, and opticians work during the day, Monday through Friday, with some Saturday and evening hours. Optometrists or opticians who own a retail outlet tend to work longer hours than if they are on salary. Optometrists and opticians who are not owners may work at more than one retail outlet. Optometric assistants work when the retail outlet is open, which is seven days a week with day and evening hours. Ophthalmic laboratory technicians work when the retail outlet is open if the glasses are made on the premises while the customer waits and if no one else is present to make the glasses. Hours are more regular for lab technicians who work for a commercial optical laboratory without an on-site retail outlet.

Career advancements occur when an ophthalmologist becomes chief of the service or advances in a research or government position. For optometrists, career advancements may occur if they are accepted into a medical practice, made supervisor of a department, or purchase a franchise to fit and distribute eyewear. For ophthalmic technicians, becoming a supervisor in a large clinic setting would be an advancement. Ophthalmic laboratory technicians may advance to manager in a large office or become a supervisor in an optical laboratory. For others, continued education to become certified or licensed is necessary to advance beyond entry-level positions.

Desired personal characteristics include the ability to work successfully with people, teach to all levels of intelligence and all ages, and communicate with sincerity and caring. Attention to detail, manual dexterity, and compliance with safety practices are other important facets of a valued worker in this field. Patience, a friendly demeanor, a sense of humor, comprehension of business practices, and an understanding of the needs of persons of all ages are also needed.

Job satisfaction comes from helping individuals to attain better vision through surgery, mechanical devices, medication, and education. It also comes from helping to maintain eye health and from fitting eyewear for the best visual and cosmetic effects. Researchers find job satisfaction in developing products and instruments that will detect flaws and improve vision. For people in sales, satisfaction arises from informing professionals and eye care workers of new products and medications that improve vision.

Career roles

Ophthalmologists are medical doctors who have spent several years in an internship and residency program after graduating from medical school. They specialize in diagnosing and treating abnormalities and injuries (Figure 20–7). Treatment options include medication, laser treatments, and surgery. They examine eyes for vision deficits, identify specific problems, and prescribe eyeglasses or contact lenses. Laser therapy or surgery may be indicated to alleviate certain problems and improve vision. Some surgeries depend on the availability of corneal tissue. Physicians work in an office setting and in the surgery of a hospital or freestanding surgical center.

Many ophthalmologists work in group practices but maintain their own patients. These physicians share office

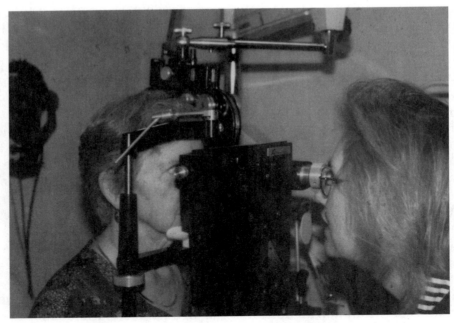

Figure 20–7   A slit lamp is used to view the back of the eye, the retina.

space and workers as well as expenses. They take turns being on call during evening and weekend hours and substitute for each other during vacations.

Optometrists are doctors of optometry who gain experience with patients while in optometry school. They examine eyes for visual acuity, depth, color perception, and ability to focus and move in coordination. They prescribe corrective lenses and contacts. In some states, they diagnose and treat certain eye diseases, such as conjunctivitis, glaucoma, or corneal infections. They prescribe medications to arrest those diseases and follow patients over time. They are not licensed to perform surgery or laser treatments. When patients have eye conditions that require surgical or Laser treatment, they are referred to the ophthalmologist. Some optometrists specialize in working with children, the elderly, or partially sighted people.

Ophthalmic technicians assist the ophthalmologist in the office, clinic, and hospital. They prepare a patient for examination, record the patient's history, and care for the office equipment. They have a broad range of duties, including performing ultrasound of the eye to measure tumors and conducting photographic imaging. Taking angiograms with dye of the front surface of the eye and the retina and assisting in surgery are other duties. Ophthalmic technicians may be cross-trained to become ophthalmic photographers (Figure 20–8). They are involved in patient education. They focus on working with the patients.

Optometric technicians work for optometrists in the office or retail store.

Figure 20–8 *The visual field analyzer is used to test for glaucoma and other defects in the field of vision.*

They are trained to match the face of the client with frames of the correct shape and color (Figure 20–9). They make glasses with the correct prescriptive lenses, cutting the appropriate lens to fit the specific frame (Figure 20–10). They focus on working with glasses and contacts.

Ophthalmic photographers prepare patients for photographing the eye after dye is administered to visualize blood vessels in the eye or the retina. Most workers in this position have graduated from an art

Figure 20–9 *Shape of the face is one factor in frame selection.*

Ophthalmic laboratory technicians make prescription lenses for eyeglasses. They cut, grind, polish edges (Figure 20–11), and finish lenses according to the specifications provided by ophthalmologists or optometrists. They review commercially manufactured lenses to see that they are curved accurately to focus light on the retina of the eye. Some ophthalmic laboratories also make lenses for telescopes and binoculars. In retail or office settings, ophthalmic laboratory technicians can dispense frames and adjust the finished eyeglasses. Ophthalmic laboratory technicians usually work a forty-hour week, but hours vary according to the employment setting. Retail shops often have day, evening, and weekend hours. In an ophthalmologist's or optometrist's office, daytime hours with some evening and Saturday hours are worked.

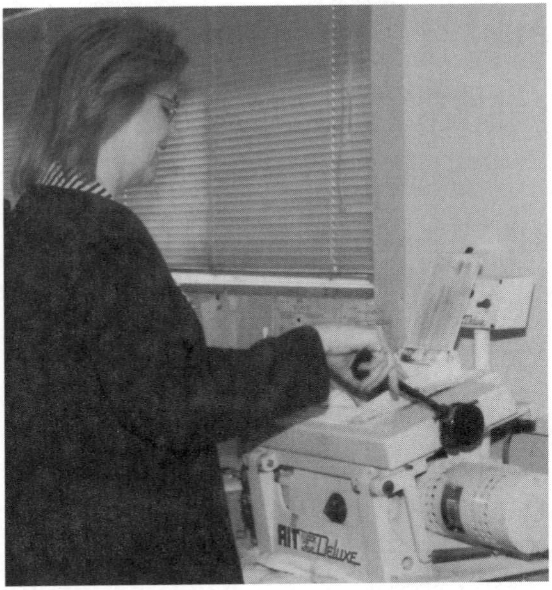

school, have photographic experience, or are ophthalmic technicians who have been cross-trained in this technique.

Figure 20–10 *The lens is cut to fit the frame.*

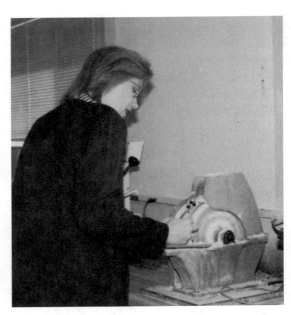

Figure 20–11 *The edger is used to smooth the rim of the lens.*

Opticians are trained to measure faces to fit eyeglass frames. They read prescriptions from the ophthalmologist or optometrist or from a lens and produce new lenses with the exact visual correction. They are licensed by the state to perform these tasks and so can own a retail outlet to dispense eyeglasses and contact lenses.

JOB AVAILABILITY

The availability for jobs for all workers in vision careers is good. Positions for ophthalmologists and opticians will grow at an average rate. Newer techniques will allow these professionals to see more patients in a day. Retail jobs for opticians will grow at a faster-than-average rate because of the increasing age of the population and fashion changes in eyeglasses. The cross-training of ophthalmic technicians as ophthalmic photographers will increase the demand for ophthalmic technicians. Optometric technician and ophthalmic lab technician jobs will be available as current workers leave the workforce or transfer to other occupations.

SKILLS

Certain skills are required to diagnose and treat visual problems and to make and fit corrective eyewear accurately. These skills are learned in school and practice is supervised until the worker can perform them competently.

Technical skills

Good technical skills are needed to perform surgery, manipulate eyeglasses, cut lenses to fit frames, and make eyeglass and contact lenses. Measurements need

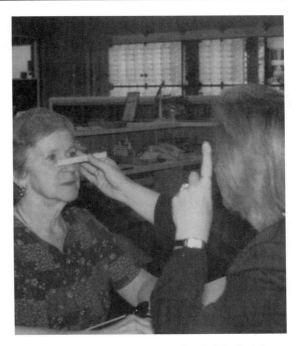

Figure 20–12 *Measuring the field of vision.*

to be taken of the face and field of vision to calculate corrective lenses (Figure 20–12). Using a lensometer to correctly interpret the lens prescription in a pair of eyeglasses is important to make another pair with the same specifications. Using machines to grind a lens to a specific curvature, smooth rough edges, and polish the finished lens to a smooth, bright finish is critical for accuracy and comfort.

Observation

Observational skills are an important part of vision careers. The ability to examine eyes with accuracy, detect flaws, and refer the patient to the appropriate professional is a significant asset. Often, customers need advice on the type and color of eyeglass frame that would look best on their faces.

EDUCATION AND CREDENTIALS

CAREER	YEARS OF EDUCATION AFTER HIGH SCHOOL	DEGREE OR DIPLOMA	TESTED BY; LICENSED BY
Ophthalmologist (M.D.)	4 years of college, 4 years of medical school, 1 year of internship, 3 years of residency, and 1–3 years of fellowship to specialize (optional)	M.D.	National board exams; State; continuing education required to maintain license
Optometrists (O.D.)	2–4 years of college, 4 years at college of optometry, and 1–2 years residency (optional)	O.D., M.S.	National board exams; State; continuing education required to maintain license
Opticians	2–4 years of on-the-job training, or 1–2 years of HOE program, or 2 year associate degree	A.A.S.D.	License or certification from A.B.O. required in some states
Ophthalmic technician (COT)	2 years or on-the-job training	A.A.S.D.	National exam by JCAHPO
Optometric technician	on-the-job training	—	—
Optometric assistant	on-the-job training	—	—
Ophthalmic laboratory technician	2–3 years of on-the-job training or 1 year of HOE certificate program	—	—
Ophthalmic photographer	2–4 years in art school or college or on-the-job training	B.A. or A.A.S.D.	Certification is optional

Key to abbreviations:

ABO—American Board of Opticianry
A.A.S.D.—Associate of Applied Science Degree
B.A.—Bachelor of Arts Degree
C.O.T.—Certified Ophthalmic Technician
HOE—Health Occupation Education

JCAHPO—Joint Commission on Allied Health Personnel in Ophthalmology
M.D.—Medical Doctor
M.S.—Master's Degree in Science
O.D.—Doctor of Optometry

Dexterity

Manual dexterity is critical when performing surgery. Surgically repairing an eye or removing and replacing a lens clouded by a cataract requires delicate and exacting technique. Dexterity is also needed in using instruments to examine eye health and to test patients' visual acuity. Other areas where dexterity is needed are in preparing eyeglasses (Figure 20–13), handling contact lenses, and taking the ophthalmic photographs.

Communication

Communication skills are important when telling patients the diagnosis and

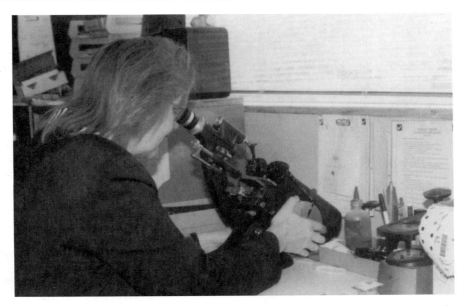

Figure 20–13 *A lensometer is used to determine a lens prescription and to check a lens to see that the prescription is accurate before cutting it to fit a frame.*

prognosis of certain eye diseases. Consumers in a retail facility will return if they are treated kindly and with genuine concern. Positive communication in the workplace makes the environment productive. Using tact when relating information about a client's appearance with glasses is essential (Figure 20–14).

Management

Management skills are essential to run a business. Ophthalmologists and optometrists may have their own offices and need to hire personnel and purchase supplies. Opticians may own a franchise of a retail outlet chain. This would entail renting space, purchasing machines and supplies, hiring personnel, paying overhead costs, and serving clients so they want to return.

Figure 20–14 *People of all ages wear glasses.*

Biography

As a child, I had severely crossed eyes. This made me see double and gave me severe headaches. My mother took me to the eye doctor many times to correct this problem. I had to wear glasses and a patch over my "good eye" so my other eye would get stronger. I had to do eye exercises to strengthen the muscles of my weak eye so that eventually my eyes would work together. If I did not do the exercises or if the exercises did not strengthen the muscles, the doctor would have to operate to shorten the muscle in my weak eye. I performed the exercises everyday, and my weak eye muscles became stronger, so I did not need the surgery. Through this experience, I learned how important it is to recognize a vision problem, know what can be done about it, gain the cooperation of the affected person, and correct the problem.

I have always liked people and had a yen to help them. Since I suffered severe headaches due to a vision problem, I wanted to prevent this from happening to others. Also, I wanted to own my own business, be my own boss, and make enough money to live comfortably. I realized that I liked being around healthy people and fellow workers who have a positive attitude. I also recognized that going to medical school to become an ophthalmologist was too long and difficult a course for me. So I became an optician. I bought a franchise from a national company, set up my retail store, and realized my dream to help people see better.

Career Search

To discover more about a career and the roles of members in the vision field, contact the following organizations for online addresses, printed information, and videotapes.

American Academy of Ophthalmology
655 Beach Street
San Francisco, CA 94109
Phone: 415–561–8500
Fax: 415–561–8533

American Optometric Association
243 N. Lindberg Boulevard
St. Louis, MO 63141
Phone: 314–991–4100
Fax: 314–991–4101

Opticians Association of America
10341 Democracy Lane
Fairfax, VA 22030
Phone: 703–691–8355
Fax: 703–691–3929

Ophthalmic Photographers' Society
213 Lorene Street, Suite 141
Nixa, MO 65714–9230
Phone: 417–725–0181
Toll-free phone: 800–403–1677
Fax: 417–725–0181

National Association of Optometrists
and Opticians
18903 S. Miles Road
Cleveland, OH 44128
Phone: 216–475–8962
Fax: 216–475–8862

Range of Annual Incomes

Ophthalmologist	$90,000–$190,000
Optometrist	$ 45,000–$85,000
Optician	$ 20,000–$45,000*
Ophthalmic technician	$ 20,000–$35,000
Optometric technician	$ 16,000–$25,000
Ophthalmic laboratory technician	$ 20,000–$40,000*
Ophthalmic photographer	$ 25,000–$36,000

*Income is higher if the individual owns the franchise or laboratory.

What's New

Combination facilities that include retail sales and a laboratory are the newest development in eyewear delivery systems. A client can bring in a prescription, select frames, and wait while the glasses are made. In a facility that has an optometrist, the client can obtain a vision test in the same visit.

School to Work

In addition to the general academic subjects and workplace skills contained in the "Job Skills" chapter, the following subjects and skills apply specifically to careers in vision.

Academic Subject	Workplace Skills
Arts	—Draw the angle of light rays on, before, or beyond the retina.
	—Learn the techniques of an eye examination.
	—Perform the steps of a vision test.
	—Select frames that are appropriate for a client.
	—Adjust glasses to fit the client.
	—Set the lens grinder for the prescribed curvature.
	—Adjust the machine to refine lens edges.
	—Fit lens into a polishing machine to finish them.
	—Set lens into the eyeglass frame.
	—Examine lens in a lensometer to be sure the curvature is accurate.
	—Dip lens into a dye if they are to be tinted or coated.
	—Repair frames and replace lenses.
	—Photograph the eye surface to check blood vessels in the iris.

School to Work—continued

Academic Subject	Workplace Skills
Arts (cont'd)	—Photograph the retina to evaluate eye problems. —Evaluate internal eye structures by ultrasound. —Reduce nearsightedness with radial keratotomy.
Business Time Management	—Schedule appointments at the customer's convenience. —Deliver the eyeglasses or contacts as soon as possible. —Give the client full attention even if someone else is waiting.
Health Education and Safety Safety	—Avoid poking the client in the eye when fitting frames. —Instruct the client in the appropriate methods of inserting contact lenses. —Teach methods of cleaning contact lenses for maximum wear. —Instruct in how to avoid eye infection. —Clean sample frames between clients. —Wear a clear plastic safety mask to cut and polish lenses. —Fit and instruct in the care of an artificial eye.
Mathematics Accounting Addition and Subtraction Division	—Measure intraoccular pressure. —Track supplies and order appropriately. —Measure the visual field in bifocals and trifocals for best sight. —Mark and measure basic frames. —Measure the distance between the eye and the lens. —Keep careful track of insurance payments. —Collect from clients what insurance does not cover. —Grind lens according to calculations. —Place bifocals and trifocals to best accommodate visual fields. —Translate a prescription into lenses. —Calculate for prisms and spheres to ensure accurate bending of light rays in each lens. —Measure eyes for the proper fitting of contact lenses.
Science Anatomy and Physiology	—Understand the parts and function of the eye. —Learn the types of astigmatic refraction errors. —Observe the optics of the cylinder in the lens that corrects the astigmatism. —Examine the retina to identify disease processes. —Learn the diseases that most commonly affect the eye. —Know the changes that the eye undergoes in older clients.

Academic Subject	Workplace Skills
Anatomy and Physiology (cont'd)	—Understand the treatments used to maintain and restore vision. —Inform clients of lens donation opportunities after death. —Explain the Eye Bank and its function. —Teach clients about cataract surgery.
Biochemistry	—Understand how chemical compounds influence vision. —Identify diseases in the eye.
Microbiology	—Identify the most common cause of eye infection. —Learn the treatment of eye infections. —Teach proper eye care to avoid infection.
Pharmacology	—Understand that certain medications cause a loss of vision. —Learn the effects of antioxidants on the eyes.

Review Questions

1. What are the goals of workers in vision careers?
2. What is the career whose members can buy a franchise for a retail outlet?
3. What are the minimum years of education after high school needed to become an ophthalmologist, optometrist, and optician?
4. What are two skills desirable in workers in visual careers?
5. List three academic subjects and two ways each is applied in vision workplaces.

BODY SYSTEMS

CARDIOVASCULAR

The cardiovascular system consists of the heart and blood vessels. Arteries come off the heart and carry oxygenated blood through the arterioles to the capillaries, where oxygen is delivered to the cells and carbon dioxide removed. The blood then passes through the venules and into veins that return the blood to the heart. The pulmonary artery comes off the heart and carries blood to the lungs; it is the only artery that carries nonoxygenated (venous) blood.

The heart is a pump that forces blood through blood vessels throughout the body. An electrical stimulus initiated within the heart muscle triggers it to contract, then relax. This stimulus keeps heartbeats strong and effective, and maintains regular rhythm.

The heart is a four-chambered, hollow muscular organ with valves that prevent the backflow of blood. It is important that the heart muscle gets enough oxygen to pump effectively and remain disease-free. When circulation to the heart muscle becomes obstructed from arteriosclerosis or a blood clot, a heart attack follows. When other conditions cause the heart to work harder than usual, it tires and begins to fail as a pump.

Blood flows through the right side of the heart, to the lungs, to the left side of the heart, and out to the body. It takes about one minute for a blood cell to make the complete trip through the body—from the heart, through the lungs, to the heart, through the body to the farthest cell, and back to the heart. The adult body has a total of about sixty thousand miles of blood vessels.

Blood flows through the cardiopulmonary system as follows (Figure A–1): through the vena cava to the right atrium; through the tricuspid valve to the right ventricle; through the pulmonary valve to the pulmonary artery, to the lungs, to the pulmonary vein, then to the left atrium; through the tricuspid or mitral valve to the left ventricle; through the aortic valve to the aorta, and then out to the body.

The coronary arteries carry blood from the aorta to the heart muscle. These coronary arteries bring a large concentration of oxygen to the heart muscle so that the heart will continue to pump effectively. Diagnostic tests to determine partially or totally clogged vessels and

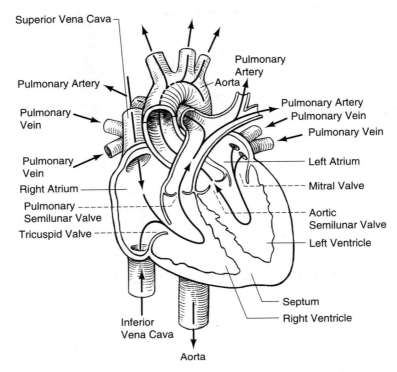

Figure A–1   *Internal heart structures and major vessels.*

abnormal heart rhythms can prevent severe symptoms and life-threatening illnesses.

Cardiac and vascular problems are increasing in the United States. Several factors are blamed. Among these factors are high-fat diets, being overweight, a lack of sensible exercise, smoking, gender, and heredity. Some of these factors can be changed with education and determination.

GASTROINTESTINAL

The gastrointestinal system is made up of the alimentary canal, which consists of the main and accessory organs of digestion. The function of this system (Figure A–2) is to take in food, prepare it for digestion, break it down into elements that can be used by the body, absorb those elements, reabsorb liquid, and expel solid waste. This complex process involves many steps and several organs.

Food passes through the alimentary canal as follows: from the mouth through the pharynx and esophagus and into the stomach; then through the small intestine, consisting of the duodenum, jejunum, and ileum; and the large intestine, consisting of cecum, ascending colon, transverse colon, descending colon, sigmoid colon, and rectum; then out the anus.

The accessory organs of digestion are attached to the main organs, but food does not actually pass into them. They contribute to the process by making di-

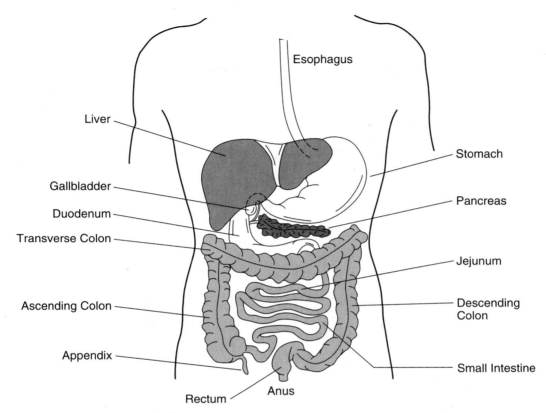

Figure A–2 *The digestive system.*

gestive juices. These organs are the salivary glands (three pairs—submaxillary, sublingual, parotid), gallbladder, pancreas, and liver.

MUSCLES (SKELETAL)
Most skeletal muscles are attached to two bones with a joint between them (Figure A–3). When contracted, they create either movement or tension. Tendons are strong, dense, fibrous, and cordlike tissues that anchor muscles to bones. When muscles are stimulated by nerves to contract, they pull one bone toward the other over the site of a movable joint. This movement is called flexion. Extension is

the movement that straightens out the bones at the joint.

Muscles need food and oxygen to work. They will atrophy if not used.

Posture depends on muscle tone. A body in natural alignment with good muscle tone will counteract the pull of gravity. Good posture allows organs such as the lungs and heart to function at full capacity.

NERVOUS
The nervous system consists of the brain (Figure A–4), spinal cord, and nerves. The neuron is the basic cell that carries

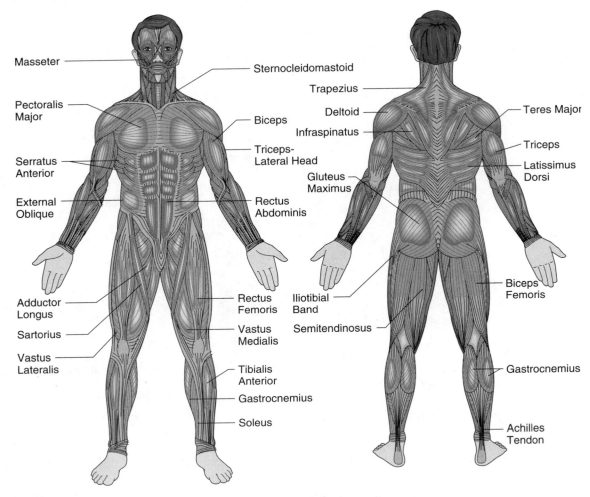

Figure A–3 *Posterior and anterior views of the skeletal muscles.*

messages throughout the body from the brain, down the spinal cord, to the periphery, and back again. There are three types of neurons, each of which receives (via dendrite fibers) and transfers (via axon fibers) messages: motor, sensory, and interdendrites. Motor neurons carry impulses from the brain and spinal cord toward the destination. Sensory neurons carry impulses from the receptor fibers to

the brain and spinal cord. Interdendrites carry impulses from one neuron to another.

The nervous system is divided into three major parts: the central nervous system, the peripheral nervous system, and the autonomic nervous system. The central nervous system is made up of the brain and spinal cord. The peripheral nervous system consists of all the nerves

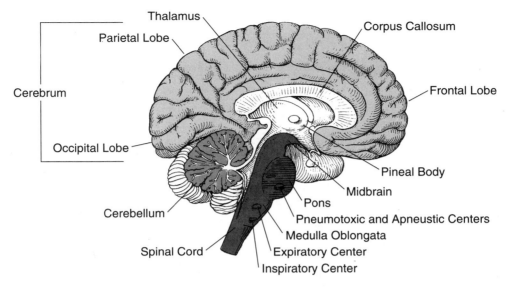

Figure A–4 *Cross section of the brain.*

from the brain and spinal cord to the body's surface. The autonomic nervous system contains all the nerves that carry messages to the vital organs of the body, such as heart, lungs, glands, eyes, and bladder.

The brain is an essential organ of the body that contains centers vital to the process of life. The brain enables awareness and conscious and automatic movements. It controls and monitors all bodily functions, including thinking, learning, memory, and speaking. If the brain does not function properly, life can be seriously disrupted. Unpleasant to life-threatening symptoms may develop. Double vision and seizures are symptoms that may indicate a neurological problem. Loss of consciousness or death can result from brain injury. The cause of problems resulting from brain disorders needs to be found and corrected, if possible. Medications may control some problems, while other conditions may require surgery.

RESPIRATORY

The respiratory system is made up of passages and parts that draw air into the body, exchange oxygen for carbon dioxide, then blow the air out of the body. When air is drawn into the body, the process is called inhale. When air is blown out of the body, the process is called exhale. One inhale and one exhale make one breath, one respiration.

The respiratory tree looks like grapes on a stem. Air flows through the air passageways as follows (Figure A–5): into the nose-pharynx, consisting of the nasopharynx, oral pharynx, and laryngeal pharynx; past the epiglottis; then

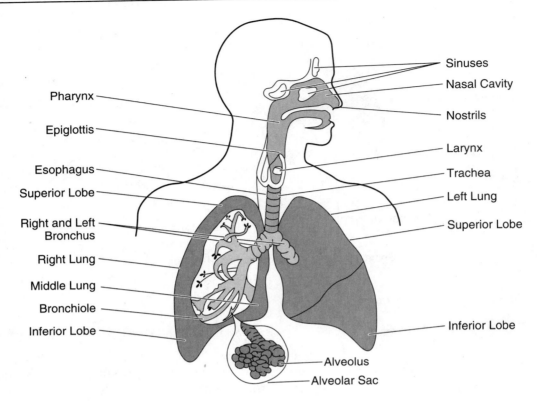

Figure A–5   *The respiratory system.*

through the larynx, trachea, bronchi, bronchioles, and alveoli.

The actual gas exchange of oxygen and carbon dioxide takes place through thin membranes in the alveoli. The bronchioles and alveoli are held together by spongy, elastic connective tissue. This combination of bronchioles, alveoli, and connective tissue makes up a lung. When air is drawn in through the mouth, it enters the oral pharynx and continues on the path to the alveoli in the lung.

The passage of air into the alveoli and the exchange of gases with the bloodstream are essential to life. If this exchange cannot take place because of obstruction or disease, the person will die. If the process of breathing stops but the parts are capable of taking in air and exchanging it with the bloodstream, artificial respiration can maintain life, provided other parts of the body continue to function. Artificial respiration can be done manually through mouth-to-mouth breathing or mechanically by using a ventilator.

SKELETAL

The skeletal system is made up of long, short, flat, irregular, and sesamoid-shaped bones that consist of minerals, special cells, blood vessels, and nerves (Figure A–6). Bones provide support for soft tissues and protection for organs.

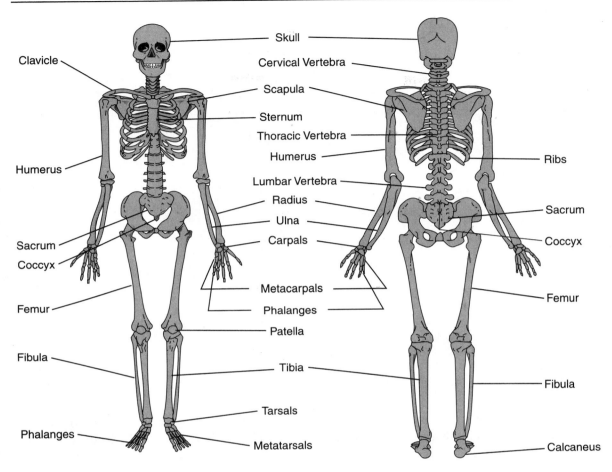

Figure A–6 *The skeleton.*

They store calcium, make blood cells (in marrow), and enable body movements by providing structure for muscles. Calcium, phosphorus, and vitamin D are important to bone health and the prevention of disease and fractures.

URINARY

The urinary system cleanses the blood of waste elements and excessive fluid. It consists of the kidneys, ureters, urinary bladder, and urethra (Figure A–7). The kidneys are complex structures consisting of nephrons that filter blood plasma from the renal artery as it passes by the nephrons and tiny tubules that select what is to be excreted and what is to be reabsorbed into the blood (Figure A–8). Elements and fluid not reabsorbed in the tubules and elements secreted directly from the blood into the tubules result in the formation of urine. After being formed in the kidney, urine drains down the ureter into the bladder. It is held there by a sphincter muscle at the urethra,

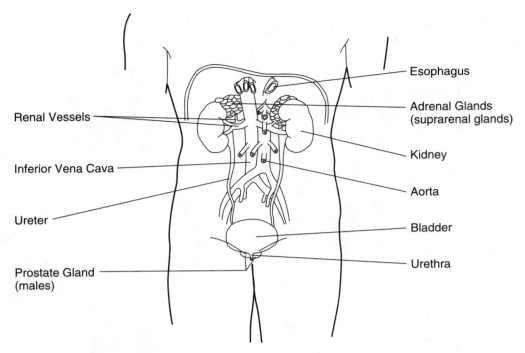

Renal Vessels

Inferior Vena Cava

Ureter

Prostate Gland
(males)

Esophagus

Adrenal Glands
(suprarenal glands)

Kidney

Aorta

Bladder

Urethra

Figure A–7   *The urinary system.*

which remains closed until voiding or urination occurs. The urinary tract is a sterile environment. The introduction of bacteria can cause an infection.

VISION

The eye is a sensory organ that allows sight (Figure A-9). It is a hollow circular structure filled with liquid. Light enters through the center hole (pupil), passes through the jellylike liquid (vitreous humor) en route to the inner lining (retina). There, it is received by the optic nerve and transmitted to the brain. The liquid bends light rays so that they focus on the retina. In front of the pupil is the conjunctiva (a clear protective membrane) and the cornea (a thick, curved covering). Behind the pupil is the lens, a clear, slightly curved structure that changes shape by becoming thicker or thinner to bring images into focus. The iris is the doughnut-shaped, colored muscle of the eye. In bright light, some fibers in this muscle contract so the pupil constricts, letting in fewer light rays. In darkness, other fibers in this muscle contract to enlarge the pupil to let in more light rays. The sclera is the white of the eye. It is part of the protective coat that surrounds the eye. The conjunctiva is the mucous membrane that covers the front of the eye and lines the lids. Muscles of the eye allow meaningful movement. Tear ducts continually release a dilute salt solution onto the front of the eyeball for lubrication.

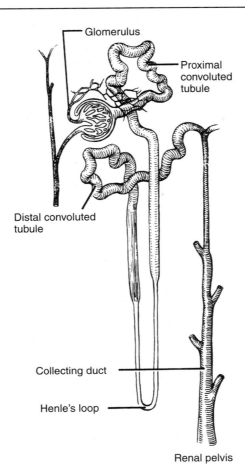

Glomerulus

Proximal
convoluted
tubule

Distal convoluted
tubule

Collecting duct

Henle's loop

Renal pelvis

Figure A–8   *Magnified view of nephron and tubule.*

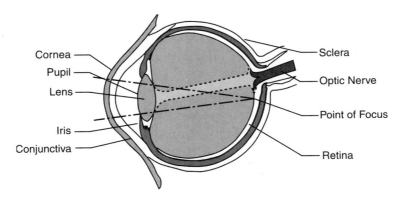

Cornea

Pupil

Lens

Iris

Conjunctiva

Sclera

Optic Nerve

Point of Focus

Retina

Figure A–9   *Cross section of the eye.*

Appendix B

OTHER CAREERS ASSOCIATED WITH HEALTH CARE

Activity therapists work with patients to provide opportunities to increase socialization, dexterity, attention span, expression, and self-esteem through projects such as arts and crafts, creative play, games, excursions, and social interaction.

Biochemists study the function of human cells and the effects of chemicals on cell nutrition, reproduction, and growth.

Bioengineers design, develop material for, and construct artificial parts (joints), and organs (heart), and electronic devices to improve the quality of patients' lives.

Building engineers maintain and repair the heavy machinery that heats, cools, and powers the facility.

Chiropractors manipulate the spinal column and other parts of the body to relieve pain and discomfort.

Clinical engineers repair machines used to monitor patients or diagnose illnesses.

Computer programmers develop systems to organize, store, retrieve, and transfer health care data.

Dance therapists use movement and dance to diagnose and treat mental illness, physical disability, brain damage, or developmental handicaps.

Ecologists study the effects of the environment on health and relate those factors to human life.

Electrical Engineers design machines to monitor patients.

Epidemiologists study the factors that might affect health and cause disease in a given population.

Forensic medicine is the study of pathology as it relates to the human body and the scene of death that may be associated with criminal behavior.

Geneticists study the effect of genes in the transmission of family traits and hereditary diseases.

Health economists act as advisors to administrators of health care agencies and develop management strategies and financial operating plans.

Health agency administrators plan, direct, and evaluate services offered, forecast future needs, and devise methods to provide and finance those new services.

Medical photographers photograph and videotape surgical procedures, set up cameras and video screens for operative procedures using scopes and microscopes, photograph patients before and after reconstructive surgery, and prepare slides for lectures.

Medical research scientists work in laboratories to test the effects of environmental elements, chemicals, drugs, artificial parts, and diagnostic instruments on living systems to improve the quality of human life.

Patient representatives communicate with patients, interpret information, act as advocates in problem situations, and help to change the health care system to be more sensitive to patients' needs and perceptions.

Pharmacologists research the effects of chemicals on cells, tissues, and diseases, and develop and refine medications for the treatment of illnesses.

Risk managers identify procedures, practices, and equipment that pose a hazard to staff or patients and make recommendations for change.

ABBREVIATIONS

Appendix

C

ā before
A/R pulse: apical/radial heart rate
AAA: aortic artery aneurysm
abd: abdominal
ABG: arterial blood gases
ac: before meals
ad lib: as much as desired
ADL: activities of daily living
AF: atrial fibrillation
AFB: acid-fast bacillus
AIDS: acquired immune deficiency syndrome
A.M.: morning; after 12 midnight
amb: ambulate; walk
amt: amount
ASAP or asap: as soon as possible
ASHD: arteriosclerosis heart disease
bid: twice a day
bm or BM: bowel movement
BP: blood pressure
BR: bed rest or bathroom
BRP: bathroom privileges
bsc: bedside commode
c/o: complains of
c̄: with
C: centigrade
Ca: cancer
ca: calcium
CABG: coronary artery bypass graft
CAD: coronary artery disease

CAT: computerized axial tomography
cath: catheterization
CBC, cbc: complete blood count
cc: cubic centimeter
CCU: cardiac care unit, coronary care unit
CHF: congestive heart failure
CO: coronary occlusion
COLD: chronic obstructive lung disease
cont.: continue
COPD: chronic obstructive pulmonary disease
CPR: cardiopulmonary resuscitation
CSR: central supply/service room
CT: computerized tomography
CV, cv: cardiovascular
CVA: cerebral vascular accident
cxr: chest X ray
d/c, dc: discontinue
DEA: U.S. Drug Enforcement Administration
diff: differential blood cell count
D.O.: Doctor of Osteopathy
DOA: dead on arrival
DRG: diagnostic related group
DSA: digital subtraction angiography
dx: diagnosis
ECG: echocardiograph
EEG: electroencephalograph
EKG: electrocardiograph

ENT: ear, nose, and throat
ER: emergency room
F: Fahrenheit
FBS: fasting blood sugar
FDA: U.S. Food and Drug Administration
FF: force fluids
Fx, fx: fracture
GI: gastrointestinal
gm: gram
gr: grain
gtt: drop
GU: genitourinary
Gyn: gynecology
h or hr.: hour
H_2O: water
HCVD: hypertensive cardiovascular disease
HDL: healthy type of cholesterol
Hg or Hgb: hemoglobin
HIV: human immunodeficiency virus
HS or hs: hour of sleep
ht: height
I&O: intake and output
ICD-9-CM: system to classify diagnoses
ICU: intensive care unit
IPPB: intermittent positive pressure breathing
IV: intravenous
IVP: intravenous pyelogram
JCAHO: Joint Commission on Accreditation of Healthcare Organizations
KUB: kidney, ureter, and bladder Xray
L: liter or left
L&D: labor and delivery
lb: pound
LDL: unhealthy type of cholesterol
LL: left lung
LLL: left lower lobe (lung)
LLQ: left lower quadrant (abdomen)
LMP: last menstrual period

LUL: left upper lobe (lung)
LUQ.: left upper quadrant (abdomen)
MDI: metered dose inhaler
med: medication, medical
meds: medications
MI: myocardial infarction
min: minute
ml: milliliter
MRA: magnetic resonance angiography
MRI: magnetic resonance imager
NA: not applicable
neg: negative
NPO: nothing by mouth (*nil per os*)
NTG: nitroglycerine
OB: obstetrics
oob: out of bed
OPD: outpatient department
OR: operating room
OT: occupational therapy
oz: ounce
p̄: after
P&R: pulse and respiration
PAC: premature atrial contraction
PAT: preadmission testing
pc: after meals
PCA: patient-controlled analgesia; self-administered pain R_x
Peds: pediatrics
PET: positron emission tomography
PFT: pulmonary function test
P.M.: evening; after 12 noon
PO, po: by mouth (*per os*)
post: after
postop: after surgery
pre: before
preop: before surgery
PRN/prn: when necessary
Psyc: refers to mental health
PT: physical therapy
PTCA: percutaneous coronary angioplasty
PVC: premature ventricular contraction

q: every
q4h: every four hours
QA: quality assurance
qd: every day
qh: every hour
qid: four times a day
qod: every other day
qs: quantity sufficient
R/O: rule out
R: rectal or right
RBC, rbc: red blood cells
RDA: recommended daily allowance
rehab: refers to returning to health
RL: right lung
RLL: right lower lobe (lung)
RLQ: right lower quadrant (abdomen)
RML: right middle lobe (lung)
ROM: range of motion
RR: recovery room
rt: right
RUL: right upper lobe (lung)
RUQ: right upper quadrant (abdomen)
R_x: prescription
s̄: without
SOB: shortness of breath
spec: specimen
SPECT: single photon emission computed tomography

stat: immediately
subq: subcutaneous
supp: suppository
Sx: symptoms
T: tuberculosis
Tbsp: tablespoon
TD filing: system of organizing medical records
TIA: transischemic attack
tid: three times a day
TLC: tender loving care
TPN: total parenteral nutrition
TPR: temperature, pulse, respiration
tsp: teaspoon
tx: treatment
UHDDS: listing of definitions of diseases and surgeries
UR: utilization review
URI: upper respiratory infection
US: unit secretary
VF: ventricular fibrillation
vo: verbal order
VS: vital signs
VTS: volunteer transport
WBC, wbc: white blood cells, white blood count
wc, w/c: wheelchair
wt: weight

Glossary

abduction: moving limb away from the body

abscess: sac filled with pus from infection

absorption: taking in nutritional elements through membranes

abstracting: reviewing charts for data to write reports

accurate: without error

active: exercise that patients do themselves

activities of daily living: usual actions to care for self (bathing, eating)

acute: severe, sharp

adaptable: able to change

addictive: substance or behavior that becomes habitual

adduction: moving a limb toward the body

ad lib: as much as desired

admission: entrance into the hospital as a patient

admitting physician: doctor responsible for a hospitalized patient's care

aerator: machine used to remove gas

aerosol treatment: breathing tiny particles of liquid in air

agility: ability to move quickly and easily

agitated: disturbed; moving with rapid, irregular motion

agraphia: inability to write

AIDS: Acquired immune deficiency syndrome; disease caused by HIV that leaves victims defenseless against malignant diseases and certain organisms

alimentary canal: gastrointestinal tract

allergist: physician specializing in adverse reactions

allergy: adverse reaction

alphabetical order: arrangement according to letters

alveoli: sacs in lungs where gases are exchanged

ambulate/amb: move about, walk

amplification: sound magnification

amputation: removal of a limb

analgesic: medication that relieves pain

aneurysm: weakening in blood vessel wall causing abnormal dilatation

angiography: pictures blood vessels

angioplasty: repair of a blood vessel

anoxia: lack of oxygen to the brain

antibiotic: medication that fights infection by killing bacteria

antigen: substance foreign to the body causing antibodies to form

antiseptic: liquid that kills bacteria

anus: sphincter at the end of the gastrointestinal tract

anxiety: feeling of apprehension or uneasiness from an unknown cause, especially related to the future

aphasia: without language; inability to communicate through speech or writing, or, possibly, to interpret sounds

apnea: lack of breathing

appendicitis: inflammation of appendix, the hollow tube on the cecum

apraxia: inability to position, sequence, and move speech muscles

aquatic: refers to marine life

arterial blood gases: test for levels of oxygen and carbon dioxide in arterial blood

arteriogram: X ray of arteries after injection of radiopaque dye

arteriosclerosis: hardening of the arteries; a thickening of arterial walls causing a narrowing of the lumen

arthritis: joint inflammation causing pain and swelling and changes in structure

articulate: pronounce

articulation: clear enunciation

artificial larynx: prosthesis that replaces the voice box to assist with communication

artificial respiration: manually breathing for a patient

asap: as soon as possible

ascending: beginning of large intestine

assess: to observe all the information about something

asthma: sudden, periodic attack of constriction of the bronchi causing dyspnea and wheezing

atrial fibrillation: quivering of the upper heart chambers

attendance: being present

attentive: observant

attitude: behavior that reflects mental view

audiogram: a graphic representation of the ability to hear

audiology: a field of evaluating and treating hearing impairment

audiometric testing: evaluating hearing levels

auditory comprehension: ability to interpret the spoken word

ausculation: listening to body sounds

autism: unable to communicate with the real world

autoclave: machine that sterilizes by steam under pressure

automatic stocking: routine delivery of supplies to present par levels

avian: refers to birds

bacteria: microorganisms

benign: self-contained tumor; does not spread

bile: liquid that helps digest fat

billing procedures: systems for informing patients of the amount due for care

biometrics: department that measures functions necessary to life

biopsy: piece of tissue surgically removed for study

bitewings: X rays of back teeth

bladder: hollow organ that holds fluid

blood: fluid that circulates in vessels; made up of cells, elements, and plasma

blood bank: lab section that supplies autologous or compatible transfusions

blood gases: test for level of oxygen and carbon dioxide in the arterial blood

blood pressure: amount of force exerted against vessel walls

blood transfusion: infusion of cells and plasma into circulation

BP: blood pressure

BR: bedrest or bathroom

brace: device that holds a joint in place

brackets: apparatus on or around a tooth; used in the straightening process

breath sounds: noise made when passing air in and out of the respiratory tree

bridge: a dental plate fastened at each end to a tooth

bronchi: tube that connects trachea with lungs

bronchial: refers to bronchi

bronchitis: inflammation of the tube between trachea and lungs

bronchopulmonary treatment: inhalation of medicated aerosol

bronchoscopy: procedure for looking into the bronchi

BRP: bathroom privileges

buccal: refers to mouth

calculus: stone; occurs in kidney and gallbladder

calorie: a unit of heat

cane: stick used to carry some of patient's weight when walking

canine: refers to dogs

caprine: refers to goats

carbohydrate: a compound composed of carbon, hydrogen, and oxygen; found in sugars and starches

carcinoma: cancer; a malignant tumor

cardiac: pertaining to the heart

cardiac arrest: sudden cessation of the heartbeat

cardiac cath: abbreviation for cardiac catheterization

cardiac catheterization: passing of a tiny tube into the heart to measure cardiac function and detect abnormalities

cardiologist: physician specializing in heart disease

cardiopulmonary resuscitation: CPR; to artificially ventilate the lungs and rhythmically compress the heart

caries: tooth decay and gradual disintegration

case management: system where one person tracks the care of patients

cast: plaster mold of part; dental casts from impressions; solid mold immobilizing a limb after fracture

CAT scan: see **computerized axial tomography**

cavity: hole in tooth from decay

cecum: blind end of ascending colon

central service: department that cleans and disinfects packages and sterilizes equipment

cerebral palsy: shaking caused by brain damage

cerebral vascular accident: stroke; interruption of circulation or bleeding in the brain

cerebrospinal: fluid around the brain and spinal cord

cervical cells: specimen from the lower part of the uterus that is used for a Pap test

charge stickers: labels applied to equipment to indicate cost

charges: cost of supplies, services, or procedures

chart: medical record

chart analysis: reviewing medical record for completeness

chemistry: lab section that identifies and measures elements in blood serum

chemotherapy: treating disease with chemical agents that are toxic to certain cells

cholangitis: inflammation of bile ducts

cholecystitis: inflammation of the gallbladder

cholecystectomy: removal of the gallbladder

cholelithiasis: gallstones

chronological order: organization according to date

chyme: mixture of food with gastric juices

clean: free from dirt

cleft palate: a congenital opening in the roof of mouth forming a passage between the mouth and nasal cavities

closed head injury: trauma to head/cranium

cobalt-60: radioactive isotope used in treatment of malignancies

coccyx: tailbone

cochlea: cone-shaped tube; auditory part of inner ear

cochlear implant: replacement of the cone-shaped tube in the middle ear

coding: identifying diagnostic groups

cognition: mental process used to acquire knowledge

cognitive: based on thinking

colectomy: removal of the colon

colitis: inflammation of the large intestine, or colon

collection: department or process for retrieving payment

colon: large intestine

colostomy: opening into the colon

common bile duct: tube that carries bile and pancreatic fluid

communication: transmission of messages through speech, hearing, and writing

compulsion: a force

computerized axial tomography: CAT scan: a noninvasive technique using X rays and a computer to visualize transverse planes of body tissue

confidentiality: respect for the patient's privacy relating to the illness

confusion: not being aware of people, place, or things

congestive heart failure: a weak heart becomes ineffective as a pump, resulting in poor circulation

contaminated: introduction of bacteria or harmful substance

contracture: muscle that has tightened and immobilized a joint

controlled substance: a drug that can become addictive or abused; includes depressants and stimulants; distribution of such drugs is monitored

conversion: admission of patient receiving outpatient treatment

coordination: parts of the body (especially limbs) working together in harmony

coronary angioplasty: repair of blood vessels in the heart muscle

coronary thrombosis: blood clot blocking an artery in the heart muscle

cough: a forceful exhale

counseling skills: ability to interview, guide, and advise

courteous: polite

critical thinking: thought processes that facilitate analyzing and problem solving

Crohn's disease: chronic inflammation of the small intestine

cross match: test of whether patient's blood will mix successfully with transfusion blood

crown: covering over the whole tooth that is made of gold or porcelain

culture: procedure for growing bacteria

cyanosis: blue skin color from a lack of oxygen

cyst: abnormal sac of clear fluid

cystitis: inflammation of the urinary bladder

cystogram: X ray of the urinary bladder

cytology: study of the formation, structure, and function of cells, using lab specimens

data: information

DEA: U.S. Drug Enforcement Administration

deafness: inability to hear

decay: degeneration of a spot on a tooth

defibrillation: electric shock to the heart to restore rhythm

dentures: artificial teeth set in a plastic mold

dependable: reliable

depression: mental state of melancholy; loss of interest in people and activities

dermatologist: physician specializing in skin disorders

descending: section of the large intestine on the left side of the abdomen

diagnosis: name of the illness

diagnostic tests: examinations to determine the illness

dialysate: fluid used in the artificial kidney machine

dialysis: procedure to cleanse blood by diffusing waste elements and excess fluid through a semipermeable membrane; used when kidney function is impaired

diapers: put on patients who cannot control the flow of urine

diastolic: amount of pressure in blood vessels when the heart is at rest; name of cardiac cycle when the heart relaxes between beats

dictation: taping information for typing

digestion: process of breaking down food into a usable form

direct: type of admission when patient comes from home or physician office

dirty: grossly soiled

disability: state or condition of physical or mental impairment from illness or injury

discharge: release from the hospital; drainage

discs: pads between spinal bones

donor: person who gives an organ

Doppler: instrument to detect blood flow/pulse by sound

DRG: diagnostic related group

drug interaction: effects of substances taken together

drug levels: test to determine the amount of chemicals in the blood

drug rehabilitation: treatment to recover from chemical use

duodenum: section of the small intestine connected to the stomach; beginning of the small intestine

dynamometer: instrument that measures hand strength

dysarthria: inability to control muscles that relate to speech

dysphagia: impaired ability to swallow; difficulty in swallowing

dysphonia: impairment of voice production; difficulty with voice

dyspnea: difficult or labored breathing

echocardiograph: picture of the heart formed by sound waves; visualizes cardiac structures by the noninvasive ultrasound procedure

ECT: electroconvulsive therapy; an electric shock to the brain sometimes used to treat acute depression

–ectomy: suffix meaning removal of an organ, part, or limb

edema: swelling

EEG: electroencephalograph

EKG: electrocardiograph, electrocardiogram

elective procedure: relieves discomfort in a non life-threatening situation

electrocardiograph: a record tracing the electrical activity of the heart

electroencephalograph: graph of electrical impulses produced by brain activity

electronic ear: device that amplifies sound

embolism: moving blood clot

emergency admission: entrance of a patient to the hospital after being seen in the ER

emergency procedures: immediate actions to save a patient's life

emergency room: place for treating sudden, serious illnesses

–emia: suffix meaning blood

emphysema: a chronic degenerative disease characterized by the loss of elasticity in lung tissue and enlarged alveoli

enamel: hard covering of the tooth

endotracheal tube: a plastic airway placed through the mouth into the windpipe to maintain airflow

enteritis: inflammation of the small intestine

enthusiastic: showing intense interest

epistaxis: nosebleed

equilibrium: balance

equine: refers to horses

esophageal speech: process of burping air to communicate with sound after the voice box has been removed

esophagitis: inflammation of the esophagus, or gullet

esophagus: tube that brings food to the stomach from the pharynx

eustachian tube: auditory tube from the middle ear to the pharynx

evacuation: removal to the outside

exchange carts: mobile shelves delivered with complete stock for department needs

exhale: to breathe out

express care: place where sudden minor illnesses are treated

expressive language: ability to convey information

extraction: removal of a tooth

extremities: arms and legs

family practitioner: physician specializing in patients of all ages

fantasy: imagination or illusion

fat: organic compound of triglyceride in fatty acid; lipid; adipose tissue

FDA: U.S. Food and Drug Administration

fear: anxiety over real or possible danger

feline: refers to cats

femur: thigh bone

fibrillation: irregular heartbeat

fibula: bone in the back of the calf

filling: restoration; process of inserting material into a prepared tooth

finance: department that manages money for the institution

flaccid: limp muscle

flexibility: capacity to bend and change

flight: helicopter crew

floss: waxed or unwaxed thread used to remove plaque and calculus from dental surfaces

fluoroscopy: temporarily pictures of organs

Foley: catheter used in the urinary bladder

fracture: broken bone

gas sterilizer: machine that kills bacteria on plastic equipment

gastrectomy: removal of the stomach

gastric: refers to the stomach

gastric juice: digestive liquid secreted by the stomach

gastritis: inflammation of the stomach

gastroenterologist: physician specializing in the stomach and intestines

GI: gastrointestinal

gingivitis: inflammation of gums; signs include redness, swelling, and bleeding

glomerulonephritis: inflammation of the kidney; a form of nephritis

glomerulus: meshwork of blood vessels in the kidney

glossectomy: removal of the tongue

glucose: a simple sugar

gums: tissue covering the bone at the base of the teeth

gynecologist: physician specializing in female organs

gynecology: branch of medicine dealing with female organs and diseases

hallucination: a false perception of sights or sounds

handicap: any mental or physical hindrance that interferes with normal activities

hand washing: most effective way to prevent infections in the hospital

health care team: several professional medical personnel working closely together to meet patients' needs

hearing: act of perceiving sound

hearing aid: instrument to amplify sound

hearing loss: decreased sound perception; degree of acuity can be detected

heart failure: diagnosis of inadequate myocardial pumping action

helpful: willing to work

hematocrit: lab test measuring the proportion of blood cells to serum

hematology: lab section that studies the number and type of blood cells

hematuria: blood in the urine

hemi–: prefix for half

hemiplegia: paralyzed on one side of the body

hemo–: prefix meaning blood

hemoglobin: red substance that carries oxygen within blood

hemorrhage: abnormal and excessive bleeding

hepatitis: inflammation of the liver

histology: lab section that studies tissue structure

HIV: human immunodeficiency virus; causes AIDS

Holter monitor: portable EKG machine

house: regular diet

humerus: bone in upper arm

humor: sense of appreciation for what is funny

hyper–: prefix meaning high, above, excessive

hyperalimentation: concentrated nutrients in IV fluids

hyperoptic: farsightedness

hypertension: high blood pressure; pressure in blood vessels that is greater than normal

hyperventilation: breathing too rapidly

hypo–: prefix meaning below, under, less

I&O: in and out; indicates the need to measure fluid intake and output

I&O surgery: one-day hospital stay for a surgical procedure

ileitis: inflammation of the ileum, the last section of the small intestine

ileostomy: opening into the distal section of the small intestine

ileum: largest and most distal section of the small intestine

immunology: lab section that studies the body's ability to resist disease

impairment: deficit

impression: outline of whole upper or lower set of teeth

impulse: a force transmitted along nerves

incentive spirometer: device used to encourage deep breathing

incomplete: medical records that need more information

indicator tape: adhesive paper that changes color in high heat

infection: condition caused by bacteria

ingestion: taking food in by mouth

inhale: to breathe in

initiative: working without being asked

inlay: a solid filling made in a mold and then placed into the tooth

inpatient procedures: system for billing for treatments on admitted patients

instrument sets: implements packaged together

insulin: important hormone in body's use of sugar

insurance claim: application for payment from medical policy

intensive care: department where critically ill patients are cared for

interest: desire to know

internist: physician specializing in medical treatments

intracranial bleed: oozing of blood into the head cavity

intravenous fluids: sterile liquids infused directly into veins to provide liquid, nourishment, electrolytes, and medication

isolation: apart from others

–itis: suffix meaning inflammation of a part, organ, or tissue

IV: intravenous

JCAHO: Joint Commission on Accreditation of Healthcare Organizations

jejunum: middle section of the small intestine

joint replacement: insertion of artificial parts at the juncture where bones meet and articulate

kidney: organ that cleanses blood and makes urine

knowledgeable: informed

KUB: X ray of kidneys, ureters, and urinary bladder

labor and delivery: area of the hospital where babies are born

laceration: irregular tear of the flesh

language: organized means of communication; method of transmitting information

language therapy: treatment of sound interpretation

large intestine: stores food waste and reabsorbs liquid

laryngectomy: removal of the voice box

larynx: voice box

laser: acronym for light amplification by stimulated emission of radiation; a device that emits intense heat and power as a beam

laser treatment: procedure used in surgery to incise and coagulate

laxative: stimulating the intestinal tract to pass waste

legal: term that describes correspondence sent to lawyers

Lifeline®: system attached to home phones to indicate that help is needed

lithotripsy: process of breaking up stones in urethra or bladder

LOC: level of consciousness

lumen: the space within a tubelike structure

lungs: spongy organs of respiration containing alveoli

macroscopic: seen by the naked eye

magnetic resonance imager: a noninvasive technique for visualizing internal organs using powerful magnetic fields

malignant: harmful tumor that can cause death if untreated

mammogram: breast X ray

manic depression: cycle of hyperactivity following melancholia

mastectomy: removal of a breast

mast trousers: inflatable pants used to raise blood pressure

mediastinum: space between lungs

Medicaid: a U.S. government program that provides reimbursement for health care given to the poor

medical: treatment of illness with medications, rest, and diet

medical asepsis: clean technique

medical referral: recommended physician

medical staff: doctors approved to work at a hospital or facility

Medicare: a U.S. government program that provides reimbursement for hospital and medical care administered to people of retirement age

medication: substance used to treat an illness

mental health: ability to cope emotionally with the stresses of life

mental illness: disorder of the mind

mentor: person who teaches and advises

metabolic: pertains to metabolism, how the body uses food for energy

metabolism: process of releasing energy when food is used by body

metered-dose inhaler: pocket aerosol treatment that mists medication to be inhaled

microbiology: lab section that studies bacteria and the substances that effectively control or kill them

microfiche: sheets of film showing microimages of pages of printed matter

microscopic: seen only with magnification

mineral: inorganic element found in food

mobility: ability to move

modulation: control of voice intensity

molar: large tooth in the back of the mouth

mood: emotional state influencing a person's perception of the world

motor: nerve sensations to muscles causing motion

mouth: buccal cavity

MRI: magnetic resonance imager

multiple sclerosis: a central nervous system disease, characterized by a loss of coordination

musculoskeletal: system of muscles and bones

myocardial infarction: heart attack; necrosis of a section of the heart muscle due to a blocked coronary artery

myopia: nearsightedness

nameplate: patient identification card

narcotic: medication that induces stupor and sleep and relieves pain

nares: openings in the nose

necrosis: death of areas of tissues or bone

nephron: basic unit of the kidney

nervous: system that relates to nerves

nervous breakdown: incapacitating, severe attack of an emotional or mental disorder

neurologist: physician specializing in brain, spinal cord, and nerves

neurology: study and care of the brain, nerves, and spinal cord, and related diseases

neurosis: mental disorder with unpleasant symptoms

nosebleed: epistaxis

NPO: not to eat or drink anything; *nil per os*

nuclear medicine: specialty that tests with radioactive substances

nuclear scan: imaging with radioactive substances

nursery: newborn care

nursing process: methods used to assess and care for patients

observation: process of viewing

obstetrics: unit that specializes in pregnancy and delivery

obstetrician: physician who delivers babies

obstetrics: process of pregnancy and birthing

obstruction: blockage, obstacle

occlusion: blockage of a blood vessel

–oma: suffix meaning tumor

oncologist: physician specializing in cancer

oncology: caring for cancer victims

operating room (OR): place where surgery is performed

oral: refers to the mouth

oral musculature: muscles around the mouth

–orrhapy: suffix meaning repair of

orthopedics: treating bone problems

osmosis: process of molecules moving through a membrane

–ostomy: suffix meaning opening into

–otomy: suffix meaning opening into

otoscope: instrument used to view the ear

outpatient: a person who is treated and released, but not admitted to a facility; a clinic providing such treatment

outpatient procedure: system for billing for nonhospitalized patients

ovine: refers to sheep

oxygen therapy: administration of the chemical element necessary to life

palate: roof of the mouth

palpation: pressing body parts to detect abnormalities

pancreas: makes insulin and digestive juice

pancreatitis: inflammation of the pancreas

panoramic radiograph: continuous X ray of the jaw and teeth

par level: number of items requested as standard stock

paracentesis: procedure for removing fluid from the abdominal cavity

parallel bars: wooden handrails used for stability when walking

paralysis: inability to move muscles voluntarily

paranoia: imagined persecution

paraphasia: using an incorrect but related word

parotid: salivary glands under the ear

partial plate: a few false teeth attached to a molded form or denture

passive: exercises or body movements carried through by a therapist without the patient's assistance

patella: kneecap

pathology: study of the nature and cause of a disease

–pathy: suffix meaning loss of normal structure and function

patient accounting: department that tracks money owed to the hospital

pediatrician: physician who specializes in the care of children

pediatrics: care of children

peptic ulcers: open sores or lesions in the stomach or duodenum

perception: awareness

percussion: process of tapping body parts

perfusion: the procedure of providing the body with blood and oxygen and removing carbon dioxide when the heart is not beating

peri–: prefix meaning around

periodontitis: inflammation or degeneration of the covering of teeth below the gum line

peristalsis: wavelike contractions that move food along

peritonitis: inflammation of the lining of the abdominal cavity

personality: the mental aspects of a person

pharmacokinetics: effect of drugs on the physical and chemical makeup of the body

pharmacology: science of drugs as they relate to medical uses

pharyngitis: inflammation of the pharynx; sore throat

pharynx: throat

phlebitis: inflammation of veins

phobias: fear of something or a situation

phonation: production of the voice by vibrations of the vocal cords

physical deficit: disabled body part

plan: individual treatment program

plaque: film on a tooth that harbors bacteria

plastic surgeon: physician who repairs and reconstructs

–plasty: suffix meaning repair of

pleural sac: tissue that surrounds the lungs

pneumonia: an inflammatory disease of the lungs, caused by infection or irritation

pneumonitis: inflammation of lungs; pneumonia

PO: by mouth; *per os*

polite: courteous

polyps: mushroom-shaped abnormal growths

porcine: refers to pigs

post–: prefix meaning after

postoperative: after surgery

pre–: prefix meaning before

precertification: approval of an insurance company before treatment

preoperative: before surgery

prescription: written doctor's order for medication

pride: justifiable self-respect

prn: when necessary

problem solving: finding the answer to a perplexing question or situation

prompt: on time

prosthesis: artificial part

protein: nutrient necessary to build new cells, heal wounds, and allow muscles to contract

psychiatry: deals with the mind and mental illness

psychosis: mental illness resulting in personality disintegration and loss of contact with reality

PT: physical therapy or patient

PTCA: percutaneous coronary angioplasty

pulmonary artery: carries unoxygenated blood from the heart to the lungs

pulmonary function test: measures the ability of the lungs to exchange gases

pulmonary vein: carries oxygenated blood from the lungs to the heart

pumps: machines that control fluid flow

pus: cloudy fluid from infection

pyuria: pus in urine

quadriplegia: paralyzed from the neck down

radiation: potentially harmful ray used for diagnostic or therapeutic purposes

radiation therapy: X-ray treatments of tumors

radiologist: physician specializing in imaging and X-ray treatments

radius: the outer, shorter bone in the forearm leading to the thumb

rales: abnormal sound produced by air passing through bronchi that contain liquid

range of motion: exercise that determines and maintains joint movement

receptive language: ability to hear and understand

recovery room: where patients wake up and stabilize after surgery

rectum: last section of the large intestine

refraction: changed direction of a light ray

registration: process of signing in before treatment or admission

regulations: rules

rehabilitation: process of a disabled person returning to maximum function

reimbursement: payment for health care

renal artery: vessel that brings blood to the kidney

renal calculus: kidney stone

requisition: order form

respiratory arrest: stopped breathing

responsible: accountable for actions

restoration: repair of tooth

restraints: appliances used to limit patients' movement

résumé: a brief summary of a person's qualifications and job history

retro–: prefix meaning behind

retroperitoneal: behind the abdominal cavity

ROM: range of movement

root canal: removal of nerve from tooth

RR: recovery room

saliva: digestive juice in mouth

same-day surgery: patients have an operation and return home in one day

scheduled: planned admission

–scope: suffix meaning instrument to look into the body

–scopy: suffix meaning procedure of looking into the body

scrub: process of washing hands, fingernails, and lower arms before performing or assisting with surgery

seizures: brief attacks of shaking movements and/or altered consciousness; convulsions

sensation: feeling or awareness of stimulus

sensory: nerve stimuli to brain

sensory receptors: nerves that carry impulses from the sense organs to the brain and spinal cord

serology: study of serum and reactions between antigens and antibodies; study of the basis of the immune system

serum: clear liquid that carries blood cells; liquid portion of blood

sigmoid: S-shaped segment of the large intestine, above the rectum

sling: arm support

small intestine: tubelike organ between the stomach and large intestine that absorbs food

sodium: element that influences retention of fluid in cells

soft: nonirritating type of diet

sound waves: vibrations that produce noise

spastic: condition of periodic muscle contractions

special diets: food ordered by physicians as part of therapy

speech: sounds that represent words

speech pathology: study of abnormal voice production process

speech therapy: process of training in verbal communication

splint: device worn to support a body part

sports injuries: athletic injuries

sputum: liquid made in trachea; spit

stapes: tiny bones in the middle ear

stat: immediately

Steri-Strips™: narrow, sterile adhesive tapes

sterile: free from living microorganisms

sterilization: process of killing microorganisms

stethoscope: instrument used to hear internal body sounds

stomach: organ that stores and digests food

stomatitis: inflammation of the mouth

stress test: EKG done during increasing exercise to determine cardiovascular fitness

stroke: cerebrovascular accident; interruption of circulation to a section of the brain; may cause paralysis and loss of consciousness

stutter: repetition of syllables when attempting to talk

sub–: prefix meaning under

sublingual: under the tongue

submandible: under the lower jaw

submaxillary: under the jaw

surgeon: physician who operates on the body structure

surgical: care of patients before and after operations

surgical asepsis: sterile technique

suture: sterile thread used to stitch a wound closed; stitching parts together

swallowing: process of moving musculature of mouth and throat; enabling the passage of something from the mouth to the stomach

swelling: edema

systolic: pressure in blood vessels when the heart contracts; name of cardiac cycle when the heart contracts

tartar: hard crust of calcium salts, saliva, and debris on teeth

TB: tuberculosis

T, C, D B: turn, cough, and deep breathe; treatment to expand lungs especially after surgery

TD filing: system of filing medical records

teamwork: actions by a number of persons in close association

terminal: final, end

thallium: diagnostic radioactive substance used after a stress test

therapeutic activity plan: appropriate actions used to facilitate adapting to a handicap

third party: a company that pays for health care

thoracentesis: procedure to remove fluid from chest cavity

thoracic: chest surgery; physician who operates in the chest

thoracic cavity: space inside the chest

thrombophlebitis: inflammation of veins with blood clots

thrombosis: formation of a blood clot; stationary clot in a vessel

tibia: shin bone

tissue: group of cells

TNP: total parenteral nutrition

TPR: temperature, pulse, and respirations

trachea: windpipe; connects larynx and bronchi

tracheostomy, tracheotomy: artificial surgical opening into the trachea, or windpipe

tranquilizer: medication taken to relieve mental tension and anxiety

transcription: typing from a physicians' tape recording

transfer: move from one nursing unit to another

transplant: surgical procedure to replace an organ

transverse: section of the large intestine under the diaphragm

trauma: serious injury from impact

traumatic brain injury: damage to the brain by sudden impact to the skull

tremors: trembling or shaking

triage: system to identify degree of illness and treatment needed

T-tube: rubber catheter placed in common bile duct to drain bile

tympanic membrane: eardrum

type: test to determine the kind of blood

ulna: the larger bone in the lower arm leading to the little finger

ultrasound: uses inaudible sound waves to outline the shape of body organs

unit-dose method: system in which medications are packaged in individual doses

Universal precautions: an accepted method of infection control

ureter: tube that connects the kidney to the bladder

urethra: tube-shaped canal that leads from the bladder to outside the body

urinalysis: test that identifies elements in urine

urine: liquid made in the kidney

urologist: physician specializing in kidney and bladder disorders

urology: urinary tract problems

utilization review: system used to monitor the use of hospital beds

vascular: blood vessels

ventricular fibrillation: quivering of lower heart chambers

vertebra: spinal bone

virology: lab section that studies disease-causing viruses and develops vaccines against them

virus: organism that is smaller than bacteria

vital capacity: maximum amount of air expelled after a full inspiration

vital signs: temperature, pulse, respirations, and blood pressure

vitamin: organic substance essential for growth and metabolism

vocalization: complex process of talking, singing, and laughing

voice prosthesis: artificial device that produces or amplifies sound

voice synthesizer: an electronic device that speaks phrases when buttons are pushed

voice therapy: treatment of speech problems

volume: amount or intensity

VS: vital signs; TPR and BP

walker: U-shaped tubular support used when walking

wax: thick substance resembling beeswax

wisdom teeth: last large teeth to come into the back of the mouth

withdrawal: withholding medication or alcohol with resulting physical and/or mental symptoms

work habits: attitude and behavior patterns in an occupation

X ray: radioactive rays used to photograph or treat the inside of the body

Index

NOTE: Page numbers in **bold** type refer to non-text material.